ESSAYS ON JOHN

STUDIORUM NOVI TESTAMENTI AUXILIA

XVII

ESSAYS ON JOHN

BY

BARNABAS LINDARS

EDITED BY C.M. TUCKETT

LEUVEN

UNIVERSITY PRESS

UITGEVERIJ PEETERS

LEUVEN

1992

CIP KONINKLIJKE BIBLIOTHEEK ALBERT I, BRUSSEL

ISBN 90 6186 520 4 (Leuven University Press)
D/1992/1869/35
ISBN 90 6831 444 0 (Uitgeverij Peeters)
D/1992/0602/81

© Leuven University Press/Presses Universitaires de Louvain
Universitaire Pers Leuven
Krakenstraat 3, B-3000 Leuven-Louvain (Belgium)
Uitgeverij Peeters, Bondgenotenlaan 153, B-3000 Leuven (Belgium)

PREFACE

I am deeply grateful to Professor Frans Neirynck, who responded so positively to my proposal to publish these essays as a single collection and who offered the project a place in the series *Studiorum Novi Testamenti Auxilia*. It is also fitting that these essays be published from Leuven. Barnabas Lindars was a firm supporter of all the work of the University of Leuven and of the Colloquium Biblicum Lovaniense. One of the essays here (no. 7) was a main paper which he presented at the 1975 Colloquium, and a summary of another essay (no. 13) was presented as a short paper at the 1990 Colloquium[1].

It proved more desirable to re-set the text of essays nos. 6, 9, 11, 12, with the original page numbers added in the margins. The essays are printed here in chronological order of publication and for the most part exactly as originally published. The only changes made are points of clarification, details of publications which were referred to as "forthcoming" originally but which have subsequently been published, and cross-references between the essays in this volume.

As one for whom Barnabas Lindars was successively parish priest, teacher and colleague, and in whose footsteps in Manchester one now somewhat fearfully treads, it is both an honour and a privilege to prepare this volume for publication. In the last words of his final book on John, he wrote that study of John "opens up the true riches of the Fourth Gospel and enables one to make them one's own"[2]. It is hoped that these essays will play their part in enabling others too to reach more deeply into the riches and treasures of the Gospel of John.

Manchester, October 1992   Christopher TUCKETT

1. See A. DENAUX (ed.), *John and the Synoptics* (BETL, 101), Leuven, University Press - Peeters, 1992, pp. 542-547.
2. B. LINDARS, *John*, Sheffield, JSOT Press, 1990, p. 101.

CONTENTS

FIRST PUBLICATION

1. The Composition of John XX.
   — *New Testament Studies* 7 (1960-61) 142-147.
   Cambridge, University Press.

2. Two Parables in John.
   — *New Testament Studies* 16 (1969-70) 318-329.
   Cambridge, University Press.

3. ΔΙΚΑΙΟΣΥΝΗ in Jn 16.8 and 10.
   — A. DESCAMPS & A. DE HALLEUX (eds.), *Mélanges Bibliques en hommage au R.P. Béda Rigaux*, 1970, pp. 275-285.
   Gembloux, Duculot.

4. The Son of Man in the Johannine Christology.
   — B. LINDARS & S.S. SMALLEY (eds.), *Christ and Spirit in the New Testament. Studies in Honour of C.F.D. Moule*, 1973, pp. 43-60.
   Cambridge, University Press.

5. Word and Sacrament in the Fourth Gospel.
   — *Scottish Journal of Theology* 29 (1976) 49-63.
   Edinburgh, T. & T. Clark.

6. The Passion in the Fourth Gospel.
   — J. JERVELL & W.A. MEEKS (eds.), *God's Christ and His People. Studies in Honour of Nils Alstrup Dahl*, 1977, pp. 71-86.
   Oslo-Bergen-Tromsö, Universitetsforlaget.

7. Traditions behind the Fourth Gospel.
   — M. DE JONGE (ed.), *L'Évangile de Jean. Sources, rédaction, théologie* (BETL, 44), 1977, pp. 107-124.
   Gembloux, Duculot - Leuven, University Press; Leuven, ²1987.

8. John and the Synoptic Gospels: A Test Case.
   — *New Testament Studies* 27 (1981) 287-294.
   Cambridge, University Press.

9. Discourse and Tradition: The Use of the Sayings of Jesus in the Discourses of the Fourth Gospel.
   — *Journal for the Study of the New Testament* 13 (1981) 83-101.
   Sheffield, Academic Press.

10. The Persecution of Christians in John 15:18–16:4a.
    — W. HORBURY & B. MCNEIL (eds.), *Suffering and Martyrdom in the New Testament. Studies Presented to G.M. Styler*, 1981, pp. 48-69.
    Cambridge, University Press,

11. The Son of Man in the Theology of John.
    — B. LINDARS, *Jesus Son of Man. A Fresh Examination of the Son of Man Sayings in the Gospels in the Light of Recent Research*, 1983, pp. 145-157, 218-222.
    London, SPCK; Grand Rapids, MI, Eerdmans, 1984.

12. Slave and Son in John 8,31-36.
    — W.C. WEINRICH (ed.), *The New Testament Age. Essays in Honor of Bo Reicke*, 1984, pp. 271-286.
    Macon, GA, Mercer University Press.

13. Rebuking the Spirit: A New Analysis of the Lazarus Story of John 11.
    — *New Testament Studies* 38 (1992) 89-104.
    Cambridge, University Press.

14. Capernaum Revisited: John 4.46-53 and the Synoptics.
    — F. VAN SEGBROECK, C.M. TUCKETT, G. VAN BELLE & J. VERHEYDEN (eds.), *The Four Gospels 1992. Festschrift Frans Neirynck* (BETL, 100), 1992, pp. 1985-2000.
    Leuven, University Press - Peeters.

Permission to reprint the articles is gratefully acknowledged.

INTRODUCTION

BARNABAS LINDARS' WORK ON JOHN

Barnabas Lindars' untimely death in 1991 brought to an end a wide-ranging scholarly career. He held academic positions in the Universities of Cambridge and Manchester and was widely respected as a scholar in the areas of both Old Testament and New Testament.

Barnabas Lindars was born as Frederick Chevallier Lindars in 1923 and attended school in Altrincham, near Manchester. He went to Cambridge University as a student in 1941 and studied for the Oriental Languages Tripos and subsequently the Theology Tripos, his studies being interrupted by war service during the period 1943-45. From 1946-48 he studied at Westcott House, Cambridge, preparing for ordination in the Church of England. In 1948 he was ordained and then served as a curate in a parish in Sunderland for four years. During this time, in 1951, he joined the Anglican order of the Society of St Francis, taking the name of Brother Barnabas. In 1952 he returned to Cambridge where he lived until 1978. In 1961 he was appointed Assistant Lecturer, and subsequently Lecturer, in Divinity in the University of Cambridge where his prime responsibility was to lecture in Old Testament studies. In 1978 he moved to Manchester accepting appointment as the Rylands Professor of Biblical Criticism and Exegesis, a post which he occupied until his retirement in 1990. Whilst at Manchester he taught primarily New Testament studies, though he always maintained some Old Testament teaching. After his retirement, he returned to the mother house of his Franciscan order in Hilfield, near Dorchester. He died from a sudden heart attack whilst walking home after visiting friends on 22nd October 1991.

Barnabas Lindars' scholarly output covered a very wide range. In the field of Old Testament studies he had a long-standing interest in the book of Judges. He had accepted an invitation in 1967 to write the new International Critical Commentary on the book and had worked on the material for several years, publishing a number of articles and essays. After his retirement in 1990 he devoted considerable energies to writing up all the material he had collected for the commentary and, when he died, he had in fact completed the commentary on the first five chapters of Judges. The task of writing the new Judges ICC commentary itself has had to be reassigned; however, arrangements have been made to publish Lindars' work on

Judges 1-5 which will appear as a separate volume[1]. In the field of New Testament studies, Lindars published widely, even during his Cambridge years when his University post involved primarily Old Testament teaching. His first full book, *New Testament Apologetic*, London, SPCK, 1961, was a study of the use of the Old Testament in the New, seeking to show how individual Old Testament texts were used in differing ways by different New Testament authors as part of their "apologetic" to explain aspects of their Christian belief. The book was in many respects significantly ahead of its time, focusing attention on the "trajectory" (though of course that word was not used in New Testament scholarly jargon at the time) of Old Testament texts, and arguing for a high level of creativity on the part of New Testament writers. As such, the book has been extremely influential and is still widely cited and used today. The significance of his work in this area was recognised in 1988 by the publication of a Festschrift to mark his 65th birthday, with all the essays in the volume dealing with aspects of the phenomenon of the use of scripture by Biblical writers[2].

It was however in the field of Johannine studies that Lindars probably made his most significant contribution to the field of New Testament scholarship. In the 1960s he was asked to write a commentary on the fourth gospel in the *New Century Bible* series. He completed the work in 1969 and the commentary was published in 1972[3]. His contribution to this and other fields was recognised the next year in 1973 by the award of the prestigious D.D. degree by the University of Cambridge. Since that time, Lindars maintained a life-long interest in the fourth gospel and published a series of articles and essays devoted to study of the gospel. It is these articles which are represented in this collection in order to enable a fuller view of Lindars' work in this area.

Lindars' work on John is slightly unusual in one respect. Many scholars who specialise in study of one particular Biblical book write a number of preliminary articles, and then collect together the sum total of their ideas into a later commentary (as indeed Lindars himself was doing with his work on Judges). In the case of Lindars' work on John, the reverse was the case. The first three of his articles on John were written before his commentary, but the majority were written later. Even his small, but highly influential, book *Behind the Fourth*

---

1. B. LINDARS, *Judges 1-5*, Edinburgh, T. & T. Clark, forthcoming.
2. D.A. CARSON & H.G.M. WILLIAMSON (eds.), *It is Written*. FS Barnabas Lindars, Cambridge, University Press, 1988.
3. *The Gospel of John*, London, Marshall, Morgan and Scott, 1972.

Gospel[4], which was published one year earlier than the commentary, was in fact written after the typescript for the commentary had been completed. All this enabled Lindars in some ways to develop his thinking and his ideas in more detail beyond what he had included in his commentary. And on at least one point he evidently changed his mind quite considerably.

Study of John remained an area of vital concern to Lindars throughout his life. He lectured regularly on John in Manchester and his work reached a fitting conclusion when in 1990 he published a small volume *John* in the series *New Testament Guides*[5]. Ostensibly this is "only" a student guide, intended for undergraduate readers to enable them to get their bearings in Johannine scholarship. Nevertheless, the book clearly represents the work of a master of his subject who knows all the problems, and the profundities, of John's gospel and yet has the gift of being able to write about them in a way that is immediately intelligible for a readership that is not quite as specialist as some. The book is a fitting tribute to much of his life's work.

Lindars remained through his life deeply committed to the historical critical method. His prime interest in studying the fourth gospel was to discover something of the thought of the evangelist himself. He was not a great believer in any "new look" (perhaps now not so new) on the fourth gospel which might enable John to be used as a source for recovering information about the historical Jesus. So too Lindars was alive and open to synchronic, literary approaches to the gospel, treating the text as an undifferentiated literary whole. Indeed much of his work was devoted to seeking to reveal John's literary skill and artistry in producing the present form of the text, and he firmly believed that the evangelist was responsible for considerably more in this respect that some scholars were prepared to credit. Nevertheless, Lindars was convinced that a synchronic approach was not sufficient by itself. In order to come to a full appreciation of John's work, one had to have some notion of the sources which were used by the evangelist to be able to see how that source material had been taken up and used by John in writing the present gospel. As a result, several of Lindars' essays are concerned in some way or other with the question of John's sources and traditions. For the most part, such concern was a means to the further end of trying to understand *John*, though in some instances he addressed the source problem more directly for its own sake. (See essays nos. 8 and 14.)

4. *Behind the Fourth Gospel*, London, SPCK, 1971.
5. *John*, Sheffield, JSOT Press, 1990.

In some respects, the scholarly climate in which Lindars wrote changed over the period of time covered by these essays. In the 1960s and early 70s, Johannine scholarship was dominated by Bultmannian-type source theories. Johannine independence from the synoptics was assumed almost without question; and theories about the existence of a Signs source, as well as a possible revelatory discourse source, abounded. Lindars remained convinced throughout his life that, in particular, these latter theories were unjustified and unnecessary; further, they failed to do justice to the richness and complexity of John's own contribution to the content of his gospel. Lindars early book, *Behind the Fourth Gospel*, was a sustained attack on the theory of a Signs Source (especially as argued for then by R.T.Fortna[6]), with a corresponding positive argument that the evangelist himself was responsible for the vast bulk of the text in its present form. So too, he argued, Bultmannian-type theories of displacements within the gospel were to be discounted since, as often as not, they played havoc with the delicately structured flow of John's argument. Lindars well recognised all the problems in John's text which displacement theories sought to solve, e.g. the position of ch. 6 between chs. 5 and 7, the presence of chs. 15-17 after the apparent conclusion to the farewell discourse in 14,31, etc. Lindars' own theory was to postulate a two-stage development in the production of the gospel whereby the evangelist added further material (e.g. ch. 6, chs. 15-17, the Prologue) in a second version of the gospel. But this was not to be seen as the adoption of a source which (according to some theories) John profoundly disagreed with and wished to correct[7].

Lindars did however believe that John had traditional material available to him, and it was here that Lindars exploited to the full the similarities between John the Synoptics. In several instances Lindars believed that the basis for a section in John was a saying attributed to Jesus which was available to the evangelist as part of his tradition. Sometimes this could be argued for independently (e.g. Jn 5,19, though cf. Mt 11,27 / Lk 10,22); at other times, this could be suggested by a parallel in the synoptic gospels (Jn 3,3 cf. Mt 18,3; Jn 8,35 cf. Mt 5,45 and 17,26; Jn 8,51f. cf. Mk 9,1). In these instances, Lindars believed that a traditional saying was taken up by the evangelist and developed

---

6. R.T. FORTNA, *The Gospel of Signs*, Cambridge, University Press, 1970. For a more recent statement of the author's views, see ID., *The Fourth Gospel and Its Predecessor*, Edinburgh, T. & T. Clark, 1989.

7. According to some, for example, the Signs Source used by John implied a Christology (of Jesus as the great triumphalist miracle worker) which John himself disapproved of and wished to modify and correct.

into a richly structured discourse in order to get across the message John wanted to develop. Many of the essays here thus represent Lindars' exposition of John's argument along these lines. In many respects it is a convincing argument, and the insights which these essays give into the progression of thought in the Johannine discourses are richly illuminating.

Times do however change. In the 60s and early 70s, the question of John's relation to the synoptics was thought to be almost a non-question, with Johannine independence assumed almost without discussion. John might well have had sources, but such sources were considered to be quite unrelated to the synoptics. In some respects, Lindars' work at this period, seeking to exploit synoptic parallels to John, represented an attempt to swim against this tide. Although he never argued at any time for John's dependence on the synoptics, and indeed in his early articles he almost assumes Johannine independence without any real discussion, nevertheless he did believe that the synoptic evidence could be used to uncover John's traditions. And he maintained consistently that it was really only the synoptic evidence which provided some sort of critical control in attempts to recover John's traditions[8]. Further, when the synoptic parallel is removed, Lindars frequently argues that the residue in John is Johannine through and through (thus obviating the need for further source theories). Yet if John's differences from the synoptic versions are so thoroughly Johannine, this raises the question of whether in fact John's traditions must be necessarily the pre-synoptic traditions or whether they might be the synoptic gospels themselves.

In the late 70s and 80s, of course, the scholarly climate on this issue has changed. Johannine independence from the synoptics is no longer the unquestioned assumption it used to be, and especially due to the work of F. Neirynck and others associated with the University of Leuven, the theory of John's dependence on the synoptics is once again a live issue[9]. Lindars was clearly aware of the change in scholarly climate. In fact he never gave up his belief in the independence of John from the synoptic gospels, maintaining consistently that John used traditions which lay behind the synoptics, rather than the synoptic gospels themselves. He addresses the problem explicitly in the essay on Jn 3,3 and the possible parallel in Mt 18,3 (essay no. 8 here), arguing

8. See his review of Fortna's more recent book (n. 6 above) in *SJT* 43 (1990) 526-527.

9. For recent discussion of the problem, see the essays in the collection A. DENAUX, *John and the Synoptics* (BETL, 101), Leuven, University Press - Peeters, 1992, especially Neirynck's comprehensive survey article *John and the Synoptics: 1975-1990*, pp. 3-62.

that John and Matthew represent independent translations of a common Aramaic form of the saying. Similarly, his very last article, completed just before his death and published posthumously in the Neirynck Festschrift (see no. 14), argues strongly for the view that John's account of the nobleman's son (Jn 4,46-54) is dependent on the story underlying Mt 8,5-13 / Lk 7,1-10 and indeed the evidence of John perhaps can and should be used in reconstructing the source underlying the accounts in Matthew and Luke.

In one respect, however, Lindars did change his views, and this concerned his beliefs about the "Son of Man" problem. In the 70s Lindars had devoted dome time to this and had published at least one article on the theme[10]. However, in the late 70s and early 80s, he appeared to change his mind quite considerably on a number of matters. After two articles, he produced a book devoted to the Son of Man problem, of which the chapter on the Son of Man in John is reproduced here (essay no. 11 here)[11]. In his book he argues that the Aramaic idiom *bar (a)nasha* has been largely misunderstood and ignored. Judaism had no "Son of Man" concept in the first century: "Son of Man" was not a title. Rather the use of the phrase, at least on the lips of Jesus, is simply a modest self-reference with a limited generic sense. It should perhaps be translated as something like "a man in my position". Any possible allusions to Dan 7,13f. are later accretions to this primitive tradition and it is only the latter which can be traced back to Jesus.

This is not the place to seek to discuss this much debated problem. However, some change of view can be seen in Lindars' own essays. In his 1973 essay (no. 4 here) he assumes that there was an apocalyptic Son of Man concept, based on Dan 7, which was taken up and developed by John. In the chapter of his later book, Lindars modifies this view considerably by effectively denying any meaning to the phrase "Son of Man" itself beyond a third-person self-reference by Jesus as speaker. He still maintains that the phrase is used in a significant way in the gospel to get over a key aspect of the message John wishes to convey, namely the importance of the revelation which is disclosed in the cross. But its origins for John may lie in the authentic sayings tradition rather than in any "Son of Man myth". In order to enable comparison to be made, both contributions relating to John are

---

10. See his *Re-enter the Apocalyptic Son of Man*, in *NTS* 22 (1975-76) 52-72.

11. The articles *Jesus as Advocate: A Contribution to the Christology Debate*, in *BJRL* 62 (1980) 476-497, and *The New Look on the Son of Man*, in *BJRL* 63 (1981) 437-462, were followed by his *Jesus Son of Man. A Fresh Examination of the Son of Man in the Gospels in the Light of Recent Research*, London, SPCK, 1983.

reprinted here, though other essays in the collection also contain important material on the topic (see especially essay no. 6, for example).

The essays reprinted here cover a period of more than thirty years of intensive study of the Gospel of John by a leading Johannine expert. Despite some changes of mind and emphasis over the years, they still show a consistency and a relevance which make them important reading for all contemporary study of the Gospel of John. Barnabas Lindars' articles and essays have made important contributions to the study of John. It is to be hoped that the republication of this material in a single volume will enable his total contribution to be more widely appreciated and better assessed.

Christopher TUCKETT

ESSAYS ON JOHN

NTS 7 (1960-61) 142-147

1

THE COMPOSITION OF JOHN XX

In *N.T.S.* II (1955), 110–14, there was a short study by A. R. C. Leaney on 'The Resurrection Narratives in Luke (xxiv. 12–53)'. He suggested that the similarities between the narratives in Luke xxiv and John xx can best be explained on the hypothesis that both have made use of the same tradition, rather than direct borrowing one from the other. His interest lay primarily in the possibility this hypothesis affords of recovering the sources of the Lukan material. But his observations deserve to be studied further from the point of view of the composition of the Fourth Gospel. They reveal John's aims and methods in handling his sources in this chapter. This may have a bearing on our estimate of the composition and purpose of the Fourth Gospel as a whole.

Apart from the two final verses, which summarize the whole book, the chapter can be divided into two sections, containing five episodes altogether. The first section is the story of the empty tomb, *vv.* 1–18. This consists of (I A) Mary Magdalene's visit to the tomb (*vv.* 1–2); (I B) Peter and another disciple at the tomb (*vv.* 3–10); and (I C) the appearance of Jesus to Mary Magdalene (*vv.* 11–18). The second section is the story of the appearance of the risen Lord to the assembled apostles, *vv.* 19–20. This consists of (II A) his appearance on Easter night (*vv.* 19–23), and (II B) the story of Thomas (*vv.* 24–9).

For the purposes of comparison we may for the moment leave out of account the narrative of the two disciples at the tomb (I B). The other two episodes of the first section are bound together by the common interest in Mary Magdalene. If we now compare Mary at the tomb (I A) and the appearance of Mary (I C) with the appearance to the apostles (II A) and the story of Thomas (II B), we can observe some significant literary features which both sections have in common.

I A, C. The first section is based on a form of the tradition of the empty tomb common to all three Synoptists. The features of the story are:

(*a*) The women come to the tomb, and find the stone rolled away and the tomb empty.

(*b*) They see a young man or angel (or two such), who says that Jesus is risen.

(*c*) They go away to tell the disciples.

(*d*) As they go, Jesus appears to them. This item is found only in Matt. xxviii. 9 f., but it is possible that it originally completed Mark's narrative after ἐφοβοῦντο γάρ.

John's handling of this material has the following characteristics:

(i) Only one woman is mentioned, Mary Magdalene, who has already played a prominent part in John's teaching on the resurrection (John xi).

(ii) She finds the tomb empty and goes to tell the disciples, but the narrative omits two features, the angels in the tomb and the appearance of Jesus as she goes to the disciples.

(iii) The *omitted matter* forms the nucleus of a *supplementary incident*, that is, I c.

(iv) This is presented with considerable dramatic skill. Mary Magdalene is a representative of the readers of the Gospel, gathering up their emotions, so that the episode brings home the desired teaching concerning the resurrection.

II A, B. The second section is based on a tradition of our Lord's appearance to the apostles, which has come down to us in a variety of forms. Luke xxiv. 36–49 bears the closest resemblance to John, but Matt. xxviii. 16–20 follows the same fundamental pattern. Mark xvi. 14–18, although it occurs in the longer ending of Mark, is not derived directly from either of these, and deserves to be taken into account as an independent witness to the same tradition.

(*a*) Jesus appears to the assembled apostles.

(*b*) They disbelieve and he upbraids them.

(*c*) He gives the apostolic commission.

(*d*) He specifies some of the effects of their work.

When John adopts this tradition, he applies the same technique as in the former section:

(i) The story is told according to the same form with the one omission of the unbelief of the disciples. Jesus displays his wounds, as in Luke, but it is not necessary for him to do so. In Luke they are shown in order to dispel the disciples' doubts.

(ii) The *omitted matter* is again the nucleus of a *supplementary incident*, II B.

(iii) The new incident is again concerned with one person, Thomas, who has figured in the same previous incident of the raising of Lazarus, xi. 16. This time the wounds are connected with Thomas's doubts.

(iv) It is presented with dramatic force, leading the reader to share in Thomas's adoration of the risen Christ and to make an act of faith.

I B. With these examples to guide us, we may now try to estimate the relationship of the episode of the two disciples at the tomb to the underlying tradition. According to Luke xxiv. 24 some of the disciples visited the tomb in response to the women's report. They found it empty, and returned without seeing Jesus. If Luke xxiv. 12 be accepted as an original part of the text, and not dependent on John xx. 3–10, it was Peter who did this, apparently alone.[1]

In this case John has not constructed a supplementary incident out of the

---

[1] Cf. I Cor. xv. 5 καὶ ὅτι ὤφθη Κηφᾷ.

tradition. But his work has some of the features observed in his handling of the other material:

(i) Specific persons are mentioned. Peter perhaps belongs to the tradition. The 'other disciple' is clearly John's own contribution to the story. It will be recalled that he had accompanied Peter to the high priest's house in xviii. 15.

(ii) The telling of the story has dramatic interest, and leads up to the 'other disciple's' intelligent belief.

This general analysis of the chapter can be made a basis for more exact conclusions by attention to vocabulary.

I A　John xx. 1–2	Matthew	Mark	Luke
1　τῇ δὲ μιᾷ τῶν σαββάτων	—	xvi. 2	xxiv. 1
Μαρία ἡ Μαγδαληνή	xxviii. 1	xvi. 1	xxiv. 10
πρωΐ	—	xvi. 2	—
εἰς τὸ μνημεῖον	—	xvi. 5	—
τὸν λίθον...ἐκ τοῦ μν.	—	xvi. 3	xxiv. 2 (ἀπό)
2　τρέχει	xxviii. 8 (ἔδραμον)	—	—
ποῦ ἔθηκαν αὐτόν	—	xvi. 6 (ὅπου)	—

It is evident that the words of these verses have most affinity with Mark. The rest of the vocabulary is distinctively Johannine, and shows a characteristic tendency of repeating phrases: *v.* 1 σκοτίας (frequent in John), τὸν λίθον ἠρμένον (cf. xi. 41 ἦραν οὖν τὸν λίθον); *v.* 2 τὸν ἄλλον μαθητήν, κτλ. (cf. xiii. 23; xviii. 15), ἦραν...ἐκ τοῦ μνημείου (*v.* 1), τὸν κύριον (cf. xi. 2).[1]

It will be best, as before, to continue with I c, the supplementary incident, and to leave I b till later.

I c　John xx. 11–18	Matthew	Mark	Luke
11　παρέκυψεν *Ev. Petri* xiii. 55–6	—	—	[xxiv. 12]
12　δύο (*omit* ℵ* *e*)	—	—	xxiv. 4 Acts i. 10
ἀγγέλους	xxviii. 3, 5	—	xxiv. 23
λευκοῖς	xxviii. 3	xvi. 5	Acts i. 10
καθεζομένους *Ev. Petri* xiii. 55	—	xvi. 5 (καθήμενον)	—
ὅπου ἔκειτο	xxviii. 6	—	—
τὸ σῶμα τοῦ Ἰησοῦ	—	—	xxiv. 3, 23
15　ζητεῖς	xxviii. 5	xvi. 6	xxiv. 5
17　μή μου ἅπτου	(contrast xxviii. 9 ἐκράτησαν)	—	—
τοὺς ἀδελφούς μου	xxviii. 10	—	—
18　ἀγγέλλουσα	xxviii. 8, 10 (ἀπαγγ.)	—	xxiv. 9 (ἀπαγγ.)

---

[1] Does the plural οἴδαμεν point to the underlying tradition of several women at the tomb?—cf. Bauer *ad loc.*

Although Luke figures quite prominently in this list, the significant words belong to Mark and Matthew (and the lost conclusion of Mark's narrative?). παρέκυψεν is probably to be taken as an example of repetition from *v.* 5, but has been included because it is used of the women in *Ev. Petri*. Johannine words and repetitions are numerous: *v.* 11 εἰστήκει, κτλ. (cf. xviii. 16 ὁ δὲ Πέτρος εἰστήκει πρὸς τῇ θύρᾳ ἔξω), κλαίουσα (cf. xi. 33); *v.* 12 καθεζομένους (cf. xi. 20 ἐκαθέζετο), πρός *c. dat.* (*v.* 11), τὸ σῶμα τοῦ Ἰησοῦ (xix. 38, 40); *v.* 13 γύναι (ii. 4), ἦραν, κτλ. (=*v.* 2); *v.* 14 ἐστράφη (i. 38), εἰς τὰ ὀπίσω (vi. 66; xviii. 6), ἑστῶτα (xviii. 18, etc.); *v.* 15 γύναι, τί κλαίεις (cf. *v.* 13), δοκοῦσα (frequent in John), κηπουρός (cf. xix. 41 κῆπος), ἐβάστασας (several times in John), ποῦ, κτλ. (cf. *v.* 2); *v.* 16 στραφεῖσα (*v.* 14), Ἑβραϊστί (*v.* 2; xix. 13, 17, 20), ῥαββουνί, κτλ. (cf. i. 38 ῥαββί (ὁ λέγεται...διδάσκαλε)); *v.* 17 οὔπω, ἀναβέβηκα (both frequent in John), πρὸς τὸν πατέρα (xiv. 6, etc.), θεόν μου (cf. *v.* 28); *v.* 18 μαθηταῖς (*v.* 10), κύριον (*v.* 2).

This leaves only one significant word not found in the Synoptic witness to the underlying source, and not used elsewhere by John, namely, ἅπτου (*v.* 17). It is possible that it existed in the source, where Matthew has ἐκράτησαν.

Taking the two episodes together, it can be seen that the material which John has in common with Matthew-Mark contains a closely similar vocabulary; whereas the rest of the material is purely Johannine.

II A	John xx. 19–23	Matthew	Mark	Luke
19	ἔστη εἰς τὸ μέσον	—	—	xxiv. 36
	εἰρήνη ὑμῖν	—	—	[xxiv. 36]
20	ἔδειξεν	—	—	[xxiv. 40]
	τὰς χεῖρας	—	—	xxiv. 39
	ἐχάρησαν	—	—	xxiv. 41 (χαρᾶς)
22	λάβετε πνεῦμα ἅγιον	—	—	Acts i. 8, etc.
23	ἀφῆτε τὰς ἁμαρτίας	—	—	xxiv. 47

The number of verbal contacts is not large, even if we accept Leaney's contention that Luke xxiv. 36*b*, 40 are genuine. The *form* of *v.* 23 shows a closer parallel with Mark xvi. 16 than with Luke. Johannine words are: *v.* 19 οὔσης οὖν ὀψίας (cf. vi. 16; xx. 1), τῇ μιᾷ σαββάτων (repetition of *v.* 1), διὰ τὸν φόβον τῶν Ἰουδαίων (vii. 13; xix. 38), εἰρήνη ὑμῖν (cf. xiv. 27); *v.* 20 ἔδειξεν (seven times in John), πλευράν (xix. 34), ἐχάρησαν (xvi. 22, etc.); *v.* 21 εἰρήνη (repetition), καθὼς... ὑμᾶς (xviii. 18; cf. xiii. 16); *v.* 22 λάβετε πνεῦμα (cf. vii. 39).

Although θυρῶν κεκλεισμένων is not represented in John except here and *v.* 26, it need not have come from the source, seeing that the following definitely Johannine phrase requires some such statement. In *v.* 22 ἐνεφύσησεν is ἅπ. λεγ in the New Testament. It is presumably a direct allusion to Gen. ii. 7, and as such may be due to John himself. The phrases in *v.* 23 are not Johannine, and may be from the source. However, non-Johannine words are few, and not such as to suggest a source differing greatly from that which lies behind the Lukan material.

IIB	John xx. 24–9	Matthew	Mark	Luke
25	οὐ μὴ πιστεύσω	—	xvi. 13, 14	—
27	ἄπιστος...πιστός	—	xvi. 11, 14, 16	xxiv. 11, 41

This meagre and inconclusive contact with the Synoptists tells us nothing further about the source. On the other hand, Johannine words and repetitions abound: *v.* 24 Θωμᾶς... ὁ λεγόμενος Δίδυμος (xi. 16), εἷς ἐκ τῶν δώδεκα (vi. 71); *v.* 25 ἑωράκαμεν τὸν κύριον (cf. *v.* 18), χερσίν... πλευράν (cf. *v.* 20), βάλλω... εἰς (frequent in John), οὐ μὴ πιστεύσω (cf. iv. 48, etc.); *v.* 26 (all significant words from *vv.* 19, 24); *v.* 27 εἶτα (xiii. 5; xix. 27), φέρε (frequent in John), ὧδε (xi. 21, 32); *v.* 28 ἀπεκρίθη... καὶ εἶπεν (frequent in John), κύριος... θεός (cf. *v.* 17); *v.* 29 μακάριοι (xiii. 17).

In *v.* 25 τύπον (τόπον), ἥλων and δάκτυλον are special vocabulary required by the context, and do not indicate source material. There is nothing distinctively non-Johannine. The only point of contact with the source is in the matter of belief and unbelief, significantly omitted in II A. We thus reach precisely the same conclusion as in the previous case.

IB	John xx. 3–10	Matthew	Mark	Luke
3	Πέτρος	—	—	[xxiv. 12]
4	ἔτρεχον *Ev. Petri* xiii. 55, 56	—	—	[xxiv. 12]
	κείμενα τὰ ὀθόνια	Cf. xxviii. 6	—	[xxiv. 12]
5	παρακύψας	—	—	—
7	ἐντετυλιγμένον	xxvii. 59	—	xxiii. 53
9	γραφήν	—	—	Cf. xxiv. 27, 32, 45 (all plural)
	δεῖ	—	—	xxiv. 7
	ἐκ νεκρῶν ἀναστῆναι	xxviii. 7	—	xxiv. 5, 7, 46
10	πρὸς αὑτούς	—	—	xxiv. 12

The rest of the vocabulary is Johannine. Of the words listed in the above table, only παρακύψας, ἐντετυλιγμένον, ἐκ νεκρῶν ἀναστῆναι, and πρὸς αὑτούς are not used elsewhere by John. παρακύψας itself may come from the tradition of the women, as we have seen. It thus becomes possible to regard the episode as a fabrication based on the kind of hint given in Luke xxiv. 24. On the other hand, Leaney's suggestion that there is a common source here is attractive and may well be right. He reconstructs this as follows: ὁ δὲ Πέτρος ἀναστὰς ἔδραμεν ἐπὶ τὸ μνημεῖον, καὶ παρακύψας βλέπει τὰ ὀθόνια κείμενα μόνα, καὶ ἀπῆλθεν πρὸς ἑαυτὸν θαυμάζων τὸ γεγονός, οὐδέπω γὰρ ᾔδει τὴν γραφήν· ὅτι δεῖ αὐτὸν ἐκ νεκρῶν ἀναστῆναι.

In the remainder there is the usual feature of repetition. Thus *v.* 3 is derived from *vv.* 1, 2; *v.* 6 repeats *vv.* 4, 5; *v.* 8 has repetitions from *v.* 4. Johannine words are: *v.* 4 ὁμοῦ (iv. 36), τάχιον (xiii. 27), πρῶτος predicatively

(i. 41); *v.* 5 ὀθόνια (xix. 40); *v.* 6 ἀκολουθῶν (frequent); *v.* 7 σουδάριον (xi. 44), χωρίς (i. 3; xv. 5); *v.* 9 οὐδέπω (vii. 39; xix. 41), τὴν γραφήν of a particular testimony (frequent). It is probably no more than coincidence that προέδραμεν and σουδάριον are found in Luke xix. 4 and 20 respectively.

The vocabulary analysis confirms the impressions gained from comparison of the form of each episode. It shows that in this chapter the material which is not derived from sources, which are also used by one or other of the Synoptists, makes use of an entirely Johannine vocabulary. This renders the possibility of *other* sources unlikely. The following conclusions thus emerge from this study:

(1) John's sources cannot be confined to one of the three Synoptic Gospels. His account of the empty tomb has affinities with Matthew and Mark, the rest with Luke. It is probable that his sources are traditions which lie behind the Synoptic Gospels, and not the Gospels themselves.

(2) The sources represent the most commonly received resurrection traditions, existing in a variety of forms. St Paul in I Cor. xv. 5 mentions both the appearance to Peter and the appearance to the Twelve.

(3) John takes these sources, rewriting them in such a way as to provide the starting-point for what he wants to teach. This is embodied in a very free development, showing recurring characteristics: (*a*) The vocabulary is simple, and there is much repetition. (*b*) Particular persons are named and circumstantial detail is provided to give verisimilitude. (*c*) The argument is worked out to a climax with great dramatic skill. (*d*) The climax thereby demands a response from the reader of the gospel.

(4) A source-criticism of the Fourth Gospel would have to begin by differentiating between the nucleus which makes the starting-point to each section, and the free development which follows. This is easily done in the case of the major signs in the first half of the gospel—the cleansing of the temple, the healing of the paralytic, the feeding of the five thousand, the man born blind.[1] The phenomena of John xx also suggest that the free development is likely to make use of some elements of the source material. On the other hand, circumstantial detail, particular persons, etc., are not evidence of the sources. John xx is particularly instructive, because its relation to the sources can be assessed with a high degree of probability. There is room for further research along these lines in other parts of the Gospel.

---

[1] For the parable of sheep and shepherd, cf. J. A. T. Robinson, 'The Parable of John x. 1–5', *Z.N.T.W.* xlvi (1955), 233–40.

NTS 16 (1969-70) 318-329

2

TWO PARABLES IN JOHN

One of the most fruitful aspects of recent study of the Fourth Gospel has been the recovery of traditional sayings of Jesus embedded in Johannine discourses. They are often the starting point of the whole argument. The classic example of this is the Parable of the Apprenticed Son in John v. 19 f. This was isolated as a parable from earlier tradition by both C. H. Dodd[1] and P. Gächter,[2] working independently of each other. In this case it is easy to see how the entire exposition of the work of Jesus as the Son of man, with which the ensuing discourse is concerned, is based on the parable. The Parable of the Son and the Slave in viii. 35 has a similar relation to the discourse in which it is enclosed, even though this may not be so obvious at first sight. These and other examples of parables in John have been conveniently collected in the popular work of A. M. Hunter, *According to John* (1968), pp. 78–89.

Traditional sayings of this kind are not confined to the discourses. Form-critical study of the Marriage at Cana (John ii. 1–11) reveals that another parable of Jesus is preserved in it, as will be shown below. Another parable has been incorporated into the speech of John the Baptist at John iii. 29. Recognition that this verse comes from pre-Johannine tradition has led some critics to conclude that it is an authentic saying of the Baptist. It will be argued below, however, that it is really to be attributed to Jesus himself. Thus two further items may be added to the recovery of traditional words of Jesus in the underlying sources of the Fourth Gospel.

I. THE PARABLE OF THE GOOD WINE (JOHN ii. 10)

It is not necessary for the purposes of this article to review the interpretation of the Marriage at Cana. It has frequently been defended as a genuine historical incident in the life of Jesus. It has also been treated as an extended allegory. Debate continues concerning the range of its symbolism and the question whether it is intended to refer to the Christian eucharist. The purpose of the story, however, is not in dispute. It is clearly a sign of the new order which is inaugurated by the coming of Jesus. It is inevitable that, in whatever way it is interpreted, it should be compared with the 'new wine in

---

[1] 'Une parabole cachée dans le quatrième évangile', *Revue d'Histoire et de Philosophie Religieuses*, XLII (1962), 107–15 = 'A Hidden Parable in the Fourth Gospel', *More New Testament Studies* by C. H. Dodd (1968), pp. 30–40.

[2] 'Zur Form von Joh. 5. 19–30', in *Neutestamentliche Aufsätze*, edited by J. Blinzler, O. Kuss, and F. Mussner, in honour of J. Schmid (1963), pp. 65–8.

old wine-skins' of Mark ii. 22 and with the additional saying on new and old wine in Luke v. 39.

A more radical criticism has been introduced by the observation that the motif of changing water into wine has a variety of pagan parallels in the Greco-Roman world. Dodd[1] draws attention to such diverse references as Pliny, *Hist. Nat.* II. 231; XXXI. 16; Diodorus Siculus III. 66; Pausanias VI. xxvi. 1–2; Plutarch, *Lysander*, XXVIII. 4; Ovid, *Metamorphoses*, XIII. 650 ff. This leads him to suggest that a similar folk-tale has been adapted to Christian use, presumably because of its thematic connection with a traditional saying of Jesus. He is careful to point out that this may have happened without any conscious realization of the pagan origins of the motif. If this is what has happened, the central feature of the miracle-story must be stripped off from the pericope as an accretion to the underlying tradition. Dodd then goes on to point out that this tradition could have been a parable of Jesus, beginning with some such words as 'A certain man made a marriage-feast', and leading up to the saying of ii. 10, 'You have kept the good wine until now'. He supports this contention by comparing the Barren Fig-tree (Mark xi. 12–14, 20–5) and the Coin in the Fish's Mouth (Matt. xvii. 27). The first of these appears to be a parable which has been transformed into an incident (cf. Luke xiii. 6–9). The second seems to be in the process of such a transformation.

Dodd puts forward these views tentatively, and does not attempt to formulate the process of accretion and transformation with any precision. He confines himself to the observation that the addition of the pagan miracle-story must 'belong to a relatively late stage in the development of the tradition', although this was 'before the material came into the hands of our evangelist' (p. 228). In fact it is virtually impossible to reach precision so long as the formation of the tradition is analysed along two different lines which are not really mutually compatible. I am convinced that Dodd is right in his two main speculative contentions, that the miracle derives from extraneous folk-lore, and that the saying of the steward in verse 10 is a relic of an authentic parable of Jesus. But he spoils his case by introducing the topic of the historicization of a parable. For the only *event* in the pericope is the miracle of the wine. To suggest that there has been historicization implies that the parable included this element, which has been turned into an event. But it is precisely this element which is to be regarded as an accretion from folk-lore. Consequently Dodd's reconstruction really contains two alternative explanations of the same motif. It has to be assumed that the tradition began as a parable of Jesus about a wedding-feast. This was later reshaped as a story about Jesus' presence at a wedding. Finally the incident was turned into a wonder-story by the inclusion of the pagan motif of changing water into wine.

---

[1] *Historical Tradition in the Fourth Gospel* (1963), pp. 224 f. All other references to the work of Dodd are taken from this book.

The difficulty with this reconstruction is that it is impossible to see what was the motive of the story in its two earlier stages, whether as a parable or as an event in the life of Jesus. There must have been some happening which has been replaced by the miracle of water into wine. Thus the original reason for the delighted approbation of the steward in verse 10 is completely lost. But is there really any need to postulate such a happening? Is it not sufficient to assume that the miracle-story, already applied to Jesus, has been fused with the parable? In this case there has been no prior historicization of the parable at all. It simply becomes part of the story in the process of fusion with the miracle.

If the Marriage at Cana is analysed in this way, there are only two elements to deal with, and both are preserved almost intact in the resulting whole. The first element is the miracle-story. This, it is assumed, was derived from pagan folk-lore, but was taken to be a genuine tradition of the early life of Jesus, and was retold from this point of view. This story is contained in verses 1–8, describing how Jesus miraculously produced a supply of wine at a wedding-feast. The story could have ended at verse 8, for nothing further needs to be said. On the other hand it is intrinsically probable that there was some form of conclusion expressing the wonder of the assembled company at what Jesus had done (see further below). The second element is the parable, derived from traditions of the words of Jesus. There is no compelling reason to suppose that this ever consisted of anything more than is actually preserved in the concluding words of verse 9 and the whole of verse 10, except that it must have had a brief narrative opening. This could either have been 'A certain man made a marriage-feast. . . ', as Dodd suggests, or else have taken such a form as 'The kingdom of God is like a marriage-feast. . .'. In either case it continues: '. . . and the steward called the bridegroom and said to him, "Every man serves the good wine first; and when men have well drunk, then the poor wine; but you have kept the good wine until now."'

Before we proceed to analyse these two elements in greater detail, something must be said about the rest of verse 9, by which the fusion has been effected. The steward has not figured earlier in the story. But he is brought in at this point, more or less as an afterthought, in order to give confirmation to the miracle. For he 'did not know where it [the water now become wine] came from', so that his testimony is unimpeachable. Thus the possibility that the transformation did not really work is excluded. On the contrary, the wine which has been produced by Jesus is actually better than the wine originally purchased for the feast. It may here be observed that the idea of the marriage-feast and the bridegroom, which has been postulated for the opening of the parable above, may be part of the linking of the two elements by means of verse 9, so that the parable need not originally have presupposed the setting of a wedding at all.

If this is so, then there really is very little relation between the miracle-story and the parable at all. The point of connection is confined to the wine. We may then well ask how it is that the fusion of the two pieces ever happened. The answer to this question is best left until the parable has been analysed. For this purpose it is desirable to emphasize the difference between the miracle and the parable, a difference which has left a certain tension, in spite of the care with which the two pieces have been fused. For the parable is concerned with the superiority of the new wine over the old. On the other hand the miracle does not require any reference to degrees of quality of the wine. It is only concerned with the miraculous way in which a deficiency was made good. There is no reason why the wine produced from the water-jars should be regarded as any better than the wine which was all spent. The whole point is the transformation of water into wine by the creative word of Jesus. This does not necessarily entail any symbolism, the water for purification representing the old order of Judaism, the wine representing the new order which comes with Jesus. That may be present to John's mind as he uses this material in his gospel, but it is not an essential feature of the underlying tale. Rather the motive of the story is nothing else than the display of Jesus' miraculous power. That Jesus should be regarded as a wonder-worker is all that is required to explain the application to him of this pagan tradition in circles where genuine traditions and extraneous items of folk-lore are not clearly distinguished. The application of this story to Jesus as a wonder-worker follows a distinct pattern, as will be shown later.

The parable, on the other hand, requires no miraculous element. It rests on an observation from life. It makes its point very effectively by reversing what is normally expected in the circumstances. It is a mistake to suppose that the reference here is to fixed wedding customs. Windisch[1] asserted that the normal practice was to reserve the best wine until a fairly late stage in the festivities, contrary to what is implied here. But, as has been observed above, we cannot be sure that the original parable actually referred to a wedding. The setting for the words in verse 10 could be any social occasion at which wine was drunk. Luke v. 39 is equally vague. Jesus seems to be referring to the shrewd habits of the poorer people among whom he lived and worked. It is perfectly natural to put the guests in a good humour first, by giving them wine of good quality, and then to make do with cheaper wine at a time when they are likely to be less critical.

The application of the parable is easy to see. It forms one of a group of sayings of Jesus which are concerned with the novelty of the Kingdom. Some of his hearers are sceptical. They cannot easily change their habits and their outlook at the bidding of a young enthusiast. The parable of New Wine in Old Wineskins (Mark ii. 22) is designed to show that the break with the past is inevitable; the old ways cannot accommodate the new order which is now beginning. Luke v. 39 adds to this saying another, which is obviously

---

[1] 'Die johanneische Weinregel, Joh. 2. 10', *Z.N.W.* XIV (1913), 248–57.

closely related to our present parable: 'No one after drinking old wine desires new; for he says, "The old is better."' Both these sayings are proverbial in type, and could be applied to many situations. Our parable in John, however, reverses the general truth, and thereby applies to something special. When a man actually tastes the new wine which Jesus gives, he discovers that, on the contrary, it is better than the old. Hence John ii. 10 is not to be taken as a proverbial saying dressed up as a parable. It needs some sort of setting like the final words of verse 9, and the second-person address at the conclusion of verse 10 is to be retained as original.

The application of the parable to the new order inaugurated by Jesus is obvious enough to us, in the light of modern study of the primitive tradition. But it cannot be assumed that it would be obvious in the oral stage of transmission, when it circulated as an isolated parable without a fixed context. It is at this point that we can see how it came to be fused with the miracle-story. For an unreflective listener would presuppose that something must have happened to make the later wine better; in other words, that the good wine is the result of a transformation. But then (it seems) there actually existed a tradition of Jesus transforming wine. The case was not really parallel, for water becoming wine is not the same as poor wine being replaced by better. But the similarity is close enough to suggest that the two pieces belong together, so that the one may be used as a comment on the other.

The fusion of the two pieces presupposes that the miracle-story has already come into being as a tradition about Jesus, even though it is derived from extraneous sources and is not related to any actual episode in his life. This study would not be complete if we did not attempt to analyse this other tradition as well. It will then be possible to form some idea of how it came to be incorporated in the Fourth Gospel.

Before we can proceed, it is necessary to remove the Johannine editing from the story. Dodd points to the following phrases as characteristic of John's pen: οὔπω ἥκει ἡ ὥρα μου (verse 4), κατὰ τὸν καθαρισμὸν τῶν Ἰουδαίων (verse 6), ἀρχὴν τῶν σημείων and ἐφανέρωσεν τὴν δόξαν αὐτοῦ (verse 11). This final verse, of course, is not part of the original story, though it probably has a basis in John's source. I suggest that the original form of this verse was much closer to that of iv. 54, using πρῶτον σημεῖον and omitting the whole of the latter part of the verse from καὶ ἐφανέρωσεν onwards.

But it would be a mistake to leave out of account verse 12. This also had a basis in John's source, and perhaps originally provided the lead-in for the Second Sign, now incorporated in John iv. 46–54. But it gives valuable assistance for the recovery of the underlying story because of the mention of the family of Jesus. Jesus 'went down' from Cana in the hills to Capernaum by the lake 'with his mother and his brothers'. The following words (καὶ οἱ μαθηταὶ αὐτοῦ) are not to be regarded as part of the true text. They are missing from א it and misplaced in W, and are clearly an interpolation to bring the verse into linewith verse 2. But then it becomes probable, on the basis of this verse, that μαθηταί in verse 2 is a Johannine change for ἀδελφοί in the original. The placing of the story immediately after the call of the first disciples in i. 35–51 is quite sufficient to account for this change. There was not the same need to make the same alteration in verse 12.

It thus seems likely that the story made no mention of the disciples, but did include Jesus' brothers. It then follows that the story does not belong to the traditions of Jesus' ministry at all. Rather it is a tradition of the early life of Jesus, before his baptism by John and the beginning of his public ministry. It could indeed be placed much earlier, even in his childhood. There is nothing in the story to suggest that Jesus is an adult. We could really put it at any stage in his life from childhood to early manhood—always remembering that it is not an historical incident, but a story which has been attributed to him after his fame has spread.

From this point of view it is evident at once that the story belongs to a special class of traditions which is very common in folk-lore. For folk-lore loves to find traditions of the childhood of a great man, in which some curious and remarkable action is seen to be prophetic of his future greatness. We do not need to look outside the gospels for a typical example of this in the case of Jesus. The Finding of Jesus in the Temple (Luke ii. 41–51) exactly fulfils this function. In it the child Jesus exhibits greater wisdom than any of the learned teachers who surround him. They are 'amazed at his understanding and his answers'. The explanation has an air of mystery about it, indicating that Jesus is no ordinary child: 'Did you not know that I must be in my Father's house?' At the same time this implies a certain distance between Jesus and his parents, who 'did not understand the saying'. The story not only points forward to Jesus' future greatness, but also contains an element of pathos, as it is clear that Jesus cannot be held by the ties of family life. We find other stories of the same type in some of the apocryphal literature. There is a whole series of them in the *Infancy Gospel of Thomas*.[1] This includes the famous tale of Jesus and the clay birds. Jesus, at the age of five, makes model birds out of clay on the sabbath day. When challenged for his breach of sabbath, he claps his hands and the birds fly off chirping—and, of course, 'the Jews were amazed...'. Other items, such as stories connected with a teacher called Zacchaeus, are evidently later elaborations of the theme of Luke ii. 41–52, which is actually reproduced as the closing episode in the collection. Another story, about the Child Jesus and the Dyer, is preserved in the *Arabic Infancy Gospel* and the Paris manuscript of *Thomas*.[2] This has a theme quite similar to that of the Marriage at Cana. For the child Jesus brings clothes out of a huge cauldron of indigo dye, each one miraculously

[1] *New Testament Apocrypha*, edited by E. Hennecke, W. Schneemelcher and R. M. Wilson, i (1963), 388–400.
[2] *Ibid.* pp. 400 f.

dyed the colour which the customers wanted. Again the pericope concludes with expressions of amazement.

The present story fits well into the same pattern. It is comparable to the Lukan story in its restraint, and also in the feature of tension between Jesus and his mother. But it sides with the later traditions of *Thomas* in being concerned with a nature-miracle, which has no moral or didactic purpose, but is simply a cause of wonder and a promise of the great things that are to be. The addition of the Parable of the Good Wine is a subsequent elaboration, which is primarily aimed at emphasizing the element of the miraculous. It would seem that it has been edited in a collection containing further miracles, including that of John iv. 46–54. But this need not have been the major Signs Source postulated by Bultmann and other critics. It did not necessarily include all the material which John has derived from earlier tradition. But that the fusion of the miracle-story and the parable had already taken place in a written document, which John has used as the basis of ii. 1–12, is the most likely explanation of the text.

2. THE PARABLE OF THE BEST MAN (JOHN iii. 29)

The second parable occurs in a little paragraph purporting to be the teaching of John the Baptist in John iii. 25–30. There is nothing new in the isolation of verse 29 as a parable derived from previous tradition. This again has been excellently presented by Dodd.[1] The question which is to be considered here is its provenance. Is it a genuine item of the Baptist's teaching, which has survived along with a few other rare fragments in the traditions concerning the relations between him and Jesus? Or is it really a parable of Jesus, concerned with a different issue, and transferred to the Baptist either in previous tradition or by John himself? Dodd takes the former view, and expounds it as the Baptist's reply to the statement of the people in verse 26, that Jesus 'is baptizing, and all are going to him'. It is then concerned with popular bewilderment at what appears to be a take-over bid on the part of Jesus. And this is more or less what it means in John's own handling of the traditional material.

On the other hand Dodd himself throws out a hint that it might have been a parable of Jesus transferred to the Baptist, or at least that it was found in a collection which did not clearly distinguish between the sayings of Jesus and those of the Baptist (pp. 283, 331). Suspicion that it really derives from Jesus is aroused by its similarity to Mark ii. 18–20:

[18]Now John's disciples and the Pharisees were fasting; and people came and said to him, 'Why do John's disciples and the disciples of the Pharisees fast, but your disciples do not fast?' [19]And Jesus said to them, 'Can the wedding guests fast while

---

[1] *Op. cit.* pp. 279–87.

the bridegroom is with them? As long as they have the bridegroom with them, they cannot fast. [20]The days will come, when the bridegroom is taken away from them, and then they will fast in that day.'

It is clear that the last verse is a later addition, designed to commend the church's practice of fasting. It could be objected that this conflicts with the Master's own teaching. So it has to be emphasized that what he said only applied to the time of the incarnate life. Now that Jesus is withdrawn from earthly life the time of feasting is over, and fasting again becomes appropriate. But it is patently obvious that this expansion of the saying has altered the interpretation. The question and answer of verses 18 ff. are concerned with an important difference between the practice of Jesus and that of other pious Jews of the time. These include the disciples of the Pharisees, as we might expect. It is more significant that the Baptist's disciples are mentioned. It might be argued that we have here a reflection of later rivalry between the church and the Baptist sect. But the evidence for such rivalry is very insecure.[1] It is, then, difficult to resist the conclusion that there was a real difference of practice in the matter of fasting between Jesus and the Baptist. In fact there is independent evidence of this in the Q passage, Matt. xi. 16–19 = Luke vii. 31–5. The reason for Jesus' laxity can scarcely be carelessness. It is altogether probable that it was a deliberate policy on his part, so as to make himself accessible to the outcasts of Jewish society. It is thus no accident that the question of fasting comes straight after a short passage about eating with tax-collectors and sinners (Mark ii. 15–17). For the two themes are very closely related. The parable in Mark ii. 19 is a defence of this practice. Jesus maintains that the present time, the time in which he preaches the good news of the Kingdom to the poor, is too full of gladness for fasting. It is comparable to a wedding-feast. If we may be allowed to allegorize the details, the guests would seem to be the disciples of Jesus, who have been referred to in the question of verse 18. The bride, who is not actually mentioned, is presumably the people in general, to whom the message of Jesus is addressed. At one level Jesus is himself the bridegroom. But at a deeper level the bridegroom is God, for whose kingdom Jesus seeks to win the outcast. For in biblical tradition Israel is God's bride (Isa. lxii. 4 f.; Hos. ii. 16). In fact the whole point of using a parable, rather than giving a direct answer, is to make a reply which has deeper implications than appear on the surface. Thus Jesus delicately indicates the real meaning of his apparently lax practice without in any way spoiling the cordial relationship which he seems to have had with the Baptist.

Returning to John iii. 29, we can see another facet of precisely the same issue in the Parable of the Best Man. Unlike the parable in ii. 10, this is a proverbial type of saying in the third person, comparable to the sayings

---

[1] Cf. J. A. T. Robinson, *Twelve New Testament Studies* (*Studies in Biblical Theology*, xxxiv) (1962), p. 49 n. 49.

collected in Mark ii. 18–22. The traditional material consists only of the following words: 'He who has the bride is the bridegroom: the friend of the bridegroom, who stands and hears him, rejoices greatly at the bridegroom's voice.' The remainder of the verse and verse 30 are to be excluded as part of John's editorial work.[1] It is not a foregone conclusion that the best man is to be identified with the Baptist. The emphatic χαρᾷ χαίρει[2] indicates that the point of the parable is to be found in these words. The best man is glad when he hears the bridegroom speak. It is clear that this refers to the actual wedding ceremony, when the bridegroom takes the bride and makes his vow. The rejoicing of the best man is not simply a matter of participation in the general festivity of the occasion, but is his pleasure at the moment when the bridegroom solemnly takes the bride to himself. The emphasis suggests by contrast that at such a moment it would be unthinkable for the best man to bear any grudge or ill will at what is done.

If this is a parable of Jesus, it can be interpreted along precisely the same lines as Mark ii. 19. The success of Jesus in winning the outcasts for the Kingdom is like a wedding. It means, at the deeper level of interpretation, that God himself gains his bride. This suggests that the best man is to be identified with the critics of Jesus. So far from grudging him his success, they should be the first to rejoice at it. Jesus does not regard them as his opponents. On the contrary, by casting them in the role of the best man, he puts himself alongside them too. He does not dissociate himself from them. They have his approval in so far as they are genuine spiritual guides. He hopes to win their support by showing that his own aims are not really far removed from their own. The parable is then an appeal to the critics to have the generosity to see beyond their criticisms and to share in the joy which he experiences in winning the outcasts for the Kingdom of God. For indeed this is precisely what they themselves most want, if only they could overcome their inhibitions. Thus the use of a parable not only allows two levels of interpretation, such as we found in Mark ii. 19, but also constitutes an appeal to the critics in such a way as to avoid any suggestion of hostility towards them.

[1] The phrase αὕτη οὖν ἡ χαρὰ ἡ ἐμὴ πεπλήρωται is typical of John, cf. xv. 11 ; xvi. 24. Verse 30 could be derived from a previous tradition, as the verbs are not used elsewhere by John. But it cannot have been part of the parable, as it makes use of the first person. Thus I cannot agree with the attempt of M. Black (*An Aramaic Approach to the Gospels and Acts* ([3]1967), p. 147) to weld these verses together as a whole from an Aramaic source, though the resulting paronomasia (kallᵉtha–νύμφη, qala–φωνή, qᵉlal–ἐλαττοῦσθαι, and kᵉlal–πεπλήρωται) is attractive. His transposition of verse 30 to precede the final words of 29 is a further count against it.

[2] The dative of the verbal noun, used in conjunction with the cognate verb, frequently represents the Hebrew infinitive absolute construction in both LXX and NT, cf. Blass–Debrunner–Funk, *A Greek Grammar of the New Testament and other Early Christian Literature* (1961), § 198 (6). This suggests that the original of the parable was in Hebrew rather than Aramaic. In his Aramaic reconstruction Black makes no attempt to translate this phrase. The Syriac versions insert an adjective to avoid the difficulty (ḥaduṯa' rabᵉta' haḏe'). The use of the infinitive absolute construction is not considered by J. A. Emerton in his article 'Did Jesus speak Hebrew?', *J.T.S.* n.s. XII (1961), 189–202. But it does seem to point to the conclusion that some of the sayings of Jesus were transmitted either in Hebrew or in an Aramaized Hebrew (cf. Luke xxii. 15).

The parable cannot have stood alone. It must have some setting in which the critics are identified, and in which the substance of their criticism is made plain. We can guess from the Markan passages that the objection was Jesus' willingness to consort with the tax-collectors and sinners. The most obvious reason for this objection is the fact that these classes were notoriously lacking in strictness over the maintenance of ceremonial purity. Jesus risks rendering himself unclean by using crockery which may have been in contact with a menstruous woman, etc.[1] The objectors to such laxity could well be the Pharisees. But, as we have seen in Mark ii. 18, they could also be the disciples of the Baptist. It seems possible, then, that the best man might be the Baptist after all, though the issue is very different from what John has made of it in his use of this material. Jesus knows that the Baptist's strictness is a barrier to the cause they both have at heart.

By this reasoning we can look afresh at the context of the parable, and see if any relic of the original setting of it survives in John's composition. It is clear enough that the whole of verses 26–8 is John's own work, composed almost entirely of phrases which he has himself used elsewhere.[2] This leaves only the enigmatic verse 25: 'Now a discussion arose between John's disciples and Jesus[3] over purifying.' The use of καθαρισμός is surprising. In view of the information in iii. 23 and the ensuing discussion in verse 26, we should expect John to use βάπτισμα. The idea of καθαρισμός can include baptism, of course, and so the expression can be allowed. But it is sufficiently curious for Dodd to regard this verse as 'an entirely detached statement', which is 'the remnant of an introduction to a dialogue which has not been preserved' (p. 280). But if the meaning of the parable is to be explained along the lines which have been argued above, there is every reason to suppose that it is the introduction to the question which this parable answers. It corresponds with the introductory information that 'John's disciples and the Pharisees were fasting' in Mark ii. 18a. What is still missing is the question which they ask, corresponding with Mark ii. 18b. This has been lost in the Johannine adaptation embodied in verse 26.[4] But the missing question can be deduced from καθαρισμός in verse 25. This word is only used by John

---

[1] Cf. *Tohoroth*, the sixth division of the Mishnah, and Appendix IV to Danby's translation, pp. 800–4.

[2] Thus πέραν τοῦ Ἰορδάνου is from i. 28 and μεμαρτύρηκας is from i. 34, deliberately referring back to these verses; βαπτίζει is a reference to iii. 22; ἔρχεσθαι πρὸς αὐτόν is used of Jesus himself undergoing John's baptism in i. 29; verse 27 embodies a cardinal point of Johannine theology, with close verbal parallels in vi. 65 and xix. 11; in verse 28 αὐτοὶ ὑμεῖς μοι μαρτυρεῖτε refers to ἡ μαρτυρία τοῦ Ἰωάννου in i. 19; οὐκ εἰμὶ ἐγὼ ὁ χριστός is from i. 20; ἀπεσταλμένος εἰμὶ ἔμπροσθεν ἐκείνου alludes to i. 15, 27, 30, but interestingly preserves more nearly the *testimonium* (Mal. iii. 1 combined with Exod. xxiii. 20, cf. Matt. xi. 10 par.) than any of these verses.

[3] Reading Ἰησοῦ (Bentley) or τοῦ Ἰησοῦ (Baldensperger) for the impossible Ἰουδαίου of the majority of texts. The plural Ἰουδαίων, read by 𝔓⁶⁶ ℵ* G Θ λ φ syr^cur and some Latin and Bohairic texts, is an attempt to ease the sense, but does little to solve the difficulties of interpretation. The error may be due to contamination from καθαρισμὸν τῶν Ἰουδαίων in ii. 6 at a very early stage of transmission.

[4] The opening may be preserved in καὶ ἦλθον... καὶ εἶπαν αὐτῷ· ῥαββί. As it stands, the title is surprising in addressing the Baptist (but cf. Luke ii. 12). It is much more likely to be a relic of address to Jesus.

elsewhere at ii. 6, where it refers to the cleansing of vessels for food. In Luke ii. 22 it refers to the period of purification after childbirth. It is used along with the cognate verb καθαρίζω in connection with clearance from leprosy in Mark i. 40–4 par. The verb is employed in connection with vessels for food in Mat. xxiii. 25 f. = Luke xi. 39, and with *kosher* meat in Mark vii. 19 (perhaps a gloss) and Acts x. 15; xi. 9. There can be little doubt that the question is to do with Jesus' attitude to the purificatory regulations, particularly those concerned with food. Jesus himself criticized the Pharisees for their extravagant concern with these rules (Matt. xxiii. 25 f.). But he was accused of disregarding the rules and of encouraging his disciples to do so (Mark vii. 5). This accusation gives the opening for the long tirade on this issue in Mark vii. 6–23. But it could almost equally be the missing question required between John iii. 25 and 29, except that it would have to make the point that it is through his association with tax-collectors and sinners that Jesus lays himself open to the charge of laxity. But we have an example of precisely this kind of charge in the Lukan anointing story (Luke vii. 39).

It may thus be suggested with some degree of probability that John iii. 25 and 29 preserve part of the introduction and the whole of the parable in a Jesus-tradition comparable to Mark ii. 18 f. The issue at stake was another point of dispute between Jesus and the Baptist, that of the risk of ceremonial contamination involved in his policy of close association with the outcasts. The parable defends this practice on the grounds that it is the work of God himself, and at the same time makes a delicate and tactful appeal for a generous understanding on the part of the Baptist and his followers.

There is no reason to suppose that the tradition had undergone any further alteration before John used it for the present context. The situation which he wishes to describe has enough general similarity to make it usable for his purpose. For the parable concerns the success of Jesus, and seeks to associate the Baptist and his disciples with his pleasure at it. According to John's understanding of the gospel traditions, the Baptist could have no other reaction on hearing of Jesus' success. The main point of the parable fits well into his presentation of the Baptist as the self-effacing witness to Christ. It describes the joy of the best man, and this is just what the Baptist feels as he hears of the progress of Jesus' mission. John could give the parable this fresh and more general application by taking καθαρισμός to refer to Christian baptism, contrary to normal New Testament usage. As the parable is a proverbial saying in the third person, it could easily be placed on the Baptist's lips without any distortion of its meaning. It was not completely suitable, because the joy of the best man at hearing the bridegroom make his vows to the bride is not quite the same thing as an unselfish acceptance of the fact that 'he must increase, but I must decrease' (verse 30, which John has added precisely because the parable only imperfectly illustrates the point he is making).

The only grave objection to this reconstruction is the need to postulate transference of a saying of Jesus to the Baptist. Is this really something which is likely to have happened? The answer, surprisingly enough, is yes. For there is another place where John has done precisely the same thing. John vii. 4 incorporates the saying 'No man works in secret if he seeks to be known openly'. It can scarcely be doubted that this is a variant of dominical sayings preserved in Mark iv. 22 = Luke viii. 17 and Matt. x. 26 = Luke xii. 2. But John has placed it on the lips of Jesus' brothers, who use it as a taunt against him. We may also compare John vi. 34, where 'Give us this bread always' is spoken by the Jews, but is almost certainly an adaptation of the Lord's Prayer. The objection, then, is not insuperable, and the suggestion argued in this paper that John iii. 29 is really a parable of Jesus, though not capable of complete demonstration, is at least worthy of serious consideration.

3

ΔΙΚΑΙΟΣΥΝΗ IN Jn 16.8 AND 10

I

Δικαιοσύνη occurs only twice in the Fourth Gospel, and as the second occasion (Jn 16.10) is resumptive of the first (verse 8), the usage can be said to be confined to a single phrase. This is remarkable, not only because of the importance of δικαιοσύνη elsewhere in the New Testament, but also because John tends to be repetitive. His vocabulary is so limited that, if he uses a significant word once, he is likely to use it again many times. It is because this word is an exception in John that the major studies of δικαιοσύνη in the New Testament pass it over very lightly [1], or do not mention it at all [2]. One cannot deduce from it a specific Johannine tendency to compare with that of Matthew, or Paul, or the writer to the Hebrews.

But its very rarity in John suggests that there is something special about it. The absence of it from the rest of the gospel is remarkable in itself. Its presence in this one context demands all the more careful explanation. Why did the author feel it to be necessary for this particular context ? Could he have expressed his meaning by using some other word, one more central to his vocabulary ? How, indeed, are the meanings of δικαιοσύνη usually expressed in the Fourth Gospel ? It is not as if the passage in which it occurs differed so much from the rest of the gospel that it would inevitably require a special range of vocabulary. Every phrase is thoroughly characteristic of the writer.

In fact the absence of δικαιοσύνη elsewhere in the gospel is the more surprising in the light of the Semitic influence which is now generally recognised in Johannine study. John has much in common with the thought and vocabulary of the Dead Sea Scrolls, notably with regard to the themes of light and darkness. But ideas of sin and righteousness are also important in the Qumran literature. צדקה/צדק is a prominent word in the Sectarian

---

[1] G. SCHRENK, in TWNT, s.v. δικαιοσύνη.

[2] D. HILL, *Greek Words and Hebrew Meanings : Studies in the Semantics of Soteriological Terms*, Cambridge, 1967, 82-162.

writings. It not only denotes that which is correct or legitimate [1],
but also the status of man before God which is the object of the
Sectarians' endeavours (in this sense usually צדקה). The Thanksgiving Hymns have a definite idea of justification, of imputed
righteousness, and even of sanctification, which fully takes into
account the inadequacy of human efforts to attain righteousness
in the sight of God [2]. It has even been claimed that these passages
are the root of Paul's thought in Rom 3.21-26 [3]. It can hardly
be said that John is uninterested in the problem of justification.
But the word δικαιοσύνη is not a normal component of his thought.

II

The use of δικαιοσύνη in the New Testament can be roughly
classified under three headings. (a) There is the usual moral
sense of *uprightness of life*, expressed in behaviour that is acceptable
to God. For the Jews this meant fidelity to the Law, for
the Christians obedience to the will of God, which may include
the Law, but also rises above it and corrects it and supersedes it.
This is the normal usage in Matthew, and is frequent also in Paul.
(b) Especially in Paul, there is the sense of *justification*, man's
status before God, the verdict at the divine tribunal. Paul's greatest
concern is to show that this verdict has already been given in
the death and resurrection of Jesus. (c) Finally there is *the righteousness of God* [4], a special application of the first sense, which is
expressed in God's fidelity to his promises, and so is applied to
his saving acts. This usage has its origins in the Old Testament,
notably in Deutero-Isaiah, where צדק is sometimes virtually
equivalent to " salvation " [5]. In the New Testament the death
and resurrection of Jesus are the culmination of the δικαιοσύνη
θεοῦ in this sense.

How does John express these concepts?

(a) Although abstract nouns abound in John, he very rarely
employs them to express human qualities. He much prefers to
express himself more concretely (and indeed more Semitically)

---

[1] This may be the meaning of צדק in the title מורה הצדק, cf. HILL, *op.
cit.*, 111.

[2] 1QH 4.30-37 ; 7.16-19,28-31 ; 1QS 11.10-15.

[3] M. BURROWS, *The Dead Sea Scrolls*, New York, 1955, 334.

[4] Rom 1.17 ; 3.21-26. Other occurrences of the phrase are better classified under
(a) or (b).

[5] Is 45.8 ; 46.13 ; 51.5,6,8 ; 56.1.

by means of verbs. One phrase of this kind is ἀλήθειαν ποιεῖν, but it occurs only once (3.21 ; cf. also 1 Jn 1.6). Nevertheless ἀλήθεια is used on a number of occasions where δικαιοσύνη might have been possible, or even expected (e.g. 1.14,17 ; 4.23f ; 8.32,44 ; 14.6 ; 17.17,19 ; 18.37) ; τὰ ἀγαθὰ ποιεῖν is also found once (5.29 ; opposed to τὰ φαῦλα πράσσειν) ; τὸ θέλημα (sc. τοῦ θεοῦ) ποιεῖν is applied to men in general at 7.17 and 9.31. We may also add to these expressions the metaphorical use of " cleanness " in 13.10f. In particular, the disciples are to " love one another " (13.34f) and to " keep " Jesus' " commandments " (14.15,21) or " words " (8.51 ; 14.23f). These are various facets of behaviour which contribute to the good life, and together would appropriately earn for a man the description δίκαιος. This word, however, is not used to describe character, except perhaps in Jesus' address to God himself (17.25). The adjective δίκαιος is applied to God in 1 Jn 1.9, and to Jesus in 1 Jn 2.29 ; 3.7. Moreover in this epistle the phrase δικαιοσύνην ποιεῖν occurs three times (2.29 ; 3.7,10). The meaning is virtually identical with ἀλήθειαν ποιεῖν, referring to the whole range of a man's activity, which should show consistently the qualities of truthfulness and uprightness (cf. Tob 4.5-7, where both expressions occur together). John might easily have used δικαιοσύνην ποιεῖν in this way in his gospel, for it would have been true to his style and outlook. But in fact he has not done so.

(b) The clearest statement of the idea of justification in the Fourth Gospel [1] is 5.24 : " He who hears my word and believes him who sent me, has eternal life ; he does not come into judgment, but has passed from death to life ". Here " life ", or " eternal life ", denotes the condition of man before God. It is reward-language rather than status-language, but this distinction should not be pressed in view of 3.36, where " the wrath of God rests upon him " is parallel to " he ... shall not see life " (cf. 1 Jn 3.14f ; 5.11-13). The use of " life " here resembles the thought of Ezekiel (e.g. Ez 18.9,21-23,32). In fact it is this word more than any other which corresponds with the Pauline δικαιοσύνη. It is a larger concept, of course, but the full reward which it denotes includes the idea of fellowship with God and acceptance by him, so that it is possible to speak of those who attain this position as God's " children " (1.12). As in Paul, so also in John, the status of justification before God is acquired through faith in Christ. This is because of the key position of Jesus as the agent of redemption — here

---

[1] Cf. T. Preiss, *La Vie en Christ*, Neuchâtel-Paris, 1951, 46-64 : La justification dans la pensée johannique.

(in 5.24) indicated by the reference to the incarnation in the word " sent ", elsewhere connected with his death and resurrection (e.g. 6.53-58 ; 10.10-18 ; 11.50 ; 14.19). As a result of this decisive act, the judgment (which to the Jews was a future, eschatological event) has already taken place (12.21 ; 16.11), so that the transition " from death to life " has already been effected in the believer. Here are the essential points of the great Pauline exposition of justification in Romans. Nowhere does John use δικαιοσύνη in any of the relevant passages — except one, the passage under discussion. And the language of 16.8-11 is so close to that of the key passages under this heading that it must at least be seriously considered whether δικαιοσύνη in verses 8 and 10 actually means " justification " in the Pauline sense [1].

(c) The righteousness of God is expressed in John, as we should expect, in terms of his will and deeds, rather than by words denoting quality. The classic passage is 3.16 : " God so loved the world that he gave... " Similarly 6.39f : " This is the will of him who sent me... " The problem of theodicy appears in 9.3 (" that the works of God might be made manifest in him ") and in 11.4 (" it is for the glory of God, so that the Son of God may be glorified by means of it "). The love of the Father for the Son is often emphasised in contexts which deal with Jesus' own functions as the agent of salvation (e.g. 3.35 ; 5.20 ; 10.17 ; 15.9f). This is the basis of the entire prayer of chapter 17. It is probable, therefore, that πατὴρ δίκαιε in 17.25 belongs to this category, rather than to (a). If Jn 16.10 is taken to refer to the righteousness of God, declared in the death and resurrection of Jesus, then it is these passages of the love and the will of God which stand closest to it in the rest of the gospel.

We thus have the ideas associated with δικαιοσύνη woven into the fabric of the Fourth Gospel, but transposed into John's own special vocabulary and adapted to his unique ideological structure. The word, as it appears in 16.8,10, could be classified under any of the three categories. All three have their champions in the commentaries. The older commentators of the modern period tended to prefer (a) [2]. According to this view the departure of Jesus (i.e. his death and resurrection) revealed for the first time the true nature of righteousness, so correcting the false ideas

[1] J. BLANK, Krisis, Freiburg im Br., 1964, 336, utters a warning (perhaps with Bultmann in mind) against « eine gewisse Gefahr, die sich in den Kommentaren zeigt, dass man es auch hier unter paulinischem Aspekt interpretiert ».
[2] WESTCOTT, BERNARD, R.H. LIGHTFOOT ; SCHRENK, art. cit.

of the world. But more recently the third view (c) has gained ground considerably [1]. In this case the world is brought to see that God has fulfilled his promises in the departure of Jesus, so that it is convicted of having opposed the righteousness of God, and is accordingly condemned. When the sense of justification (b) is brought into the discussion, it is usually combined with (c) : The victory of Christ is the vindication of the one whom the world has condemned, so that the world now finds itself self-condemned [2].

III

The above interpretations have one point in common, that δικαιοσύνη is not applied to the world as such. Righteousness is entirely on the side of Jesus and God. The world is convicted on three counts, sin, righteousness and judgment — or, rather, the world is convicted of sin, and this fact is pressed home by consideration of two further factors, righteousness and judgment [3]. It must be admitted that they are an odd trio. 'Αμαρτία and κρίσις apply to the world, as the ὅτι clauses of verses 9 and 11 make clear. It is the world that has sinned, and it is the ruler of the world who has been judged. But δικαιοσύνη is an intruder, and it is concerned with what is just about to happen to Jesus. A first reading of verse 8 — καὶ ἐλθὼν ἐκεῖνος ἐλέγξει τὸν κόσμον περὶ ἁμαρτίας καὶ περὶ δικαιοσύνης καὶ περὶ κρίσεως — would suggest that all three nouns are related to ἐλέγξει τὸν κόσμον in the same way, that the work of the Paraclete is concerned with the world's sin and the world's righteousness and the world's judgment. It is only when we reach verse 10 that we get into difficulties. But if this verse can be explained satisfactorily, there is at least a *prima facie* case for applying δικαιοσύνη to the world. In making this proposal I am aware that it will entail a way of understanding ἐλέγχειν περί which some may regard as dubious at best, if not actually impossible. But in view of the fact that the phrases here have no precise parallel elsewhere, and that the resulting interpretation falls into line with some of the key passages of the gospel, it is at least worthy of consideration before being rejected out of hand.

---

[1] HOSKYNS, BULTMANN, BARRETT, STRATHMANN, MARSH, BLANK.

[2] BULTMANN, BLANK.

[3] According to Bultmann's source criticism, the original saying consisted only of verses 8a, 9, and verses 8b, 10-11 are the work of the later editor. But this scarcely solves the problem, for the editor must have thought of his expanded form as an intelligible whole. He has hardly completed the original in the most natural way.

In the first place, the Paraclete " will convict the world of sin ". This at least has an exact parallel at 8.46 : " Which of you convicts me of sin ? " [1] The original meaning of ἐλέγχειν in classical Greek was " to scorn ", but it then came to mean " to expose as evil ", and finally " to expose " in general. In the Septuagint it frequently means " to reprove ". When the meaning " to convict of " is required, περί is the usual construction to specify the fault (e.g. Lk 3.19). But we should not forget that this is literally " to expose someone with regard to his fault ". Jn 8.46 is thus really " Which of you exposes me with regard to sin ? " It is natural to take ἁμαρτία here to be actual sin, just as the devil in the same context is accused of telling lies (8.44). But the meaning of ἁμαρτία in the Fourth Gospel oscillates between " actual sin " and " guilt " (cf. 9.41). As the fault is not specified, the emphasis falls on the verb, and the notion of guilt is at least implicit. It is, then, possible to translate the verse " Which of you exposes me with regard to guilt ? ", i.e. " for the verdict of guilty ".

Accordingly we may translate Jn 16.8 " He will expose the world for the verdict of guilty ", and the ὅτι clause of verse 9 will be causal : " because they do not believe in me " [2]. This interpretation fits in well with the primarily forensic function of the Paraclete [3]. It now becomes clear that a similar forensic interpretation can be given to περὶ δικαιοσύνης : " He will expose the world for the verdict of innocent ". It is the well known juridical use of δίκαιος and its cognates, found in the Septuagint, and derived from the idiomatic use of צדיק in the Hebrew [4]. But of course this involves a slight change in the meaning of ἐλέγχειν. It has lost its pejorative sense, and gained the notion of approval. But in fact ἐλέγχειν is so broad in its range of meanings [5] that it can

---

[1] Barrett regards this parallel as decisive against the rendering " He will convict the world (of its error) in regard to sin ".

[2] If verse 9 stood alone, it would be natural to take ὅτι as explicative of ἁμαρτίας (= " that "). So Büchsel, in TWNT s.v. ἐλέγχω, says " to take ὅτι causally is artificial ". But this cannot be sustained in verses 10 and 11, so that nearly all commentators take it causally in all three verses.

[3] For discussion of παράκλητος as a forensic term, cf. Blank, Krisis, 317ff.

[4] For references, cf. Bultmann (KommNT Meyer), 434, note 7.

[5] For the classical usage, cf. Büchsel, art. cit. In the LXX ἐλέγχω regularly represents הוכיח, which has the same kind of oscillation between " condemn " and " prove " in general, though the latter meaning is much less frequent. It certainly means " give a favourable verdict " in Is 11.4 : καὶ ἐλέγξει τοὺς ταπεινοὺς τῆς γῆς (והוכיח במישור לענוי־ארץ). There is also a case of ,, decide one way or the other " in Gen. 31.37 : καὶ ἐλεγξάτωσαν ἀνὰ μέσον τῶν δύο ἡμῶν (יוכיחו בין שנינו). As the LXX elsewhere uses other words for הוכיח (e.g. Gen 24.14,44 ἑτοιμάζω), it must be assumed that the neutral meaning of

be taken as neutral here, requiring the additional words with περί to specify the nuance (cf. below on 3.20).

The ὅτι clause of verse 10 gives the grounds on which this favourable verdict can be given. It is because " I go to the Father, and you will see me no more ". It is not, then, on the grounds of anything which the world has done, though it must be understood that the world is here regarded as believing in Jesus, for otherwise it would come under the condemnation of verse 9. It is on the grounds of an event, Jesus' departure, i.e. his death and resurrection, the event (still in the immediate future from the standpoint of the Supper Discourses) which the disciples find it so hard to understand. Why this event should constitute the justification of the believer is not explained at present, but it will become clearer in verse 11. Along the line of interpretation here proposed, the sense of δικαιοσύνη is very close to the Pauline idea of justification. Those in the world who believe will be shown to be in the right before God, because the decisive event has already taken place in the death and resurrection of Jesus.

According to this interpretation ἁμαρτία and δικαιοσύνη are exact opposites, the negative and the affirmative possibilities respectively. There seems to be no room for a third alternative. But although κρίσις often has the negative sense of " condemnation ", it is capable of being neutral (like ἐλέγχειν). It can almost mean " the criterion " or " the deciding factor " (cf. below on 3.19). Thus it need not be taken here to denote a third possibility, but can be taken to refer to both the preceding alternatives simultaneously. So " he will expose the world with regard to judgment " means that " he will expose the world for a verdict one way or the other ". He will do this " because the ruler of this world is judged " — *already* judged *(κέκριται)* in the decisive event of Jesus' departure (verse 10). There is no middle course. The effect of the Paraclete upon the world " when he comes " (verse 8, i.e. in the mission of the disciples in the future) will be decisive, precisely because the decisive action has already been taken.

IV

Two passages earlier in the gospel support the interpretation of Jn 16.8-11 which has just been given. These are 3.16-21 and 5.25-29.

ἐλέγχω was not impossible in the Koiné, so that the translation is not a stereotyped rendering, regardless of meaning.

(a) Jn 3.16 is the gospel in miniature. The reason why God's Son was " sent " was so " that whoever believes in him should not perish but have eternal life ". This is the purpose of the incarnation, but it does not stop with the event in which Jesus is the protagonist. It is also the object of the mission of disciples (17.20), for which the guidance of the Paraclete is given (14.16f,25 ; 15.26 ; 16.7-15). It is the positive object of imparting eternal life, but this is expressed negatively as well (" should not perish "). The following verses, 3.17-21, expand this simple statement in a way which corresponds with the triadic structure of 16.8-11. In 3.17 the positive and negative aspects are repeated : God's Son was sent " not to condemn (κρίνη) the world, but that the world might be saved through him ". Structurally this verse corresponds with 16.8, which sets out the possibilities of the Paraclete's work of " exposing " the world. Then follows the explication : first the positive aspect — " he who believes in him is not condemned (οὐ κρίνεται) ", 3.18a, corresponding with 16.10; secondly the negative aspect — " he who does not believe is condemned already (ἤδη κέκριται), because he has not believed in the name of the only Son of God ", 3.18b, corresponding with 16.9 ; thirdly the criterion — " and this is the judgment (κρίσις), that the light has come into the world, and men loved darkness rather than light, because their deeds were evil ", 3.19, corresponding with 16.11. It is to be observed that here, as in 16.11, κρίσις has a neutral sense, though it inclines towards a bad sense because of the emphasis of the latter part of the verse.

So far the passage has revealed the same triadic structure as 16.8-11, but with inversion of the positive and negative aspects. Here, however, the third element (the κρίσις) forms the starting point for a further development. The positive and negative aspects are repeated in 3.20,21, but in the reverse order (as in 16.9,10), so that verses 18a,b and verses 20, 21 are balanced chiastically : " Everyone who does evil hates the light, and does not come to the light, lest his deeds should be exposed (ἐλεγχθῇ). But he who does what is true comes to the light, that it may be clearly seen (φανερωθῇ) that his deeds have been wrought in God (literally, that his deeds may be revealed that they have been wrought in God) ". It is significant that ἐλεγχθῇ and φανερωθῇ are synonymous, and the meaning of both is " expose " [1].

[1] Cf. R. Schnackenburg, Das Johannesevangelium (KommNT Herder), I, 431, note 1.

The whole passage makes much the same point as 16.8-11, using a high proportion of the same vocabulary. Δικαιοσύνη does not appear, but its meaning is expressed negatively in verse 18a (οὐ κρίνεται). Similarly ἁμαρτία is missing, being represented by ἤδη κέκριται in 18b. The good and bad behaviour which corresponds with these verdicts is expressed by ὁ ποιῶν τὴν ἀλήθειαν (21), and by πονηρὰ τὰ ἔργα (19b) and ὁ φαῦλα πράσσων (20). But the verdict is not based on behaviour, but on the response of faith (verse 18). The final verses merely point out that a right response is normally accompanied by good deeds, and a wrong one by evil deeds, because of the ramifications of the opposing forces of light and darkness.

(b) Jn 5.24-29 begins in the same way with a simple statement : " Truly, truly, I say to you, he who hears my word and believes him who sent me, has eternal life ; he does not come into judgment (εἰς κρίσιν), but has passed from death to life ". As in 3.16, the verse is making a positive statement about the salvation of the believer, but the point is stressed by means of the negative aspect of judgment and death. In this case κρίσις is not the criterion but the judicial act itself. In the verses which follow this is specified as the eschatological judgment. But the point is that it does not await a future time, but is already present : " The hour is coming, and now is, when the dead will hear the voice of the Son of God... " (verse 25). The Son's authority to perform this judgment is then explained in verses 26 and 27. It is " because he is the Son of man ". We are dealing, then, in apocalyptic-eschatological categories of thought. So in the next verses the situation is described again in terms of the general resurrection (cf. Dan 12.1-4). The dead will " come forth, those who have done good (οἱ τὰ ἀγαθὰ ποιήσαντες) to the resurrection of life, and those who have done evil (οἱ τὰ φαῦλα πράξαντες) to the resurrection of judgment (κρίσεως, i.e. condemnation) ". Here again, as in the final words of the other passage, it seems as if the criterion is good or bad behaviour, but this impression is only superficial. The content of " to do good " and " to do evil " needs to be specified. But it has already been shown in verse 24 that " he who hears my word and believes him who sent me " is the man who " does good ". It may be assumed that to refuse belief is the content of " to do evil ".

Although this passage does not exhibit a formal similarity to 16.8-11, and so has less value for comparative purposes than 3.16-21, it supports the general lines of the argument. It confirms John's use of forensic ideas. It expresses in Johannine terms the classic Pauline argument that man's final status before God is determined, not by a future act, but by the historic act of God in Christ, which is referred to in two ways in 16.10 and 11. The use of both δικαιοσύνη and ἁμαρτία is avoided, moral quality being expressed by the participial phrases οἱ τὰ ἀγαθὰ ποιήσαντες and οἱ τὰ φαῦλα πράξαντες. On the other hand it is notable that δικαία is used in the very next verse to define Jesus' verdict (ἡ κρίσις ἡ ἐμὴ δικαία ἐστίν, 5.30). Finally, the whole passage is concerned, not only with the coming event in which the judgment will be performed, but also with the permanent condition which will result from it (verse 24). The mission of the disciples as outlined in the Supper Discourses, and in particular the function of the Paraclete who will be with them, is to bring this new situation to bear upon the world after Jesus' withdrawal. Their preaching under the Spirit's guidance will bring men to the point where the judgment actually applies to them.

V

The interpretation of Jn 16.8-11 which has been put forward in this paper allows the possibility that the world may not be condemned but acquitted. In the later chapters of the gospel there is a tendency to regard the world as entirely hostile to Jesus and to the church. This no doubt reflects the actual situation of John's own church, faced with growing opposition on the part of both Jews and Gentiles. But from time to time the author corrects this one-sided emphasis by pointing out that the possibility of salvation always lies open. Otherwise the gospel would deny its own purpose. From the Prologue onwards the salvation of the world has always been a possibility (cf. 1.10-12). Nothing could be more explicit than 3.17 : " For God sent the Son into the world, not to condemn the world, but that the world might be saved through him ". So also in the Supper Discourses the disciples are told how they may " bear much fruit " (15.8,16). Jesus prays " also for those who believe in me through their word " (17.20), and the unity of the disciples is essential " so that the world may believe that thou hast sent me " (17.21,23). So, according to the above interpretation of 16.8-11, the Paraclete will condemn the world in so far as it does not believe ; on the other hand he will acquit it where there is belief ; thus in one way or the other a decision will be made wherever the Spirit is active in the world.

The reason why δικαιοσύνη appears in this one place in the gospel is that here, and only here, it was necessary to use a word which could express the exact opposite of ἁμαρτία in its judicial sense of guilt. None of the ways in which John usually expressed the δικαιοσύνη range of ideas would have been suitable. It is a usage which depends upon Semitic thought-forms, and the resulting phrase ἐλέγχειν περὶ δικαιοσύνης is scarcely good Greek. John could have used δικαιοσύνη in another phrase of Semitic origin, δικαιοσύνην ποιεῖν, as he has done in the First Epistle, but it does not occur in the gospel. In fact John is not interested in purely ethical matters, nor is he concerned to correct the false ideas of the world (according to a common interpretation of 16.8-11). The whole point of his gospel is to bring men to a decision, and this is what he is concerned with in these verses.

In conclusion I give a paraphrase of the passage :

> *For if I do not depart, the Paraclete will not come to you ; but if I go away, I will send him to you.*
> *And when he comes, he will expose the world*
> *so as to give the verdict of guilty,*
> *the verdict of innocent,*
> *the verdict one way or the other ;*
> *the verdict of guilty, because they refuse to believe in me ;*
> *the verdict of innocent, on the grounds of my departure to the Father, so that you see me no longer ;*
> *the verdict one way or the other, because the judgment of the ruler of this world has actually taken place.*

4

THE SON OF MAN
IN THE JOHANNINE CHRISTOLOGY

The perennial debate on the figure of the Son of Man tends to leave the Fourth Gospel on one side. Interest centres on the problem of Jesus and the Son of Man, how far the Synoptic sayings may be accepted as authentic, whether Jesus used the title as a self-designation, and how far he is indebted to a distinct concept of the Son-of-Man figure in contemporary Jewish apocalyptic. For all these questions the Fourth Gospel is dismissed as providing no help.[1] When the Fourth Gospel itself is considered, the questions asked are whether the Son of Man truly belongs to John's christological thought or represents an alien element in the later editing of the gospel;[2] or, if it is conceded that the references come from his hand, whether he is influenced byHellenistic or incipient gnostic speculations.[3]

Attempts have been made to rehabilitate John's use of the Son-of-Man figure by finding a traditional basis in the words of Jesus for all the places where the title occurs.[4] But this scarcely does justice to the Johannine cast of the great majority of the sayings. Nor does it take into account the larger context in each case. The subtle interplay of John's use of different titles within a single context goes largely unrecognised.

[1] Thus H. E. Tödt, *The Son of Man in the Synoptic Tradition* (London, 1965), does not find it necessary to use the evidence of the Fourth Gospel; A. J. B. Higgins, *Jesus and the Son of Man* (London, 1964) thinks that the Johannine sayings are partly derived from earlier tradition, but discounts them for his main purpose; F. H. Borsch, *The Son of Man in Myth and History* (London, 1967), is more positive, in that he sees in them evidence for an early Christian debate which points to the fact that Jesus *did* apply the Son of Man to himself in some sense. For a full survey of work on the Son of Man in John, see E. Ruckstuhl, 'Die johanneische Menschensohnforschung 1957–1969', in *Theologische Berichte* i, ed. J. Pfammatter und F. Furger (Zürich, 1972), pp. 171–284.

[2] Bultmann ascribes the sayings to the Evangelist, or (in the case of 5: 27) to the ecclesiastical redactor.

[3] For the debate on this issue see R. Schnackenburg, 'Der Menschensohn im Johannesevangelium', *NTS* xi (1964–5), pp. 123–37.

[4] The case is well presented by S. S. Smalley, 'The Johannine Son of Man Sayings', *NTS* xv (1968–9), pp. 278–301.

In fact John's variation between 'the Son of God', 'the Son', and 'the Son of man' is never accidental, but is carefully chosen in accordance with the needs of his argument.[5]

It will be argued in this essay that the concept of the Son of Man holds a key place in John's thought. Whatever may be the origin of the designation and the source of his ideas, John makes use of the concept because it provides him with the means to express the relationship of Jesus to God, which is his major concern. His use of it is not simply a kind of local colour, derived from the tradition of the words of Jesus, without much bearing on his real thought. It is essential to his task as a creative thinker, an indispensable element in the constructive christology which is his unique contribution to Christianity. Whether other Son-of-Man christologies existed in the early church is a question which cannot be answered without first taking into account the fact that such a christology exists at least in the Fourth Gospel. This also has a bearing on the problem of the Son-of-Man figure in first century Judaism.

The title first occurs in John 1: 51. Thereafter it occurs in 3: 13, 14; 5: 27; 6: 27, 53, 62; 8: 28; 9: 35; 12: 23, 34 (twice); 13: 31. It thus belongs to the first half of the gospel, in which traditions of the ministry of Jesus are employed for the unfolding of John's christological argument. It never occurs in the passion narrative, except for 13: 31, which picks up the theme of 12: 23 to provide the link between the two halves of the gospel.

Any attempt to analyse the argument of the first twelve chapters inevitably encounters the vexed question of the composition of the book. The question is too large to be treated within the confines of a short study. So I must content myself with briefly summarising what I have written elsewhere on this subject.[6] I hold that the division of the gospel into two major sources, the *Semeia-Quelle* and the *Offenbarungsreden-Quelle*, with the elaborate redactional theory which this entails, is mistaken. Also the case for accidental displacements has not been made out. But the gospel cannot have been written straight off just as it stands, because of the glaring breaks in the continuity and abrupt

---

[5] The argument of E. D. Freed, 'The Son of Man in the Fourth Gospel', *JBL* lxxxvi (1967), that John uses these titles indifferently for stylistic variation, is wholly unconvincing.

[6] *Behind the Fourth Gospel* (London, 1971); *The Gospel of John* (*The Century Bible: Revised Edition*, London, 1972). For a similar theory, see R. E. Brown, *The Gospel according to John* (*The Anchor Bible*, Garden City, N.Y., 1966; London, 1971), vol. i, pp. xxxiv–xxxix.

changes of theme. I believe that John wrote the gospel in two principal stages, making use of a number of shorter pieces which he had composed earlier, possibly as self-contained homilies. The first edition did not include the Prologue (1: 1–18), the Discourse on the Bread of Life (chapter 6), the Raising of Lazarus (11: 1–44), the second Supper Discourse (chapters 15 and 16), and the Prayer of Jesus (chapter 17). All these items were added at the second stage. At the same time some further adjustments were made, the most important being the transference of the Cleansing of the Temple from its original position in chapter 12 to its present position in chapter 2.

One observation can be made at once on the basis of this theory. The Son-of-Man title is confined to material which belongs to the first edition of the gospel, with the notable exception of chapter 6. This is important, because the christological argument of that chapter, and the special use of the Son-of-Man figure within it, interfere with the main argument of the rest of the book. This argument is complete, and stands out more clearly, when attention is confined to the sections which belong to the first edition. On the other hand the argument in chapter 6 presupposes the total argument of the rest and confirms it.

The christological argument of John begins with a series of scenes (1: 19–51), in which the various titles of Jesus are introduced. The reader's interest is engaged at the outset by the questioning of the Baptist, which may be an adaptation of the questioning about Jesus preserved in the Synoptic tradition.[7] Here 'the Christ', 'Elijah', and 'the prophet' are mentioned. Though repudiated by the Baptist, the possibility that they could be applied to Jesus is not excluded. Then the first title actually applied to Jesus is 'the Lamb of God' (1: 29, 36).[8] This introduces a reminiscence of the baptism of Jesus, including a traditional reference to him as one who 'baptizes with Holy Spirit' (1: 33). This in its turns leads to the affirmation that Jesus is 'the Son of God' or 'the Elect of God' (1: 34).[9] Then follow 'the Messiah' (1: 41), the one 'of whom Moses in the law and of whom the prophets wrote' (1: 45), and 'the Son of God ... the king of Israel' (1: 49). All

---

[7] Cf. Mark 6: 14f.; 8: 28f. The Synoptic tradition also contains questioning about the Baptist, cf. Matt. 11: 7–15; Mark 11: 29–32; Luke 3: 15.

[8] The interpretation of this title remains uncertain. For the principal views see R. E. Brown *ad loc.* In any case it plays no further part in John's argument.

[9] Read probably ὁ ἐκλεκτός with 𝔓⁵ ℵ* e ff² syˢᶜ sa, as the harder reading. Then ὁ υἱὸς τοῦ θεοῦ is reserved until the climax of the sequence at verse 49.

these titles have been spoken by others. Finally Jesus himself promises a sight more compelling than any that has evoked the preceding confessions of faith: 'Amen, amen, I say to you, you will see the heaven opened and the angels of God ascending and descending on the Son of man' (1: 51).

Several points about this saying are highly important for the present discussion. In the first place it has long been recognised that it is an addition to the original composition of 1: 19–49, linked to it by means of verse 50. Thus the underlying homily, which John has used as the first section of his gospel, originally ended with the climax of Nathanael's confession in verse 49. The Son of Man was not mentioned in this homily. But when John set about composing a complete gospel, he added this saying as a further climax, so as to introduce the argument which will follow. As such it anticipates what is to be unfolded in the ensuing chapters. Of the numerous interpretations offered for the meaning of the saying,[10] there is much to be said for the contention that this is a symbolic description of the baptismal experience of Jesus (for τὸν οὐρανὸν ἀνεῳγότα cf. Matt. 3: 16 and parallels), in which Jesus' future glory as the Son of Man is disclosed, and the link between his earthly ministry and his heavenly status is established (here represented by the ascending and descending angels).[11] But as it refers to a future event, and the baptism has already taken place (verses 32–4), John's thought cannot be confined to this. In fact the saying will be fulfilled in a deeper and fuller sense in the passion of Jesus, which is the hour when the Son of Man is glorified (12: 23). The saying thus points forward to the conclusion of the whole of the argument which John is about to expound.

In the second place it is noteworthy that John uses the arthrous form of the phrase (τὸν υἱὸν τοῦ ἀνθρώπου) in common with the Synoptic tradition. This is sufficient to establish the fact that it is a title, and not the common Aramaic בר אנשא. The significance of this will appear when we reach 5: 27, the only place where John uses the anarthrous

---

[10] Cf. Higgins, pp. 157–71; Borsch, pp. 278–80.

[11] As Borsch, p. 280 n. 5, points out, the glorification of the Son of Man is not mentioned as such. He remains on earth, and the opening of the heavens allows the passage of the angels upon him, just as in the baptismal vision the Spirit comes down upon Jesus. That this is the correct interpretation, so that it is wrong to suppose that the Son of Man is at this point seen in heaven, is indicated by the biblical allusion to Gen. 28: 12. John's text follows the Hebrew of this verse exactly.

form. As the form with the article occurs only in the words of Jesus (and Acts 7: 56), the conclusion is inevitable that John derives it from the Jesus-tradition, rather than from Jewish or Hellenistic sources.

Thirdly the Amen-formula is an indication that John is drawing on the sayings of Jesus.[12] He not only derives the title from this tradition, but has formed the verse by adapting a traditional saying, such as Mark 14: 62 (which may also lie behind Acts 7: 56). The christological argument in John constantly draws on traditional sayings in this way.

After the symbolic tale of the Marriage at Cana, in which the new dimension of the coming of Jesus is expressed, John resumes the christological argument in the discourse with Nicodemus in chapter 3. Starting from another Amen saying (verse 3),[13] Jesus insists on the necessity of rebirth, which is nothing less than birth from above.[14] Nicodemus is nonplussed. His rabbinic training has not prepared him for this. Jesus then explains that he is himself the source of divine knowledge (verse 11, again an Amen saying).[15] It will appear subsequently that Jesus is also the giver of the spiritual life which comes through the birth from above. But for the moment attention is confined to the question of the divine knowledge. Jesus asserts that it is only accessible through the Son of Man (verse 13). To those who have pondered the implications of 1: 51 this should occasion no surprise. For if there is a link between earth and heaven through the earthly ministry of him who is to be glorified as Son of man, then it is through Jesus that the divine knowledge is mediated to men.

It is the aim of John at this point to state that Jesus is the sole mediator of eternal life. It is tempting to see the influence of Hellenistic

---

[12] The Amen-formula probably does not go back to Jesus himself, but is rather a very early form of asseveration to guarantee an apocalyptic statement, extended in Mark and John to denote the legitimation of the Jesus-tradition. It is thus a sure sign that the words which it introduces are based on authentic logia of Jesus. Cf. K. Berger, *Die Amen-Wörter Jesu: eine Untersuchung zum Problem der Legitimation in apokalyptischer Rede* (*BZNW* xxxix, 1970).

[13] The saying is a variant of Matt. 18: 3.

[14] Following Schnackenburg, I take ἄνωθεν to mean 'from above' each time it occurs (verses 3, 7, 31). Verse 4a shows that it is the kind of birth which is the point at issue. It is only at 4b that Nicodemus points out that Jesus' statement entails rebirth of some kind. As the birth from above is not the same thing as physical birth, it is not strictly rebirth at all.

[15] There is no Synoptic parallel, but the proverbial character of the verse, with the sudden change to plural verbs and parallelism of the first two clauses, suggests a traditional saying.

religion here, but this is probably a mistake. In fact man gains eternal life not through gnosis, but through belief in Jesus crucified and exalted (verse 14). The divine secret is nothing else than the vindication and glorification of Jesus. The 'heavenly things' which Nicodemus is not ready to believe are precisely this vindication and glorification. They are accessible now, because he who is to be the Son of man has come down in the incarnation of Jesus. The background to this idea is probably not the myth of the descent of a heavenly revealer, but the Wisdom christology presupposed by John elsewhere, and developed by him in the Prologue.[16] Jewish seers may claim to have been admitted to the divine secrets, and indeed they have been so admitted inasmuch as they have seen the future glory of the Son of Man (cf. 12: 41). But they cannot reveal God's plan with such clarity as the Son of man himself, by whom it is accomplished.

Before going further, it will be worth while to consider why John found it necessary to use the Son-of-Man theme at this point. It is because this theme, as already implied in 1: 51, enabled him to express the relation between the earthly ministry of Jesus and his heavenly glory in which God's purpose for mankind is achieved. And the crucial act in this process is the cross. John states this fact immediately (verse 14), though it will have to be worked out in detail in the ensuing chapters. It is not at once obvious why the cross should most fully reveal the future glory of the Son of Man. For the moment John is content to express it by a play on words, using the double meaning of ὑψωθῆναι, reinforced with the typology of the serpent in the wilderness. It will appear in the end, however, that the glory of Jesus as the Son of Man consists in his union with the Father, and the cross most fully reveals this because it is the ultimate expression of the union of his will with the Father's. This is to anticipate matters, for it is the climax of John's argument. But it is important to see that John is using the Son-of-Man theme in chapter 3 in order to lay out the terms in which his argument is to be expressed.

[16] It is important to notice that John never says that the Son of Man has come down from heaven. All he does here is to identify the one who has come down from heaven with the Son of Man. In other words, *descent is not part of the Johannine Son-of-Man myth, though it is an essential feature of his christology.* Normally he uses the idea of sending to express this, in line with Paul (cf. Rom. 8: 3; Gal. 4: 4) and some Synoptic sayings (e.g. Mark 9: 37). Apart from 3: 13, καταβαίνω is only used of the incarnation in the discourse of chapter 6, where it is probably dependent on the typology of the manna miracle. See further the article of Schnackenburg cited above.

Even if the serpent typology is taken to be an original contribution of John himself, there can be little doubt that he is indebted to the important work of apologetic in early Christianity with regard to the passion of Jesus. John's δεῖ is reminiscent of the first prediction of the passion (Mark 8: 31 and parallels). It was necessary that Jesus should suffer, because it was written in scripture. John is familiar with this argument from scriptural fulfilment, and shares the predestinarian outlook which it implies (cf. 19: 28–30), and indeed the allusion here to Num. 21: 9 is the fruit of further biblical work along the same line. But the necessity of the passion is much greater than this. It is indispensable for the salvation of men, because they cannot reach the level of faith required for eternal life without it (verse 15). And the irony of this is that John knows only too well that it is at the cross that the faith of the Jews stumbles (12: 31–6; cf. 1 Cor. 1: 23).

Direct reference to the Son of Man in the discourse is now concluded. But there are two supplementary pieces (verses 16–20 and 31–6) which add further features to John's argument.[17] These two paragraphs are important for two reasons. (a) They introduce two new themes, which will play a major part later on. These are the themes of *judging* and of *giving life*. The judgment is not a judicial verdict in the literal sense, but the inevitable consequence of belief or unbelief. Belief leads to life, whereas unbelief renders a man self-condemned (verse 18). Belief is necessary in order to appropriate life, because Jesus gives life by conveying the *words* of God unstintingly, being himself fully endowed with the Spirit (verse 34).[18] (b) These paragraphs also introduce new descriptions of Jesus, which have not been used before in the first edition of the gospel. These are τὸν υἱὸν τὸν μονογενῆ, τὸν υἱόν, and τοῦ μονογενοῦς υἱοῦ τοῦ θεοῦ (verses 16–18). Moreover in verse 35 ὁ πατήρ is correlated with ὁ υἱός for the first time. Although it is natural to regard these titles as variants of ὁ υἱὸς τοῦ θεοῦ, and it may well be legitimate to do so in the light of the full spectrum of John's christology, in the present context the thematic connection with verses 11–15 strongly suggests that they are alternatives to ὁ υἱὸς τοῦ ἀνθρώπου.

---

[17] The use of material of a very different type between these two paragraphs presents a difficult problem. Theories of transposition (Bernard, Bultmann) or subsequent addition (Schnackenburg) have been suggested. But it can be accounted for equally well on the theory that John first composed this discourse as a self-contained homily, which he then broke up in the making of the first edition of his gospel (see my commentary *ad loc.*).

[18] Taking God to be the subject of δίδωσιν (so Bernard, Bultmann, Barrett).

The adjective μονογενής emphasises the uniqueness of Jesus in his capacity as God's agent of salvation.[19] The simple ὁ υἱός expresses his personal relationship with God, but in an open way, without tying down the meaning to the special implications of either ὁ υἱὸς τοῦ θεοῦ or ὁ υἱὸς τοῦ ἀνθρώπου. It has often been observed that John regularly uses 'the Son' in correlation with 'the Father'. It has not always been noticed that John does this deliberately, in order to leave the further implications open. In the present context it is virtually an abbreviation of 'the Son of Man'. But the subject of the discourse has run out into more general considerations, for which it is desirable to keep open the full range of meaning implied by *both* titles. The significance of this observation will appear when we turn to the argument in chapter 5.

The discourse with the Samaritan woman in chapter 4 has figured prominently in recent work on the Fourth Gospel, because of the interest among scholars in early Christian contacts with the Samaritans.[20] The chapter stands apart from the main christological argument nevertheless. The themes already adumbrated are developed further, it is true. The function of Jesus as the giver of life is expounded in the conversation on the water of life, and is demonstrated in the healing of the officer's son at the end of the chapter. Jesus' capacity to reveal the divine knowledge is also represented in the second part of the conversation, where the woman recognises in him the Prophet-Messiah of Samaritan expectation. This is given wider significance in the people's affirmation that he is 'the saviour of the world' (verse 42). But these thoughts are not resumed in the sequel. The chapter gives impressive testimony to the results of belief in Jesus, but does not bring any new insight into the nature of the relationship between Jesus and God, which is the real issue in the Johannine christology.

When we turn to chapter 5, however, the idea of 'the Son' becomes prominent once more. The argument begins with the Parable of the Apprenticed Son (verses 19–20a),[21] where the words 'father' and

---

[19] Cf. D. Moody, 'God's Only Son: the Translation of John 3: 16 in the Revised Standard Version', *JBL* lxxii (1953), pp. 213–19.

[20] Among recent studies see especially W. A. Meeks, *The Prophet-King: Moses Traditions and Johannine Christology* (*Supplements to Nov. T.* xiv, Leiden, 1967).

[21] Cf. C. H. Dodd, 'Une parabole cachée dans le quatrième évangile', *RHPR* xlii (1962), pp. 46–50 (= 'A Hidden Parable in the Fourth Gospel', *More New Testament Studies* (Manchester, 1968), pp. 30–40); P. Gächter, 'Zur Form

'son' are ambiguous. They might refer to any father and son. But they could be intended to refer specifically to God and Jesus. The ambiguity remains unresolved in the verses which immediately follow. But as the craft which the father teaches turns out to be the eschatological functions of giving life and performing judgment, it is (at least) clear that the father is God. It is only at verse 24, when Jesus suddenly adopts the first person, that we are made aware that he is himself the son.

We are already familiar with the functions of giving life and judging. But there is also here a new theme, which has not been mentioned before, and which will have profound consequences for the progress of the christological argument. This is the idea, already hinted at in verse 18, and explicitly stated in verse 23, that the Son has the right to equal 'honour' with the Father, so that those who withhold honour from him *ipso facto* withhold it from the Father himself.

It is only in the second paragraph of the discourse (verses 25–9) that the Son is identified as the Son of Man, though this is the natural conclusion to which the argument has been leading. To begin with there is a surprise. Verse 25 reads: 'The dead shall hear the voice of the Son of God...' In view of what follows, we should naturally expect 'the Son of man' (it is actually read by KS 28 *al.*). But that can hardly be right, as it would spoil the climax in verse 27. 'Son of God' must either be retained as an intentional variation in the styling of the argument, designed to hold back the climax at the same time as giving a hint of it; or, more probably in my opinion, it should be regarded as a very early corruption of the text due to the influence of the Lazarus story in chapter 11.[22] It must be admitted that 'the Son' alone best fits the flow of the argument. Then in the next verse the Father and Son correlation is employed, recalling the Father's delegation of his prerogative of giving life. Finally, in verse 27, the other function of judging is mentioned, and at last the reason for the delegation of these powers is given. It is because the Son is υἱὸς ἀνθρώπου. The anarthrous form, unique in the New Testament, can only be intended to be a

von Joh. 5: 19–30', in *Neutestamentliche Aufsätze*, edited by J. Blinzler, O. Kuss and F. Mussner (Regensburg, 1963), pp. 65–8.

[22] To overcome the difficulty, Wendt conjectured the omission of ἀνθρώπου in verse 27. But this makes nonsense of the verse. Variants for αὐτοῦ at the end of verse 28 attest confusion at an early date. Thus sy^c reads *da'lāhā'*, Origen τοῦ υἱοῦ τοῦ θεοῦ, and Irenaeus *filii hominis*. The latter reading is probably influenced by verse 25 (hence the addition of *mortui* in the same verse). It thus seems likely that both τοῦ θεοῦ and τοῦ ἀνθρώπου are attempts to elucidate an original τοῦ υἱοῦ.

direct allusion to the foundation text, Dan. 7: 13. Notice also the unmistakable allusion to Dan. 12: 2 in the next two verses. The conclusion can now be drawn that the acts of Jesus in his earthly life anticipate his functions at the End of the Age, when he will be glorified as the Son of Man. The rest of the discourse does not take this point further, as it is taken up with the testimony to this claim.

One further feature of this passage should not be missed. The biblical allusion to Dan. 7: 13 is the clue to the argument, but it is not the origin of John's use of the Son-of-Man title. That comes, as we have seen, from the tradition of the sayings of Jesus. But of course John knows perfectly well that the title comes in the first instance from Daniel. So here he takes the title from the tradition, and builds his argument on it with conscious reference to the biblical passage from which it is ultimately derived. We shall see a comparable literary feature in connection with the phrase ἐγώ εἰμι.

Passing over chapter 6, we come to the composite assemblage of teachings at the Feast of Tabernacles in chapters 7 and 8. The problem of Jesus' credentials is still the main topic in chapter 7. Doubts are expressed whether he fulfils the conditions for a genuine messianic claimant. In chapter 8, however, the thought fastens once more on the subject of Jesus' relationship to God. In other words, the argument passes from consideration of the physical origin of Jesus to the question of his heavenly origin.

To begin with, Jesus does not use a title to refer to himself, but speaks in the first person. First he announces the theme: 'I am the light of the world' (8: 12). It quickly becomes clear that the reference of τὸ φῶς is not to revelation of esoteric knowledge, but to the Jewish concept of exposing good and bad, truth and falsehood, by illuminating the mind. The argument in verses 13–19 is taken up with Jesus' claim to do this. His ἐγώ εἰμι is refuted on the grounds that it is self-witness. Jesus counters this on the grounds that he knows his own origin and destiny, which the Jews do not know (verse 14). Jesus here adds a disclaimer. He does not pass this sort of earthly, ill-informed judgment. This rather artificial disclaimer acts as a bridge to the next point in the argument, that the *content* of what Jesus claims to be, the judge (or light) of the world, cannot be denied, because it has the twofold witness required by the canons of Jewish legal practice. For his own judgment is confirmed by the Father who has delegated this function to him.

So far no title for Jesus has been used. But at verse 21 the discussion is reopened on a fresh occasion, and now the issue is brought to a head. In covert language Jesus forecasts the passion, which, as we have already seen, is a crucial item in the Son-of-Man themes. This in fact will be the decisive act, whereby Jesus' heavenly origin is revealed and the unbelieving world is judged (verse 23f.). The thought is moving in the categories of the Son-of-Man christology, as may be seen by comparison with 3: 11–15, where the heavenly origin of the Son of Man and the passion are both referred to. The language of the present passage keeps harping on the ἐγώ εἰμι of verse 12. It has been taken up in verse 18, where the self-witness which it implies (verse 13f.) is given formal justification. Now it comes again in verse 23 to express Jesus' heavenly origin in contrast with all other men. At the same time the predicate (τὸ φῶς) is not forgotten. It is implied in the phrase 'you will die in your sins' (verses 21 and 24 twice), which is the consequence of exposure to the light of judgment, as explained in 3: 18–21. This, Jesus asserts, is inevitable, *unless* the Jews believe that ἐγώ εἰμι. The predicate is not expressed. But it is clear from the whole tenor of the argument that it is all that Jesus has been claiming about himself. And this is at least what he has claimed in the immediate context, that he is the light of the world, the one who judges, the one who comes from above, the one who must mysteriously 'go away'. But all these are things that can be said of the Son of Man, according to John's use of this title. With his customary skill, John leaves the matter open for the moment. Naturally the lack of a predicate in verse 24 draws the question 'Who are you?' Jesus' reply is indirect, and may seem evasive.[23] But it becomes unmistakably clear that the predicate should be the Son of Man, when Jesus magnificently concludes the argument with a further allusion to 3: 14 in verse 28: 'When you have lifted up the Son of man, then you will know that ἐγώ εἰμι . . .' The allusion to the argument in 5: 19–30 in the remainder of the verse should also be noted.

It is at this point that we may observe how John's technique has a certain similarity to his use of scripture in 5: 27. There a title from the tradition was elucidated by reference to the actual biblical passage from which it was derived. Here a phrase which John is using christologically

---

[23] For the problems of this verse see commentaries. The translation turns on the meaning of the idiomatic τὴν ἀρχήν. The lack of classical style elsewhere in the gospel scarcely favours the meaning 'at all', cf. F. N. Davey in E. C. Hoskyns, *The Fourth Gospel* (London, ²1947), pp. 335f.

is treated in a similar way. Whether ἐγώ εἰμι was already in use as a title is disputed.[24] But John's very special use of it does not require a prior history in the tradition. In fact, if it arises simply from ἐγώ εἰμι τὸ φῶς τοῦ κόσμου at the beginning of the section,[25] we can see how it has come into being from John's adaptation of a quite different saying in the tradition.[26] But when John reaches the climax of the argument he introduces a striking allusion to a biblical passage in which ἐγώ εἰμι occurs, Isa. 43: 10: γένεσθέ μοι μάρτυρες, κἀγὼ μάρτυς, λέγει κύριος ὁ θεός, καὶ ὁ παῖς, ὃν ἐξελεξάμην, ἵνα γνῶτε καὶ πιστεύσητε καὶ συνῆτε ὅτι ἐγώ εἰμι ... We may notice how this also includes the theme of joint witness (cf. verses 13–20), and how the context may account for the troublesome τὴν ἀρχήν of verse 25 (cf. Isa. 43: 9, 13). The force of this allusion is to deepen immeasurably the awe-inspiring implications of Jesus' claim to be the Son of Man. It lays stress on his relationship to the God of incomparable majesty, who is to accomplish salvation. This prepares the way for the breath-taking climax of the whole section in 8: 58, where once more the ἐγώ εἰμι is used.

The rest of the chapter is concerned with paternity. It answers the question Who is Jesus' Father? Though it begins with another parable, comparable to 5: 19f., in which a 'son' figures,[27] the sonship titles are not actually employed. That Jesus is the Son is presupposed throughout. The argument is consistent with his claim to be the Son of Man, for it is concerned with his heavenly origins, in this case especially with the aspect of pre-existence. But the special themes associated with the Son of Man – judging, giving life, the passion and exaltation – are not

---

[24] See Bultmann's valuable note on 6: 35, and the discussion in Appendix IV of the commentary by R. E. Brown, vol. i, pp. 533–8.

[25] ἐγώ εἰμι has occurred previously at 6: 20, 35, 51, but if this chapter is taken to belong to the second edition of John, 8: 12 must be regarded as the first use of the formula. The absolute ἐγώ εἰμι is found eight times in John. 6: 20 comes from John's source (cf. Mark 6: 50), and it is not certain that he intends deeper overtones to be read into it. 8: 24, 28 acquire these overtones from the allusion to Isa. 43: 10. 13: 19 is a cross-reference to 8: 28, and 18: 5, 6, 8, by the unnecessary reference to Judas in 5b, probably intends an allusion to 13: 19 to explain the awe-inspiring effect of the phrase on those who have come to arrest Jesus. 8: 58 cannot be regarded as a title, because it requires the meaning 'I am in existence'. Again, although the nuance is different, the awesome effect of the words has been prepared for by the allusion to Isa. 43: 10 in 8: 28.

[26] Cf. Matt. 5: 14. It is not to be supposed that John has created the saying on the basis of this or a similar logion without taking into account the vast ramifications of the theme of light in late Judaism and the ancient world.

[27] Cf. C. H. Dodd, Historical Tradition in the Fourth Gospel (Cambridge, 1963), pp. 379–82.

under consideration. The theme of life, or rather of escaping death, appears, it is true, in verse 51f.,[28] but only as a lead-in to the climax in verse 58. It is thus not surprising that the Son-of-Man title does not occur in this discourse. John only uses it when the special themes are present. True to his aim, he pursues the grand unfolding of the relation of Jesus to God, for which he has indeed employed the Son-of-Man title at crucial points, but for which he is never dominated by the various titles at his disposal.

The christological argument reaches its conclusion in the discourse of 10: 22–39. In order to pave the way for his final statement, John uses two originally independent sequences, the Man Born Blind in chapter 9 and the Allegory of the Shepherd in 10: 1–18. The first of these reverts once more to the theme of judgment. The blind man, illuminated by the creative hand of Jesus, is capable of recognising him as the one who is to perform the eschatological judgment. The Pharisees, on the other hand, are self-condemned by their unbelief. It is thus no accident that 'the Son of man' is used in 9: 35.[29] The man now has the evidence that Jesus is the Son of Man, and only needs to make his act of allegiance. His illumination has prefigured the devastating clarity of the day of judgment, and has been done with that precise intention. Hence the assertion that his blindness from birth was ἵνα φανερωθῇ τὰ ἔργα τοῦ θεοῦ ἐν αὐτῷ (verse 3). It is no accident that there is a cross-reference to 8: 12 in verse 5: ὅταν ἐν τῷ κόσμῳ ὦ, φῶς εἰμι τοῦ κόσμου (note the avoidance of ἐγώ εἰμι here). The man's profession of faith is not just the reaction to a miracle-worker, but the acknowledgment of the true meaning of what has been done.

The Allegory of the Shepherd has a passing allusion to the judgment theme in the figure of the thief, but all the emphasis goes on to the other main function of the Son of Man, that of giving life. The title itself is not used. When Jesus abandons the allegory, he uses the first person. John is leading up to the climax that Jesus is the Son of God (10: 36). The allegory brings to expression what is to John the essential point of his christology, i.e. the perfect unity of will between Jesus and the Father, which justifies the use of the various titles. So, when the question of Jesus' identity is raised (verse 24), the allegory is resumed

---

[28] An Amen saying, which may well be a variant tradition of Mark 9: 1.
[29] The reading of the best manuscripts. The majority reading 'the Son of God' is probably due to the influence of the baptismal confession of faith.

so as to prepare the way for the most concise expression of exactly this point: 'I and the Father are one' (verse 30).[30]

In what follows, John uses once more the feature which has been observed at 5: 27 and 8: 28. A biblical quotation provides explication and confirmation of what has been argued. Jesus 'makes himself God' (verse 33) in the sense that, as the one 'whom the Father consecrated and sent into the world', he is 'the Son of God' (verse 36). This accords with scripture (Ps. 82: 6, quoted in verse 34). But even this title is not to be taken as exhausting the meaning of his relationship to the Father. No title by itself is sufficient to express this. But the point is that this and all the other titles contribute to the full understanding of the grand affirmation to which the whole work of Jesus has been directed, 'that you may come to know and continue to know that the Father is in me and I am in the Father' (verse 38).[31]

The main argument is now finished. But it remains to describe the final act whereby the work of Jesus in obedience to the Father is accomplished. This is the Passion, as we know already from 3: 14 and 8: 28. So, in preparation for the Passion narrative, to ensure that it is understood correctly, John is at pains to show that it is the moment, the hour, when the Son of Man is glorified (12: 20–36). All the Son-of-Man themes are now drawn together. The glorification takes the form of a death which is fruitful for eternal life, and so fulfils the Son of Man's function of giving life (verses 24–6, based on traditional sayings). The cross is inevitable, and indeed is the Father's will. It is the decisive act, whereby 'the ruler of this world' is judged, but 'all men' are attracted. It can only be understood when it is recognised that Jesus is the Son of Man. To the people's puzzled question on this point, Jesus replies with a challenge to walk in the light while it is still with them (verse 35f.). The allusion to 8: 12 is obvious, and so warns the reader to ensure that he has grasped the argument which followed from it. If he will only accept now, while he has the light, that Jesus is the Son of Man, who is destined to be glorified, but must first be lifted up, who is the giver of life and the judge of the world, then he will have the faith which will

---

[30] Verses 27–9 certainly belong to the allegory in its original form as an independent homily, but John has reserved them deliberately for their present position in writing the gospel. Transposition theories miss the point. See my commentary *ad loc.*

[31] Reading γνῶτε καὶ γινώσκητε. The repetition of the same verb adds a note of urgent appeal to the reader to accept this crucial statement.

make him one of the sons of light, those who escape the judgment of the world.

It is only after this full explanation of his meaning that John can speak of Jesus' death as his glorification, without further discussion, in the setting of the Last Supper at 13: 31f. But the idea is now laden with the whole range of the Son-of-Man christology, which has been unfolded since the first mention of this theme in 1: 51. And it is not without significance that, in this last mention of the Son of Man, Jesus speaks of the reciprocal glorifying of the Son of Man and God. For the Son-of-Man christology has always been at the service of John's most treasured idea of the unity that subsists between the Father and the Son.

It is not the object of this paper to discuss in detail the origin of John's thought about the Son of Man. He takes over the title from the sayings of Jesus. But the picture which immediately springs to his mind when he uses it is the glorification of the Son of Man in Dan. 7 (cf. the allusion in 5: 27). This is a vision in which the Son of Man is given royal power and honour. John accordingly regards the exalted Jesus as worthy of such honour, indeed of equal honour with the Father. John also holds that the exaltation of Jesus as the Son of Man follows his passion. This idea has its precedent in the Synoptic passion predictions. John does not give evidence for solving the problem of the origin of this idea, though it remains possible that it was deduced in the first place from the explanation of the vision in Dan. 7: 15–27.[32] But it is clear that he is indebted to the scriptural exegesis of the early church, in which the necessity of the Passion was worked out. In this connection it is possible that his use of ὑψοῦν in 3: 14; 8: 28; 12: 32, 34 depends on the employment of Isa. 52: 13 in the course of this work.

It is more difficult to see how John arrived at the idea that the Son of Man has the delegated functions of God's prerogatives of giving life and performing the eschatological judgment. But for the latter at least he had precedents in the Synoptic tradition,[33] and redaction criticism

---

[32] This is not to deny the correctness of H. H. Rowley's observation that only the people suffer, and the Son-of-Man figure is exclusively concerned with the subsequent stage of glory (*The Servant of the Lord*, Oxford, ²1965, p. 64 n. 3). But the equation Son of Man = Saints of the Most High could lead to this interpretation. See A. J. B. Higgins, 'Son of Man-*Forschung* since "The Teaching of Jesus"', *New Testament Essays*, edited by A. J. B. Higgins (Manchester, 1959), pp. 119–35.

[33] In Mark only at 8: 38. But the Q variant (Matt. 10: 32f. = Luke 12: 8f.) shows the wide diffusion of sayings of this type.

points to the conclusion that the idea became increasingly important in at any rate some circles of early Christianity.[34] And once the notion of the Son of Man's activity in performing the judgment has been reached, it is only a short step to the idea that he is actively concerned in the general resurrection that precedes it. That this is how some thought about the Son of Man is indicated by the Similitudes of Enoch, which is probably neither a direct influence on the New Testament nor on the other hand directly dependent on the New Testament, but an independent example of the development of Son-of-Man mythology.[35] It has to be remembered that the Son of Man was not primarily thought to be a man in the strict, earthly sense. He was 'one like a son of man', a heavenly being. As he was superior to the angels, it was inevitable that the description of his glory and his activity should be borrowed from those of God himself. The real difficulty is, then, not to see how the Son of Man should do these acts at the End of the Age, but how he can be a man on earth, whose acts already anticipate them. But here again there are precedents for John's ideas in the Synoptic Gospels (Mark 2: 10, 28, etc.). However we explain these sayings, John did not doubt either their authenticity or their truth. What he did was to take the idea that Jesus' miracles are works of the Son of Man and transform it into a systematic doctrine. The earthly ministry of Jesus declares in advance, to those who have eyes to see it, what is to be at the End of the Age, and so provides the means whereby men may already pass from death to life through faith.

It is against this full background of John's thought that we must consider the discourse on the Bread of Life in chapter 6, the only place where he uses the Son-of-Man figure in the additions for the second edition of his work. It is well known that the idea of the renewal of the manna miracle was current in Jewish eschatological thought, but that there is no precedent for the idea that the Son of Man will actually perform it. In fact this is only stated in verse 27. In the rest of the discourse Jesus is the bread himself, and the giver of it is God to begin with (verse 32f.). When the Son of Man is mentioned again (verses 40 –

---

[34] Strenuously denied by Borsch, who regards Matthew as preserving the more primitive form of the relevant logia. But Borsch's thesis, that the Son of Man is original in the Jesus-tradition and progressively disappears from it, is not spoilt by the possibility that there was some development of the Son-of-Man christology for a while in the Matthaean circle, just as in the case of John.

[35] This is the thesis of Morna D. Hooker, *The Son of Man in Mark* (London, 1967).

on which see below – and 53), the idea of the eschatological renewal of the manna is not the point at issue. It is probable that the original form of the discourse, before John reworked it for inclusion in the gospel, began with the people's question in verse 28, as they are not aware that Jesus has already given a sign (verse 30). Verse 27, then, belongs to an artificial dialogue, contrived to link the opening narrative with the ensuing discourse. The purpose of mentioning the Son of Man in this verse is to set the eschatological perspective for it (hence Jesus adds τοῦτον γὰρ ὁ πατὴρ ἐσφράγισεν ὁ θεός).

The other references to the Son of Man are completely consistent with John's use of the idea elsewhere. The discourse is really an exposition of the manna text in verse 31. The purpose of the eschatological bread is to 'give life to the world' (verse 33). This is expressed in terms of the consistent eschatology of resurrection on the last day. And those who recognise the Son now, and believe in him, already have eternal life, which anticipates this future resurrection (verse 40). The idea is quite similar to 5 : 24, where the present activity of Jesus as 'the Son' anticipates the final work of the Son of Man. But John will not allow that this is possible without acceptance of the necessity of the passion. It is for this reason that he adds verses 51b–58, which should not be deleted as an interpolation. The Son of Man must suffer before he is glorified, and so also the believers must receive his flesh and blood before they can participate in the life he gives (verse 53). This is the scandal of the cross (61b), which is only resolved when men see the Son of Man rise to glory (62).[36]

The central aim of the Johannine christology is to expound the intimate relationship of Jesus and God. For this purpose John takes over the idea of the Son of Man, already current in the gospel tradition. He works creatively on this basis, in full view of the primary text in Dan. 7, and in the light of developments from it in Jewish apocalyptic. His use of the term keeps strictly within the categories of Jewish apocalyptic, and does not show any influence of the syncretistic mythology of the Primal Man. John has no hint of Paul's Adam christology. When forced to expound his cosmology, he drops the theme of the Son of Man in favour of a Wisdom christology, which appears as the Logos in the Prologue.

John's constructive use of the Son-of-Man figure is unique in early

---

[36] Following the interpretation of Bauer and Odeberg, against Bultmann.

Christian literature.[37] Elsewhere, with the possible exception of Matthew, there is a tendency to drop the title, even where the concepts associated with the Son of Man are used and developed. Thus Paul never uses the title, nor does it appear as a title in the Book of Revelation, in spite of its large debt to Daniel and Jewish apocalyptic and actual allusions to Dan. 7: 13 in 1: 13; 14: 14. Justin uses it, but only to prove that Jesus fulfils the vision of Dan. 7, just as he fulfils all the other Old Testament types. Other writers use the phrase sparingly, but their purpose is to express the humanity of Jesus, following a Jewish usage derived from the Psalms. The Son of Man appears much more frequently in the Gnostic literature, sometimes in dependence on John. But here there is no interest in apocalyptic, and the thought is wholly dominated by cosmological speculations. As so often in Gnostic writings, we are faced here with a complex amalgam of ideas and literary influences, including Jewish cosmological speculations and apocalyptic ideas, compounded with reminiscences of Synoptic and Johannine sayings in which the Son of Man figures. These works scarcely provide evidence for a constructive Son-of-Man christology within more orthodox Christian circles, to which the writers might have been indebted. John's work remains without parallel.

The Son of Man is not a title in the true sense, like the Messiah or the High Priest. In so far as it is to be distinguished from the Aramaic בר אנשא, it is the designation of a particular figure, first described in Dan. 7. He is a mythological figure, capable of expansion and contraction in the hands of different practitioners. This myth may have been a fundamental influence on Jesus himself, inspiring him with his sense of mission and destiny.[38] Consequently Son-of-Man sayings have been preserved in the most primitive gospel strands. John, with his unerring capacity to pierce through to the inner meaning of the primitive logia, has the unique distinction of bringing to expression on the basis of them the deepest and most compelling interpretation of Jesus' self-understanding before God.

In conclusion, it is a pleasure to record how much this essay owes to discussion of the tantalising problems of the Son of Man with Professor C. F. D. Moule, to whom it is dedicated with admiration and affection.

[37] For what follows in this paragraph, see the full discussion in F. H. Borsch, *The Christian and Gnostic Son of Man* (*Studies in Biblical Theology*, second series xiv, London, 1970).

[38] Cf. Borsch, *The Son of Man in Myth and History*, pp. 402ff.

SJT 29 (1976) 49-63

5

WORD AND SACRAMENT IN THE FOURTH GOSPEL

I

WORD and sacrament belong together in the Christian life. It has been one of the achievements of the renewal of Christendom in the present century to overcome the deep-seated sense of opposition between them. This opposition can be traced to the polarisation of theological emphases in the Reformation of the sixteenth century. The divine activity in performance of the sacraments was stressed to such a degree that they appeared to be almost magical acts, encouraging a superstitious approach on the part of the people. The Protestant reaction placed all the emphasis on the word of God, appealing to the heart and the mind. There could be no operation of the grace of God in the soul except through the opening of the heart to God, through personal assent to his word and through the commitment of faith. Now it is recognised that sacramental acts have a social function in the organic life of the church, that they preach to the people through symbols and actions, so that they require (and also evoke) the proper dispositions for receiving the grace of God, and that the inclusion of scripture readings and a homily in the course of sacramental services produces a fruitful interaction between them. This recovery of the balance between word and sacrament has proved beneficial for the life of the church. It has also marked a return to the perspective of the New Testament.

This is not to say that the New Testament contains anything that can be termed a sacramental theology. It is not possible to ask whether the religion of the primitive church is a sacramental or a non-sacramental religion. The New Testament does not know the word 'sacrament'. There is no special category of thought which would enable the early Christians to think of the sacraments as a distinct concept in Christian faith and practice. What the New Testament does show, however, is that the church had certain practices which later became known as the sacraments.

But it would be a mistake to take these too closely together. If it could be proved that a certain group of Christians rejected the practice of baptism, it would not follow that they were opposed to sacraments in principle, and therefore rejected the eucharist too. References to these practices need to be examined for the information which each can give in respect of the actual practice mentioned, not for light on sacramental theology in general.

This observation is especially important in any attempt to understand the use and meaning of sacraments in the Johannine church.[1] Though it is generally admitted that baptism and the eucharist were practised in John's church,[2] and also that the Fourth Gospel does not contain a specific polemic against the sacraments,[3] it is often asserted that John has an anti-sacramental tendency. This can hardly be true, for the reasons just stated above, unless it is taken to mean that John evinces a wish to reduce the importance of either baptism or the eucharist or both. We are entitled to ask what is his attitude towards these two practices, and what meaning he attaches to them. This will illuminate at least one area of thought about these sacraments in the days of the New Testament, before sacramental theology as such had begun to exist.

It is not without significance that the observation of an anti-sacramental tendency in John is usually associated with the view that he is deeply indebted to incipient Gnosticism. As the name implies, the key concept of Gnosticism is the revelation of saving knowledge. Salvation consists in acceptance of this knowledge. In the Gnostic systems this is chiefly a matter of celestial cosmology, revealed to man so that he may be freed from the ignorance of fleshly existence and raised to immortality and the divine life. Such a religion is addressed to the individual and makes appeal primarily to the intellect. Though its adherents may form a social group, their common life is not likely to find expression in sacramental acts. The cosmic dualism which it entails leaves no room for a sacramental theology. If John has a tendency in this direction, he is likely to be uninterested in the sacraments and ecclesiastical institutions at least, if not actively opposed to them.

[1] H. Klos, *Die Sakramente im Johannesevangelium* (Stuttgart, 1970), p. 9f.
[2] E. Käsemann, *The Testament of Jesus* (London, 1968), p. 32.
[3] E. Lohse, 'Wort und Sakrament im Johannesevangelium', *NTS*, 7, 1960/1, pp. 110-25, especially p. 124.

The Bultmann school, which is chiefly identified with this view, admits, however, that the content of the saving knowledge in John differs from that of the Gnostic systems in a very important way. Jesus in the Fourth Gospel is not only the revealer of this knowledge. He is also its content. It is thus not possible to define salvation in this gospel purely in intellectual terms. What is required of the reader is not acceptance of knowledge, but *belief into* (*pisteuein eis*) Jesus. This puts the matter in terms of personal relationship.[1] Christian life consists in establishing and maintaining this relationship. The response of the whole man is required, not just his intellect. There can be no objection to sacramental acts, if these enable the worshippers to realise their fellowship with Jesus and to adhere to him more closely. John is very emphatic that actual sight of Jesus is not essential for personal response to him (20.29). He also dispenses with the need for intellectual propositions. It is sufficient to know Jesus personally, in spite of not seeing him, and such personal knowledge is like the mutual knowledge of friends (15.1-10, 15). It is indeed a closer bond, because it is not limited by the conditions of earthly life which inevitably set people apart. In the new conditions which prevail after the resurrection the relationship can be described in terms of mutual indwelling. And because of the similar relationship between Jesus and the Father, communion with Jesus automatically entails communion with God (14.18-24). Furthermore, this communion is not just a private affair between the believer and his Lord. The individualism of the Fourth Gospel has often been stressed, and indeed this is inevitable, because it is impossible to speak in terms of personal relationship except from the standpoint of the individual. But the Fourth Gospel has a social dimension too. Discipleship is revealed in the love of the brotherhood (13.34f). It is to be expected in such circumstances that the common meal of the disciples will have spiritual importance as the most characteristic expression of their reunion with one another in which the communion of each one with the one Master and with God is realised. Even without the words of institution of the eucharist, chapter 13 certainly describes a sacramental act.

[1] It is possible to describe this personal relationship in Bultmannian terms as 'existential confrontation', but John is in no sense an 'existentialist'. He thinks in realistic personal categories, which should not be dissolved into subjectivism.

It follows that, even with the presuppositions of the Bultmann school, it is not necessary to assume that the Fourth Gospel is opposed to sacraments. A British scholar may perhaps be permitted to suggest that this conclusion owes not a little to the polarisation at the time of the Reformation, mentioned at the beginning of this essay. The Reformation in England did not take these issues to the same extremes which they reached on the Continent.[1] Consequently British commentaries on John have generally been more ready to allow the existence of sacraments in the Johannine church.

II

It is the purpose of this paper to look briefly at the evidence of the Fourth Gospel for the practice and meaning of baptism and the eucharist in the Johannine church. They will have to be considered separately, because there is no overarching category (i.e. 'the sacraments') to bring them together. Moreover it is a mistake to seek illumination by pointing to sacramental themes in the gospel.[2] What we know as baptismal or eucharistic themes from more developed theology and liturgy were not necessarily recognised as such in John's day. Thus it is doubtful whether the marriage at Cana (2.1-11) should be regarded as embodying eucharistic themes.[3]

We begin with baptism. There can be little doubt that the Christian practice of baptism, as an initiation ceremony, was derived from that of John the Baptist, whatever other precedents it may have had in contemporary Judaism. The baptism of Jesus himself is not necessarily relevant, because that is recorded as a revelatory experience, not as a precedent for the disciples to follow. However, some reference to it is required, because John's strange description of it (1.29-34) has been taken as evidence for devaluation of the sacrament of baptism in John's circle.[4] It is not actually stated that Jesus was baptised. On the other hand, the Baptist commits himself to the surprising statement that his activity of baptising with water was under-

---

[1] For Luther's more moderate view, cf. Lohse, p. 117 and note 1.
[2] As is done, for instance, by O. Cullmann, *Urchristentum und Gottesdienst* (Zürich, 1962), and by P. Niewalda, *Sakramentssymbolik im Johannesevangelium?* (Limburg, 1958).
[3] For the interpretation of John 2.1-11, cf. B. Lindars, *The Gospel of John* (The New Century Bible) (London, 1972), pp. 123-28.
[4] Lohse, art. cit., p. 124.

taken precisely in order to reveal the coming Messiah (verse 31). This can only mean that the revelation was made at the moment when he baptised Jesus.[1]

More important for our purpose is the assertion in 3.22 that Jesus himself undertook a ministry of baptising along with his disciples.[2] This statement is unique in the four gospels. The Synoptists never mention that either Jesus or the disciples baptised. It is widely held today that John here reproduces a genuine historical tradition which is unknown from other sources. This is not absolutely certain, because Jesus' baptising activity is necessary to John's narrative at this point, to prepare for the contrast between Jesus and the Baptist in verses 26-30 (note especially verse 26). However that may be, the fact remains that John sees nothing wrong or incongruous in the idea that Jesus was baptising. It may thus be inferred that baptism was a normal practice of the Johannine church.[3]

The meaning of the rite is not referred to. John does not mention the washing away of sins associated with the Baptist's ministry (Mark 1.4). All we are told is that to baptise is the same thing as to 'make disciples' (John 4.1). This at least shows that baptism was a rite of initiation into the fellowship of the disciples of Jesus. But in order to discover the meaning of it in John's circle we must turn our attention away from these few references to baptismal practice. We must also be wary, as mentioned above, of looking for specifically sacramental themes. The clue has been provided by the observation that to baptise is to make disciples. The meaning of baptism can then be found by examining what the gospel has to tell us about becoming disciples. From these observations it may be deduced that baptism in the Johannine church is a cleansing rite, anticipating the eschatological cleansing which precedes the final consummation; that, besides the ritual washing, it includes confession of faith in Jesus as the Son of God; and that the neophyte is promised blessings which anticipate the blessings of the coming kingdom.

(a) John takes over from earlier tradition the distinction between baptism *en hudati*, practised by the Baptist, and

[1] So also Bultmann, ad loc.
[2] John 4.2, limiting this activity to the disciples, is almost certainly a gloss.
[3] Lohse, art. cit., p. 123.

baptism *en pneumati hagiō*, which will be performed by the coming Messiah (1.33; cf. Mark 1.8. Matt. 3.11; Luke 3.16 add *kai puri*). Although the word *baptisma*, which properly means immersion, is applied to both acts, in the second case it must be used figuratively for a process which achieves the same object as washing with water, i.e. purification. The rite of baptism prepares men for a further purification, which it symbolically anticipates. This further cleansing may be a catastrophic act (hence the mention of fire in Matthew and Luke), but it may also be thought of as an act of mercy. It depends on the condition of the persons concerned. For the wicked it entails burning and destruction, but for the righteous it is a gracious act of cleansing from defilement.[1] John is only concerned with the latter aspect, because he has the believing disciple in mind. He can speak of this in terms of pruning by the vinedresser in the allegory of the vine (15.2). This has taken place already in the case of the disciples because of the cleansing effect of Jesus' words (15.3). For John this means response to the message of Jesus about himself. Thus those who refuse to accept his word cannot belong to the group of his disciples (5.38; 8.37), whereas the keeping of his word is a true mark of discipleship (17.6, 14).[2] In the allegory of the vine the cleansing may seem to be a repeated process, as pruning has to be done regularly. But John makes it clear that he thinks of it as an act done once and for all in his comment in 15.3. Similarly the whole purpose of the *pedilavium* in 13.1-11 is to assert that the act of cleansing does not need to be repeated.[3] This, of course, refers to the atoning

---

[1] cf. Ezek. 36.25f, and especially 1QS 4.20f: 'Then God in his truth will make manifest all the deeds of man, and will purify for himself some from mankind, destroying all spirit of perversity . . ., and purifying him with a spirit of holiness (cf. Rom. 1.4) from all deeds of evil. He will sprinkle upon him a spirit of truth like waters for purification . . .'

[2] Hence Käsemann speaks of the Johannine church as 'the community under the word'. It is important to remember, however, that to John Jesus is the content of the word as well as its author, so that response to the word is never merely an intellectual assent, but a fully personal response leading to the establishment of a lasting personal relationship.

[3] The *pedilavium* is primarily an example of humble service, but John has added into the original tradition a dialogue in verses 6-10 which draws attention to the *effect* of the washing. As this is something that cannot be understood now, but only at a later stage (*meta tauta*, verse 7), it is clear that the primary reference of the dialogue is to the cleansing effect of the passion. It remains possible, however, that John also intends a secondary reference to baptism, whereby men 'have part with Jesus' (*echeis meros met' emou*, verse 8). For the literary analysis of the pericope and the text of verse 10, cf. B. Lindars, *The Gospel of John*, pp. 446-52.

efficacy of the sacrifice of Jesus on the cross, which can never be repeated. But it is equally appropriated in a single act by the disciple, for his act of faith has the effect of taking him beyond the eschatological judgment, so that he has already passed from death to life (5.24). There is one act of atonement, and in the life of the individual there is one act whereby its effect is appropriated. This act of the disciple is his response to the message.

It would be a mistake to suppose that John does not see any further need of cleansing after the initial act of faith. He is aware that the disciples will still be exposed to the attacks of the devil (17.15) and will still have to confess their sinfulness (1 John 1.5-2.6). But he writes of the act of faith from the point of view of conversion.

(b) The water-baptism practised by Jesus and the disciples (3.22,26; 4.1), and therefore presumably by the Johannine church, anticipates the eschatological cleansing because of its decisive character as a positive response to the word of Jesus. This response can be called the confession of faith, because the neophyte assents to the message which Jesus has spoken about himself. It is a major purpose of the Fourth Gospel to expose the full implications of the confession of faith. This can be expressed very simply as belief that Jesus is the Messiah, the Son of God (20.31)—a statement which may well be precisely the form of the baptismal confession in John's circle. But to understand the full meaning of this, it is necessary to review all that Jesus says about himself in the preceding chapters. For the purpose of this essay it will be sufficient to indicate this very briefly. Faith that Jesus is the Son of God starts with the fact that he comes from God (3.13), bringing all the fullness of God (3.34f). He is the true teacher (4.25f), the saviour of the world (4.42). As the designated Son of Man (1.51; 3.13f) he performs now, for those who make confession of faith in him, the eschatological functions of the general resurrection and the judgment (5.21-9).[1] He is the eschatological bread from heaven, which supersedes the Law of Moses, represented by the manna in the wilderness (6.32-51). Though known as a man upon earth, and a possible messianic claimant according to current Jewish expectations (7.25-52), he is affiliated to God as

[1] There are no secure grounds for assigning 5.28f to an interpolator (against Bultmann).

a son to a father (8.30-47), which means that he has a supra-historical dimension (8.58). To those whose eyes are enlightened[1] to understand the truth (9.1-34), he is known not only as the designated Son of Man (9.35),[2] but also as the Son of God, whose sonship consists in perfect moral unity with the Father (10.30, 33, 36-8). Above all, this relationship with the Father is expressed in his death (12.27), which paradoxically is the moment of his glorification as Son of Man (3.14; 8.28; 12.28, 32; 13.31f; 17.1), and makes possible a permanent relationship of fellowship with the disciples for all time (14.18-23; 15.1-10; 16.16-22; 17.26). Thus it is absolutely essential that the confession of faith in Jesus should include acceptance of the necessity of his death. Without that the confession of faith would be defective (6.53-8; 7.33-6; 8.21-9; 10.11,15,17f; 12.23f; 16.5-7). Many of these facets of the confession of faith are introduced in the Prologue (1.1-18). The importance of a correct understanding of its full implications is further emphasised in 1 John 4.1-6.

(c) Belief in Jesus, formally expressed in this way, enables the disciple to avail himself of the eschatological cleansing, which is symbolised by baptism in water, without waiting for the consummation. Baptism is a spiritual act whereby men are brought into the realm in which the Spirit is operative (3.5-8).[3] It is a transference from the old order to the conditions of the new age which follows the judgment. It marks so radical a break with the past that it can even be described as a fresh birth, a birth from above (3.3, 5, 7). It results in life under the Spirit, comparable in its fecundity to a never-failing spring of water (4.4-14; 7.38).[4] John has to explain that this only applies

---

[1] In chapter 9 John uses a tradition of the healing of a blind man to teach the need for the enlightening of the mind, in preparation for the full revelation of the identity of Jesus which will be given in chapter 10. This suggests that he has the experience of conversion in mind (cf. Acts 9.17f), and therefore the possibility of an allusion to baptism here cannot be excluded (cf. Heb. 10.32; 1 Pet. 2.9).

[2] The reading 'Son of God' in this verse is probably due to the use of this chapter in connexion with baptism, so that the words have been conformed to the baptismal confession (hence also the interpolation of verses 38, 39a, which are missing from some important manuscripts).

[3] This is another passage where the primary reference is to spiritual cleansing in preparation for the coming kingdom, but a secondary reference to baptism is possible, even probable. There is no warrant for the omission of 'water' in verse 5 (held by Bultmann to be an addition by the ecclesiastical redactor). It can, of course, be interpreted of spiritual cleansing (cf. the quotation from 1QS 4.2 of above) without requiring any reference to baptism (so Lohse, art. cit., p. 116).

[4] Water is not only a symbol of purification, but frequently represents a source of life (cf. Ps. 36.9; Isa. 12.3; 55.1; Ezek. 47.1; Zech. 14.8).

after Jesus has been glorified (7.39).[1] This is because the revelation of Jesus about himself is not complete until he has passed through death to be glorified as Son of Man, and therefore the full confession of faith cannot be made until then (hence the belief of Jesus' hearers during his ministry, often referred to by John in the course of his narrative, is partial and awaits completion before it can be effective). By the shedding of his blood the eschatological fountain of water has been opened (19.34, 37; Zech. 12.10; 13.1).[2] The Spirit is actually imparted to the disciples when they are in a condition to make full confession of faith, i.e. when they see him after his resurrection, and thus know that his death has led to glory (20.19-23). Then he shows them his pierced side (verse 20), and, breathing upon them just as God breathed on the first man to bring life into his nostrils (Gen. 2.7),[3] says, 'Receive Holy Spirit' (verse 22).[4]

The Spirit is rarely mentioned in John.[5] More often he speaks of the effect of the confession of faith in terms of 'life' or 'eternal life' (3.15f, 36, etc.). 'Eternal' (*aiōnios*) can be taken in a timeless way, but probably carries with it the idea of belonging to the Age to Come (*hā-'ōlām hab-bā'*), as the present age is passing away and therefore cannot rightly be called eternal. This is clearly indicated by 5.24, a verse which is of crucial importance for understanding John's eschatology. John does not repudiate the categories of Jewish eschatology in favour of a timeless 'realised' eschatology. Rather, the blessings of the Age to Come are available now through the confession of faith, so that it is more correct to speak of an anticipated eschatology. It is thus natural to speak of the new life with the

---

[1] It is tempting to treat this verse as an explanatory gloss, but it is (rightly, in my view) accepted by Bultmann.

[2] Here again Bultmann brackets the operative words (*kai exēlthen euthus haima kai hudōr*) as a gloss intended to introduce a sacramental allusion. But 'blood' here can hardly refer to the eucharist. Rather, it refers to the death of Jesus considered as a sacrifice, so that 'water' is to be taken as a hint of its atoning and cleansing effect, cf. 1 John 1.7; 5.6-8. Once more, an allusion to baptism is possible, but not certain. See further Klos, op. cit., pp. 74-81.

[3] cf. also Ezek. 37.9, where the same word (*enephusēsen*) is used.

[4] This is the mission charge of the risen Christ to the apostles as representatives of all the disciples (cf. Matt. 28. 19f; Mark 16.15f), and there is no necessary reference to ecclesiastical ordination as a sacrament. Similarly verse 23 refers to the response to the mission preaching, rather than to the discipline of penance, as in Mark 16.16, cf. J. N. Sanders and B. A. Mastin, *The Gospel according to St. John*, Black's New Testament Commentaries (London, 1968), ad loc.

[5] For further references cf. 3.34 and the Paraclete passages (14.16f, 26; 15.26f; 16.5-15).

imagery of resurrection, which is anticipated in the believer
(4.46-54; 5.25-9; 11.21-7).

If it is right to assume that baptism in water was actually
practised in the Johannine church, it is certainly an act
which can be regarded as sacramental. It is not merely a
symbol of something that awaits realisation in the future. Its
range of reference extends to the full revelation of Jesus concerning himself, his life, death, glorification and gift of the
Spirit. By confession of this faith the disciple acquires the
benefits of Christ's finished work. The future blessings are
available from that moment. Baptism is thus both a symbolic
act and the moment when what is symbolised is effected. This
Johannine approach to baptism illustrates two important tendencies which were operative at the time when the Fourth
Gospel was written. One of these is the concentration of interest on Christology in face of the proliferation of heretical
teachings, which accounts for the great importance which is
attached to the confession of faith. The other is the shift of the
centre of gravity with regard to eschatology. Consistent
eschatology is not denied, but the emphasis now falls on the
idea that the individual believer may have present possession
of future blessings. For him the decisive moment in the passage
from the present order to the Age to Come has already passed.

<h1 style="text-align:center">III</h1>

When we turn to the eucharist, we are faced with a very
different problem from that of baptism. Here it is not enough
to prove that the Johannine church had a common religious
meal, comparable to that of the Qumran Sect. It is, indeed,
virtually certain that their common life included a meal of this
kind, as already indicated at the outset of this essay. No doubt
that can be regarded as sacramental in some sense. But later
(and possibly already by the time John was writing) a clear
distinction was made between the *agapē* and the eucharist.[1]

---

[1] The liturgy of *Didache* 9-10, which shows literary dependence on the Fourth
Gospel, and may perhaps emanate from the Johannine circle, is best explained as an
instruction for the *agapē*. Only at the end do we have the opening of the eucharist,
including the *maranatha* invocation (10.6). Hence the eucharistic words are not included. The omission of the eucharistic liturgy is almost certainly due to the *disciplina
arcani*. In this document *eucharistia* is used in its proper sense of 'blessing'. The eucharist proper (as opposed to the *agapē*) is called *thusia*, thus indicating the connection with the passion, which is not mentioned otherwise in the *Didache* (14).

There seems to be only one distinguishing feature between them, and that is that the eucharist necessarily included some form of the eucharistic words of Jesus in the blessing of the bread and of the cup. Ignatius (*Smyrn.*, 6) complains that the Docetists abstain from *eucharistias kai proseuchēs*, but it appears in chapter 8 that they held their own schismatic assembly, in which the eucharistic blessings were defective because they denied the flesh and blood of Jesus which these blessings affirm.

In dealing with the Fourth Gospel it is thus not sufficient to look for evidence of a common meal, and, as before, little help can be gained by looking for eucharistic themes. The whole question hinges on the eucharistic words of Jesus. If John contains no reference to them, it cannot be claimed that he knows and approves the Christian practice of the eucharist. This consideration throws into sharp relief the surprising absence of the eucharistic words from John's account of the Last Supper in chapter 13. It is difficult to deny that the eucharistic words lie behind the last section of the discourse on the Bread of Life (6.51b-58), but this section is held by the Bultmannian school to be an interpolation by the ecclesiastical redactor. Before we tackle these points in detail, it should be pointed out that, even if John does not accept the eucharist, his reason cannot be the same as that of the Docetists. They were concerned to evade the tradition of the physical death of Jesus, but John is most insistent on the reality and the necessity of the passion, as we have seen in considering the confession of faith. On the other hand no other reason for the rejection of the eucharist is known at this period. It is an anachronism to suggest that anti-sacramentalism was a factor at this time. Nowhere in the New Testament is the eucharist classed among the human ordinances, like the Jewish food laws, which the spiritual man can treat with contempt.[1]

It is obvious that the problem of the omission in chapter 13 cannot be decided unless we first settle the question of 6.51b-58. For if this passage is an integral part of John's composition, then the omission in chapter 13 cannot be explained on the grounds of an objection to the eucharist on his part, but will have to be explained in other ways. But although the claim that these

[1] On Col. 2.16 see M. D. Hooker, 'Were there False Teachers in Colossae?', in *Christ and Spirit in the New Testament: Studies in Honour of C. F. D. Moule*, edited by B. Lindars and S. S. Smalley (Cambridge, 1973), pp. 315-31.

verses are an interpolation has had many advocates, the opposite view has been steadily gaining ground in recent studies.[1] They have not been added simply in order to relate the discourse on the Bread of Life to the eucharist. They are needed in order to make an essential point of the discourse, which John could not make if he confined himself to the terms of reference used up to this point. This is the fact that Jesus, who is the Bread of Life, must die.[2] The theme of the manna in the wilderness (verses 31-4), and the Wisdom invitation in terms of food and drink (verse 35), are not sufficient to make this point. The eucharistic words, however, maintain the metaphor of eating and drinking and also provide the required reference to the passion. The case is no different from the Shepherd allegory of 10.7-18, where the idea of the shepherd's sacrifice of his life for the sheep is introduced at a late stage in the exposition, although there has been nothing to prepare for it in the opening parable (10.1-5). The object of these verses is thus, not to relate the discourse to the eucharist, but to exploit the eucharistic words for the needs of the discourse. Those who feed on Jesus as the Bread of Life must accept the fact that they feed on one who was bound to die in order to accomplish the divine purpose. This is the 'hard saying' (verse 60) which gives offence (*skandalizei*, verse 61; cf. 1 Cor. 1.18-24).[3]

Besides this general point of interpretation, it should also be noted that there are no decisive points of style to suggest that these verses are the work of any other writer than John himself.[4] Moreover the formal structure of the whole discourse positively requires them. The discourse uses the techniques of Jewish midrashic exegesis, whereby a scriptural quotation is broken down into its separate elements, which are then treated successively. In this case the quotation is to be found in verse 31 (*arton ek tou ouranou edōken autois phagein*). These verses are required for the exposition of *phagein*.[5] Finally an allusion to the

[1] See the survey in Klos, op. cit., pp. 11-44.
[2] cf. H. Schürmann, 'Joh. 6.51c—ein Schlüssel zur johanneischen Brotrede', *BZ*, N.F. 2 (1958), pp. 244-62.
[3] Thus the scandal is not the supposed 'carnal' idea of the sacrament in these verses (Lohse speaks of 'eine so krasse sakramentale Auffassung'), but the passion. Hence Bultmann transposes 6.60-71 to follow 8.40.
[4] Lohse, art. cit., p. 118f, lists a few small points which are contrary to John's usual style, but none is without parallel elsewhere in the gospel.
[5] This analysis of the discourse was worked out by P. Borgen, *Bread from Heaven*, Supplements to *Novum Testamentum* 10, Leiden, 1965.

eucharist is at least possible already in verse 35, where Jesus identifies himself with the bread from heaven, and then promises satisfaction not only of hunger but also of thirst. For, although these ideas can be explained sufficiently from texts of the Old *Testament* Wisdom tradition,[1] so that reference to the eucharist is not positively required, it should not be forgotten that in the eucharistic words Jesus does in some sense identify himself with the bread.[2]

Turning back to chapter 13, we may well comment in passing that the failure of the ecclesiastical redactor to insert the eucharistic words in this chapter is eloquent testimony to the integrity of the text in general and its freedom from major interpolations. The omission of the eucharistic words cannot be explained by anti-sacramentalism. The *disciplina arcani* can scarcely be the reason, if John has already made such open use of these words in 6.51-8.[3] In any case it is doubtful if this was operative at the time when John was writing.[4] The most simple and natural explanation is that he wished to concentrate on other interests in his account of the Last Supper, and so reserved the eucharistic words for separate treatment. It is charactersitic of his literary technique to single out particular items from the traditions which are available to him, and to blow them up into larger units.[5] Here he wishes to concentrate on the theme of discipleship. The treachery of Judas at the supper table, which John regards as the most terrible breach of the obligations implicit in a common meal, is turned into a dramatic episode as an object-lesson for the contemporary church. By placing the emphasis on this aspect of the tradition, John has neglected the eucharistic words, which could have been the basis for a very different development, if he had wished to use them at this point. What that development would have been we have already seen from our consideration of chapter 6. John values the eucharistic words as a means of inculcating his

[1] The verse constitutes a reversal of Ecclus. 24.21. Cf. also Prov. 9.5; Isa. 55.1 (the latter may well be in mind, in view of the quotation of Isa. 54.13 in verse 45).
[2] If the Aramaic underlying *sōma* is *gūph*, then 'this is my body' (1 Cor. 11.24) could mean 'this [bread] is myself'. It is thus possible that 'I am the bread' is an intentional allusion to the eucharistic words, adapted to the needs of the discourse at this point. On the other hand John's *sarx* in verses 51ff does not support interpretation of *sōma* in this sense in his circle.
[3] This view is taken by J. Jeremias, *The Eucharistic Words of Jesus*, revised edition, London, 1966, pp. 125-37.   [4] cf. Lohse, art. cit., p. 122.
[5] For examples of the technique, cf. B. Lindars, *The Gospel of John*, p. 595.

very important theme of the necessity of the passion. As he had already treated this theme in different ways all through chapters 7-12, he did not need to treat it afresh in his account of the Last Supper. In fact he chose to use the supper traditions as the starting-point for extended treatment of another very important theme, the meaning of discipleship (chapters 13-17). This holds good, even if chapter 6 was not part of the gospel as originally planned.[1]

Finally, even Bultmann admits that there is evidence that John knew the eucharistic words in 17.19 (*huper autōn (egō) hagiazō emauton*).[2] Here the two themes of discipleship and of the necessity of the passion come together. There is certainly some truth in Bultmann's contention that the Prayer of Jesus in this chapter is to be regarded as John's substitute for the missing institution of the eucharist in chapter 13.

The meaning of the eucharist in the Johannine church embraces both these themes. In any case it can be assumed without hesitation that these Christians held a religious meal of the Jewish type, in which their union with one another and with the glorified Lord was vividly realised. But there is no serious reason to doubt that the celebration included the eucharistic words also, so that the blessing of the bread and the cup always made reference to the death of Jesus, which is so important to John. The bread and wine are symbols of Christ's flesh and blood, which he gave 'for the life of the world' (6.51). He is present with the disciples, though he cannot be seen (20.29). But their joy in acknowledging his presence (20.20) can never let them be forgetful of what it cost him to achieve the place of glory. For, just as in the practice of Paul, the eucharistic blessing of the bread and cup continually makes *anamnēsis* of Christ's death. As the disciples recall this sacrificial act, they are reminded of the obligation laid on each of them as disciples to display a similar quality of love (15.13; 13.34f). The eucharistic words have not yet acquired the status of a sacramental 'form', effecting a hidden change of substance in the sacred elements. But they define the act of breaking the bread and sharing the

---

[1] Chapter 6 was added in the second edition of the gospel, according to the two-stage theory of composition advanced in B. Lindars, *Behind the Fourth Gospel* (London, 1971).

[2] cf. I Cor. 11.24 *huper humōn*; Mark 14.24 *huper pollōn*; also John 6.51 *huper tēs tou kosmou zōēs*.

cup in relation to the central act of redemption, the sacrifice of Christ. They thus constitute a proclamation (1 Cor. 11.26) of the word of the gospel, no doubt further elaborated in a homily or in the extempore prayer which accompanies them.[1]

The eucharist of the Johannine church thus maintains the life of the Christian brotherhood which is entered by baptism. It recalls the most solemn item of the confession of faith, and it provides a setting in which the abiding presence of the glorified Christ is realised. At such a moment the disciples are conscious that, through their union with him, they already possess the blessings of the Age to Come (6.36-40). They are also inspired to follow out the moral consequences of communion in mutual love.

John has no wish to belittle the importance of either baptism or the eucharist. They are practices with which his readers are expected to be familiar, so that he can simply take their existence for granted. What does concern him is that those who are brought into fellowship with Christ through baptism should have a true understanding of what is implied by the confession of faith; and that those who meet for the celebration of the eucharist should fully comprehend the moral obligations implicit in the act of communion with one another and the glorified Christ. To this end the preaching of the word in connection with these sacramental acts is indispensable.

---

[1] cf. *Didache*, 10.7, where, immediately after the *maranatha* which opens the eucharist, the instruction continues: 'But permit the prophets to offer thanksgiving as much as they desire.'

This article was first published as 'Parola e sacramento nel quarto vangelo' in *Chiesa per il mondo*: miscellanea teologico-pastorale nel LXX del card. Michele Pellegrino (Bologna, 1974), Tom. I, pp. 105-19.

6

THE PASSION IN THE FOURTH GOSPEL

I

The christology of the Fourth Gospel has two poles, which can be summed up as incarnation and exaltation, or as the sending of the Son of God and his going to the Father. Between these two is the passion of Christ, but it is by no means clear what significance is attached to it in the Johannine scheme. Modern interpreters tend to reduce its importance[1]. They observe that, when John wishes to speak of the death of Jesus, he uses the language of exaltation or glorification. This belongs to the stage beyond death, so that the impression is given that John tends to skate over it. When John employs such an expression as 'to go away', it points to the passion merely as a mode of transition, the passage from this world to glory. John says that 'the Son of Man must be lifted up' (3,14), but, although this clearly refers to the cross, it is couched in the language of exaltation, and John never says that Jesus must suffer. In fact he appears to have no interest in the death of Jesus for what it is in itself. He does not value it as Paul does, as the unique act of atonement for sin. Such few references in the gospel as do point in this direction merely reflect the common theology of the church and are not central to John's thought[2].

That John should have so little interest in the passion is surprising, when we consider the importance of the passion in the structure of the gospel as a whole. No less than eight chapters (12-19) are devoted to the events following the decision of the Sanhedrin to put Jesus to death (11,53). This can, of course, be attributed to John's choice of the gospel form, combining a collection of traditions about Jesus with a passion narrative, but this is in itself significant, because he could have adopted some other type of treatise for his purpose, if he had wished to do so. Moreover in the earlier part of the gospel he has broken down the Markan chronology so as to bring Jesus to Jerusalem on a number of occasions. Each time there is some indication of the march

---

1. Notably BULTMANN, cf. his *Theology of the New Testament* II, London, 1955, pp. 52-55.
2. BULTMANN, *op. cit.*, p. 54, even calls them 'a foreign element in his work'. W.G. KÜMMEL, *The Theology of the New Testament*, London, 1973, pp. 296ff, is more positive, but speaks of a 'recession of the idea of the expiation for sin through Jesus' death'.

of events towards the passion, which thereby becomes a more insistent theme than in the Synoptic Gospels. It may be objected that the structure of the gospel cannot be used as an argument, because it remains an open question how far it agrees with the evangelist's intentions or only represents the interests of a redactor. In fact the importance of the passion has penetrated the gospel far more deeply than in the arrangement of the contents. The repeated references to attempts to arrest Jesus cannot all be regarded as editorial comments. They are closely integrated into the progress of the christological argument of the first ten chapters. When this reaches its climax in 10,22-39, and the final challenge is given to Jesus concerning his identity, his answer provokes the charge of blasphemy, which is precisely the charge levelled against him in the Synoptic trial narrative. Moreover the themes of the lifting up of the Son of Man and of Jesus' going to the Father certainly include reference to the passion in some sense, and are found exclusively in the discourses.

It is already clear from these facts that the passion is a matter of the greatest importance to John. If he seems to pay little attention to its significance as a sacrifice for sin, it is not because he undervalues it, but because he concentrates on another side of it which is central to his purpose in writing the gospel as a whole. This is, as we shall see below, that he regards a proper understanding of the relation of Jesus to the Father as the crucial issue for faith, and the passion is the point at which this relationship is definitively expressed. The passion is so important to John from this point of view that all other considerations are subordinate to it. The passion is a revelatory act, but it is also the actual moment of transition from the time of the ministry of Jesus to the time of his lordship in heaven in the era of the church. Thus, although we shall be largely concerned with its revelatory aspects, its importance as an historical event is not to be minimised. As far as Jesus himself is concerned, it marks the transition from earthly life to heavenly glory. But because Jesus is who he is, and because of the continuing relationship of the disciples to him which is established by faith, it also marks the transition from the present world order, which is under the domination of sin, to the era of grace which belongs to the coming age. Fom this point of view Jesus 'takes away the sin of the world' (1,29), because he effects this transference. The death of Jesus is like a sacrifice, which removes the taint of sin and so renders a man capable of fellowship with God. Though this thought is not actually stated in the Fourth Gospel, it finds expression in 1 Jn 1,7; 2,2; 4,10.

Before going on to our main theme, it may be well to say something further about the sacrificial interpretation of the passion in

John. For although it is a secondary issue, it is not wholly unintegrated into his thought, and it is unsafe to try to excise it as due to the hand of a redactor. In the first place, the appellation 'lamb of God', which is certainly connected with sacrificial expiation of sin in 1,29, is picked up again in 1,36, thereby encapsulating the account of the baptism of Jesus in verses 30-34 and imposing upon it some connection with his death as a sacrifice. Bultmann is satisfied that 'the lamb of God' alone, even without the rest of verse 29, is sufficient to indicate Jewish Christian provenance and a sacrificial interest[3], though he regards it as belonging originally to verses 35-36 and not to the baptism account. Be that as it may, the text as it now stands makes the sacrificial interest explicit at the outset of the baptism story. This is told in such a way that the tradition is presented as a signal to the Baptist concerning Jesus' identity. Jesus is the one 'who baptizes with Holy Spirit' (verse 33). True to the underlying tradition, John presents the Baptist material in an eschatological mould. The Baptist baptizes with water in preparation for the coming baptism in Holy Spirit. Jesus is singled out as the actual agent of this baptism. It is evident that the eschatological cleansing is the major theme. If Jesus, who is to perform this, is the Lamb of God, it may be concluded that the act which effects this cleansing is his sacrificial death.

Secondly, this reference to sacrificial cleansing is not isolated, but reappears at a much later stage in the gospel. In his account of the Last Supper in chapter 13 John uses a tradition in which Jesus washed the disciples' feet. The main point appears to be the Master's example of humble service (verses 13-18), but this only throws into greater relief the extraordinary conversation between Jesus and Peter in verses 8-11. Here the point is the necessity of cleansing, and it is made clear that this is something that is done once and for all, though Judas Iscariot is incapable of receiving its effect. It is normal to see in these verses a reference to Christian baptism, and this may very well be true. But the lack of an overt allusion to the sacrament, and the position of this pericope within the setting of the passion narrative, certainly compel a reference to the death of Jesus as a sacrifice done once and for all, whether there is allusion to baptism or not. If, as I believe to be the case, John has himself introduced this conversation into his source, it is reasonable to suppose that he has taken advantage of the theme of washing in order to bring in this particular aspect of the

---

3. Other explanations — a messianic title (Dodd), an Aramaic confusion between 'lamb' and 'servant' (Burney) — have not won acceptance with scholars. John's timing of the passion on the eve of the passover may also be intended to imply a sacrificial interpretation.

meaning of the passion[4]. There may perhaps be a further allusion to
it in 19,34, though here the reference may be to the eschatological
effusion of the Spirit rather than to the cleansing associated with it[5].
Both cleansing and effusion are *effects* of the death of Christ, and
there is no emphasis on the mechanics of sacrifice as such in
connection with them.

But, thirdly, this does appear in another class of references to the
passion, where the preposition *hyper* is used. In these cases death is
suffered on behalf of others. Though the language of sacrifice is
certain, or virtually certain, only at 6,51 and 17,19, it is natural to
include in this class 10,11.15; 11,50-52; 18,14, in which the death of
Jesus is mentioned, and also 13,37-38 (of Peter seeking to emulate
Jesus) and 15,13 (the general principle). In all these cases the
emphasis goes on the death, which is held to be necessary for the
object which is to be achieved. Further, John states this as a general
principle in 12,24, probably quoting an authentic saying of Jesus.

In the light of these references it can be justifiably claimed that
John is neither ignorant of nor uninterested in the idea of the passion
as a sacrifice for sin. Moreover two points in particular suggest that
his thought on this subject is closely related to his main argument in
connection with the passion. Firstly, the notion of cleansing is
conceived in eschatological terms rather than in Pharisaic terms of
personal holiness. The passion opens up the conditions of the coming
age, when the judgment is past and there is no blockage to the
abundant life of the Spirit (cf. 5,24). Secondly, the sacrificial idea of
a death on behalf of others is always expressed in terms of voluntary

---

4. This opinion is based on John's technique in handling traditional material
elsewhere in the gospel. For details see B. LINDARS, *The Gospel of John* (The New
Century Bible), London, 1972, pp. 446-452.

5. The question depends on whether there is intended to be an allusion to 7,38-39
or not. Bultmann attributes verse 34b to the ecclesiastical redactor, on the grounds that
it is an allusion to the sacraments and that only the transfixion is referred to in the
following Old Testament quotations. But the second (Zech 12,10) is from a verse which
begins 'I will pour out ... a spirit of compassion and supplication, so that, when they look
on him whom they have pierced, they shall mourn...': and then the context continues 'On
that day there shall be a fountain opened ... to cleanse them from sin and uncleanness'
(13,1). The first quotation (Ex 12,46, Num 9,12 or Ps 34,21) is probably intended to
allude to the passover, which included in its ceremonial the apotropaic sprinkling of the
blood. Thus both quotations, which formally refer only to the transfixion, carry with them
overtones of the ritual use of blood and water. Even if verse 35 be excluded as the work
of the final redactor, the presence of these quotations underlines the fact that the
effusion of blood and water was felt to be significant, and it is most natural to suppose
that this has something to do with the *consequences* of the passion, seeing that the
preceding presentation of the death of Jesus has placed the emphasis on the idea of
completion (19,28.30).

self-sacrifice, so that moral considerations are uppermost. If the 74
passion is a revelatory act, it is not one in which Jesus is merely a
passive agent or the powerless victim of hostile forces. It has all the
solemnity of ultimate moral decision.

II

John's main argument with regard to the passion is closely bound up
with his presentation of the meaning of Jesus for faith, which is the
major purpose of the whole gospel. Thus his interest in the passion is
primarily christological rather than soteriological. If we leave out of
account the Prologue, which has its own inner logical structure, but
stands outside the gospel narrative through which John presents his
interpretation of Jesus, we find ourselves faced in the first chapter with
a series of titles of Jesus which immediately pose the question of
christology. These include the title Lamb of God, which can, then, be
regarded as one of a number of possibilities for exploring the meaning
of Jesus for faith. But apart from this there is no reference to the
passion until we reach the cleansing of the temple (2,13-22). John has
turned this tradition into a symbolic act, pointing to a future event of
destruction and restoration. Though Jesus speaks of the destruction of
the temple, it is his own death and resurrection that is meant. The
present position of this pericope, at the very beginning of the ministry
of Jesus, gives it a broader significance in relation to his mission as a
whole. The renewal of Israel (typified by the cleansing of the temple)
will be achieved by his death and resurrection.

It is tempting to regard this pericope as the starting point of
John's argument concerning the passion, but further inspection shows
that this is not so. The next reference to the passion (3,14) belongs to
a totally different range of thought and expression. It enunciates the
theme of the lifting up of the Son of Man, and this turns out to be a
recurring theme of great importance in the gospel (cf. 8,28;
12,23.32.34; 13,31-32; 17,1.5; 18,32). But though the idea of renewal
precedes the cleansing story in the marriage at Cana (2,1-11), and
continues in the discourse with Nicodemus in chapter 3, the ideas of
2,13-22 are not taken up again. In fact it is altogether probable that
John has transferred this pericope from chapter 12 to its present
position after the christological argument of the intervening chapters
had already been completed. It is significant that the only place where
the theme of destruction and renewal is taken up again is in the
traditional saying of Jesus in 12,24, immediately after the point which
this pericope is likely to have occupied in his original scheme. In spite

of this, the theme is not foreign to John's interests. Moreover it fits once more the eschatological orientation of his thought, inasmuch as the renewal is to be a condition which follows the death of Jesus, so that a programmatic idea of the future is implied by it.

Our attempt to find the starting point of John's passion argument has brought us to a range of verses in which the Son of Man figures. In spite of all the difficulties which surround this obscure phrase, it is to be taken seriously in all its occurrences in the gospel, and the apocalyptic ideas which appear to be associated with it are to be given their full weight. Bultmann denies that John understands it in its Jewish and early Christian sense of a future coming. The presence of Jesus in the incarnation (according to his view) *is* the future coming: in his passion Jesus reveals his glory, which belongs to his celestial origin, but reveals it through the paradox of humiliation: and the believer, thus compelled to abandon all earthly ways of appropriating salvation, gains eternal life through the decision of faith which this entails, and so has passed through the eschatological judgment to share in Jesus' glory. It is true that Bultmann has arrived at this view as a result of his dialectical understanding of the Fourth Gospel. For the emphasis on the present actuality of the future coming is derived from the presupposition that the primary influence on John is the Gnostic redeemer myth. The evangelist has, however, drawn on the apocalyptic myth of early Christianity in order to give it its specifically Christian content. And it is this confrontation of two modes of thought which has produced the gospel's 'dualism of decision'[6] in place of the underlying cosmic dualism. This avoids the difficulty that the Gnostic myth is not really compatible with the Christian kerygma, but it is equally destructive with regard to apocalyptic, which is deprived of its characteristic attachment to the historical process. Indeed, the confusion is so great that apocalyptic has been claimed as one of the stages in the process of the rise of Gnosticism, to which indeed it may well be a contributory factor[7]; and Käsemann's thoroughgoing apoc-

6. The phrase is taken from the introduction by W. Schmithals to the English edition of Bultmann's commentary, *The Gospel of John*, Oxford, 1971, p. 9.

7. Thus J.M. Robinson writes of a 'gnosticizing trajectory' which runs 'from the pre- or proto-Gnosticism of Qumran through intermediate stages attested both in the New Testament and in part of Nag Hammadi into the full gnostic systems of the second century A.D.', J.M. ROBINSON and H. KOESTER, *Trajectories through Early Christianity*, Philadelphia, PA, 1971, p. 266. However it must be pointed out that the point on this 'trajectory' at which it becomes legitimate to speak of 'the Gnostic redeemer myth' is by no means clear. The apocalyptic myth can be identified with certainty in the New Testament, and is sufficiently well documented for the Jewish background of the times. But, in spite of increasing documentation from Mandean texts and from Nag Hammadi,

alyptic interpretaion of the Fourth Gospel has produced a docetic Christ as 'God striding over the earth' which can find no place for the reality of the passion at all[8].

The mistake in all this is the failure to understand the proper meaning of the apocalyptic myth in primitive Christianity, and when this is put right it will not seem so scandalous or impossible that John retains consistent eschatology as one of his underlying presuppositions. The dominating influence of the Son of Man vision in Dan 7 has obscured the real centre of gravity in apocalyptic thought. According to Dan 7 the Son of Man receives glory as a result of God's judgment, and this is in some way identified with the struggle of the loyal Jews against Antiochus Epiphanes on earth and their coming vindication[9]. On this basis it is assumed all too easily that the exaltation of Jesus is the final act in the process, at least as far as his personal history is concerned. For, of course, the working out of his victory on earth still waits to be completed. This is in effect the position which John, and also Paul and other New Testament writers[10], come to, but it should not be taken as the most primitive view. This, as I have shown elsewhere[11], is that the exaltation of Jesus puts him in the position of God's designated agent, who will perform the divine task of the judgment and the general resurrection in its proper time, which still lies in the future. The groundwork of early Christian apocalyptic is thus not the glorification of the Son of Man, which is by no means the

the Gnostic redeemer myth is still largely inferential in the New Testament, and its influence on New Testament writers remains unproven.

8. E. KÄSEMANN, *The Testament of Jesus*, London, 1968, especially pp. 4-26. His view depends on the implications of Jn 17,5, from which he draws the conclusion that the incarnation of Jesus is an episode of revelation involving temporary descent from and return to his normal position of heavenly glory.

9. Great caution is required in using this chapter, which has been far too readily pressed into service by scholars to support their solutions of the Son of Man problem. The supposed equation between the 'one like a son of man', 'the saints of the Most High' and the loyal Jews, or *hasidim*, does not appear in the literature based on this chapter, and is in any case probably mistaken, as 'the saints' denotes the angels (cf. M. NOTH, »Die Heiligen des Höchsten«, in *Festskrift til Prof. Dr. S. Mowinckel*, Oslo, 1955, pp. 146-161; = *The Holy Ones of the Most High*, in M. NOTH, *The Laws in the Pentateuch and Other Essays*, Edinburgh and London, 1966, pp. 215-228; L. DEQUEKER, *The "Saints of the Most High" in Qumran and Daniel*, in *OTS* 18 [1973] 108-187). In the New Testament only verses 13 and 14 of this chapter are quoted or alluded to (apart from the Apocalypse, which draws heavily on its imagery), and then always with reference to the personal exaltation of Jesus.

10. 1 Cor 15,24-28; Phil 3,20-21; Heb 2,6-8.

11. In a lecture at Aberdeen University, 'Re-enter the Apocalyptic Son of Man', *NTS* 22 (1975-76) 52-72, and in the T.W. Manson Memorial Lecture for 1974 at Manchester University, 'The Apocalyptic Myth and the Death of Christ', *BJRL* 57 (1975) 366-387.

centre of interest in the contemporary Jewish apocalyptic, but the
divine intervention at the transition of the ages. But the early
Christians had a vivid sense of belonging to the Lord who was to
perform this task and of already participating in the blessings of the
Age in anticipation of the coming event. It is in this sense that
Christianity alters the perspective of Jewish apocalyptic, and reaches
its characteristic vital tension of the 'now — but not yet'. And it is in
this context that the appeal for immediate personal decision of faith
becomes a matter of pressing urgency.

Before we can proceed on this basis, however, the question of pre-
existence must be faced, as it poses the most formidable objection to
the use of the apocalyptic myth as the basis of John's thought and
explains the continuing hold of the Gnostic redeemer myth in post-
Bulmannian study. It is frequently asserted that it is incompatible with
the apocalyptic myth on the grounds that apocalyptic employs the
concept of pre-determination rather than pre-existence[12]. On the other
hand the notion of the pre-existence of Christ had certainly been
reached in Christianity prior to John, as it is already apparent in the
writings of Paul. It is in fact possible to see the confluence of several
factors behind this pre-Pauline development. In the first place, there
is the determinist attitude of the apocalyptic mind itself. It is characteristic of this way of thinking to imagine that God has prepared
everything in advance, and if he has foreseen the agent of the final
intervention it is only natural to suppose that he has also foreseen the
earthly person who is designated for this task. This at least reaches
ideal pre-existence, though not actual pre-existence. However, secondly,
rabbinic speculation knows of seven things which were in existence
before the creation of the world, and these include the name of the
Messiah[13]. Although later[14] the name of the Messiah is distinguished
as one item which did not have actual as opposed to ideal pre-
existence (by contrast with the Law), it is clear that behind this
discussion there is the assumption that it did so. In fact the naming of
the Messiah can be regarded as bringing him into existence, and if the
one was done before the foundation of the world so was the other, as
witness 1 Enoch 48,3-6, which treats the naming of the Son of Man in
this way. Thirdly, the actual pre-existence of the Law was supported in

12. Cf. T.W. MANSON, *The Son of Man in Daniel, Enoch and the Gospels*, in M.
BLACK (ed.), *Studies in the Gospels and Epistles by T.W. Manson*, London, 1962, pp. 123-
145. For what follows, cf. R.G. HAMERTON-KELLY, *Pre-existence, Wisdom and the Son of
Man*, Cambridge, 1973.
13. Pes. 54a; Ned. 39b.
14. Genesis Rabba 1,4.

rabbinic discussion by Prov 8,22[15] and other Wisdom passages, and this correlation has been an influence both on Paul and on the Prologue of John. But, fourthly, it is probable that the notion of Christ's pre-existence does not begin with these theoretical considerations, but with a conviction which these make intellectually respectable. This is the profound impression of a special personal relationship between Jesus and God, expressed in the Father/Son terminology, and the fact that Jesus claimed to have been 'sent' (though that need have meant no more than an awareness of a prophetic calling). The idea that Jesus had been exalted to heaven, to be kept in reserve for his eschatological function, placed him securely on the most exalted celestial plane, which was then regarded as his proper setting as God's Son, and put him in relation with the whole sweep of history under God[16].

John's theology of the passion is inextricably bound up with statements which show the influence of the apocalyptic myth. In the light of what has been said above, it is reasonable to take this as the starting point in the tradition from which John develops creatively his own interpretation of the passion. To this we now turn.

III

John derives his use of the Son of Man as a title from the tradition 77 of the words of Jesus[17]. How this came to be used in a seemingly

---

15. Quoted in the above passages, cf. also STRACK-BILLERBECK II, pp. 353-357. R. AKIBA (d. 137) calls the Law 'the precious instrument by which the world was created', Aboth 3,15.

16. It is unsafe to assume that the *Abba* address in itself points to a personal conviction on the part of Jesus concerning his divine sonship, which he imparted to the disciples, and which therefore accounts for the unexpected frequency of the title 'Son of God' in early Christianity. But even allowing for other factors (the occasional use of 'a son of God' = one whom God approves, by contrast with 'a son of Belial'; the sparing Messianic use of 'Son of God', based on Ps 2,7, etc.; the influence of pagan hellenistic religion), the *Abba* address may still be the ultimate reason why this title came into use so widely and so rapidly. For the effect of belief in his exaltation is to put the Father/Son relationship, which is vividly remembered as a feature of his earthly life, onto the celestial plane, and it thereby acquires new status as a description of an eternal reality. The usage of the Father/Son correlation in John is consistent with a development along these lines, building on items in the sayings tradition in which it is expressed. For the problems in connection with the title Son of God, cf. G. VERMES, *Jesus the Jew*, London, 1973, pp. 192-213.

17. The argument which now follows to some extent overlaps with my article *The Son of Man in the Johannine Christology*, in B. LINDARS and S.S. SMALLEY, *Christ and Spirit in the New Testament: Studies in Honour of C.F.D. Moule*, Cambridge, 1973, pp. 43-60 [in this volume, pp. 33-50]. It will be seen, however, that I have modified some of the

titular way to denote the agent of God's intervention, and whether it had this meaning on the lips of Jesus himself, are questions which need not concern us for the purpose of this paper[18]. What is certain is that it possessed, or acquired, this apocalyptic meaning in the process of transmission of his sayings, and that it thereby forms a conventional feature of apocalyptic sayings in the style of Jesus, not only in John but also in Matthew.

When John mentions the Son of Man, there is always a future reference to the functions of Jesus at the End Time. The title is applicable to Jesus during the time of the ministry only in so far as he is the designated Son of Man, who will perform these functions according to the predestined plan of God. But his actions in the present are 'signs' or 'the works of God', because they are revelatory acts, indicating who he is (christology) and what he is destined to achieve (soteriology). It is a matter of the utmost importance to John that the significance of these acts should not be missed. The act which demonstrates that Jesus is the designated Son of Man is, surprisingly at first sight, not the resurrection but the passion.

A hint of this already appear in 1,51, the first place in which the Son of Man is mentioned. There is much to be said for the contention than John is here making use of a Jewish interpretation of Jacob's ladder, known from rabbinic sources, in which the ascending and descending angels join the earthly Jacob to his archetype in heaven[19]. But it is a mistake to read into the present context speculations concerning the destiny of the Primal Man, or of Jesus as the inclusive

views which I there expressed.

18. The principal problem is the consistent use of the arthrous form ὁ υἱὸς τοῦ ἀνθρώπου in these sayings (except Jn 5,27), and no advance can be made in deciding these questions until this problem has been solved. C.F.D. Moule has suggested that the article has demonstrative force, as in the Similitudes of Enoch (cf. 2 Esdras 13,3, *ille homo*). On this basis he argues that the phrase always refers to a particular 'son of man', i.e. the 'one like a son of man' of Dan 7,13-14 (*Neglected Features in the Problem of "the Son of Man"*, in J. GNILKA, *Neues Testament und Kirche: Rudolf Schnackenburg zum 60. Geburtstag*, Freiburg-Basel-Wien, 1974).

19. Genesis Rabba 68,18. The interpretation is attributed to R. Yannai (c. 240 A.D.), and it is impossible to tell whether it really goes back as far as New Testament times.

But new evidence for the antiquity of the interpretation has now appeared in Targum Neofiti at Gen 28,12. This reads: And he dreamed, and behold, a ladder was fixed on the earth and its head reached to the height of the heavens, and behold, angels that had accompanied him from the house of his father ascended to bear good tidings to the angels on high, saying: Come and see a just man whose image is engraved in the throne of the glory, whom you desired to see. And behold, the angels from before the Lord were ascending and descending and observed him. (A. DIEZ MACHO, *Neophyti I*, Madrid/Barcelona, 1968, p. 572).

representative of redeemed humanity, which depend on ideas that are assumed to be latent in the title, but are nowhere brought to the surface by John. The one thing that is clear is that the Son of Man means Jesus himself. The reference is to a future occasion, when Nathanael will have a glimpse into heaven. But the whole point of the saying, and the thing which stands out all the more clearly when the rabbinic interpretation of Jacob's dream is recalled, is that on this occasion the Son of Man will be still on earth, or rather Jesus on earth will be seen to be joined to his heavenly archetype as the designated Son of Man[20]. The saying thus points forward to a revelatory act in which Jesus, while still on earth, will be seen to be the predestined Son of Man, already existing in heaven in the plan of God. What this revelatory act will be is not specified, but we have a right to expect John to make this clear as he unfolds his christological argument later on. It is evidently something that surpasses the indications of Jesus' identity that have so far been given (1,50).

The nature of this act begins to become clear in 3,14. This refers to the necessity of the lifting up of the Son of Man. It is plain enough that at one level of meaning this denotes the exaltation of Jesus to the position of divine glory appropriate to the apocalyptic Son of Man. All the emphasis, however, falls on the implied allusion to the passion. The lifting up of a serpent on a pole is meaningless as a comparison for exaltation to heaven, but makes an excellent type of the crucifixion. It had a healing effect, according to the tradition in Num 21, and in

78

20. The importance of deciding whether the Gnostic redeemer myth or the apocalyptic myth is the primary influence on John is well illustrated here. Odeberg, accepting the interpretation of R. Yannai as a guide, takes the title Son of Man to refer to Jesus as the earthly man, who is to be united with his heavenly archetype in glory. Bultmann summarizes his view with approval, as follows: 'In the Gnostic and in the Johannine view the "Son of Man" must be "glorified" (i.e. in Gnostic terms: be united with its heavenly archetype)'. This is almost the exact opposite of what is implied by the apocalyptic myth, according to which the Son of Man is the heavenly archetype, being the pre-determined agent of God reserved in heaven for the End Time, and Jesus is an earthly man who will eventually be discovered to be identical with him at his ascension. In fact this identity exists all along, because it was God's plan that Jesus should be the Son of Man when he created the Son of Man in the first place, just as Enoch first sees the Son of Man as an existing heavenly reality long before he discovers that he is himself to *be* that Son of Man (cf. note 22 below). It is this illogical situation which is presupposed by Jn 1,51. It becomes easier to grasp when we remember that the primary thought is that of the elevation of a righteous man (Jesus) to be God's future agent. The idea that that agent was created before the world is a further refinement, which then makes it necessary to think of Jesus *either* as descending from heaven for a temporary sojourn on earth *or* as being in both places at once for the period of his earthly life. It is my impression that the thought of John oscillates between these alternatives, and that he is not troubled by the logical difficulty involved.

the same way the lifting up of the Son of Man will lead to saving belief. It is an act which expresses God's love for all mankind (verse 16). Nevertheless, although it follows inevitably from this that the passion is the act which reveals that Jesus is the designated Son of Man, John does not say so directly. His language is intentionally ambiguous. The precise meaning is still held in reserve for a later point in the argument. It is instructive to follow through the references to the same theme before making further comment on the double meaning of 'lifted up'. In 8,28 the passive is replaced by the active, and the subject is the Jews: 'When you have lifted up the Son of Man...'. Hence the exaltation is an act done by the Jews, which can only mean the crucifixion. Moreover the result is that 'than you will know that I am he'. It is not necessary to make a decision on the meaning of ἐγώ εἰμι at this point. It is sufficient to observe that, having made it unmistakably clear that the lifting up is the passion, John at once asserts that it is a revelatory act, revealing something of profound importance about Jesus. The theme occurs once more in 12,32-34. Here the crowd to whom Jesus is speaking correctly understand that the lifting up means his death. The contrast in verse 34 is unintelligible on any other view, and John has inserted the comment of verse 33 to ensure that it is so understood[21].

The full meaning of what John intends cannot be deduced simply from the lifting up theme. John is playing on a comparison between exaltation to heaven and the act of crucifixion. In none of the passages in which this theme occurs is there any notion of humiliation. There is no suggestion of a paradoxical identity between humiliation and glory. From the point of view of apocalyptic the death of Jesus is his translation to the place of God's throne, so that he is lifted up from the plane of earthly existence to the celestial sphere in readiness for his functions as the Son of Man at the End Time. The passion is necessary, because there must be some definite act whereby Jesus passes from his earthly position to his heavenly position. The idea is comparable to that of Enoch in the Similitudes of Enoch, who, besides being a seer privileged to have a preview of the divine arrangements, is translated to heaven and declared to be the Son of Man whom he

21. Bultmann moves 12,34-36a to follow 8,29, on the grounds that the Son of Man has not been mentioned in 12,32. But 8,28 does not include δεῖ, so that if this reasoning is to be accepted the passage ought to be moved to follow 3,14. The comment of verse 33 is typical of John's style, as in 11,51; 13,28; cf. also 18,32; 21,19.

has seen predestined in God's plan[22]. It may well be that, in making use of this theme, John is building on one of the earliest forms of christology in primitive Christianity. Within this frame of thought the passion has significance in itself, quite apart from its implications for a doctrine of atonement, simply as the transition from the earthly to the heavenly sphere. But John also ascribes to it the significance of a revelatory act, which must now occupy our attention.

IV

We may begin by observing that a fresh theme overlaps the theme which we have just considered. It is the glorifying of God and of the Son of Man. The meaning of δοξάζειν in John oscillates between 'to give honour, respect or praise' and 'to bring to a position of honour and clothe with splendour'[23]. The former sense is to be expected when God is the object, the latter when the earthly Jesus is referred to as the designated Son of Man. Thus, when Jesus is the object, it can be virtually equivalent to the notion of exaltation (7,39; 12,16). On the other hand there can be no formal difference between the two meanings, for δοξάζειν is used of both Jesus and God in very close connection. The raising of Lazarus is done 'for the glory of God', i.e. to win the praise that is due to him, because it is not only a demonstration of divine power but also a declaration of his will to bring men to eternal life; it will also be the means whereby 'the Son is glorified', i.e. wins his own share of praise, because as the one who performs the miracle, it reveals his own eschatological position as the agent of God's plan (11,4).

It is in a sense similar to this that the passion can be called a revelatory act. So, when Jesus announces that 'the hour has come for the Son of Man to be glorified' (12,23), and continues to speak of his death, the implication is not only that the passion is part of the

22. The order of material at the end of the third Similitude is manifestly dislocated on account of the insertion of an extraneous Noah apocalypse, 1 Enoch 65-69.25, which ends with a request that Michael should reveal 'the hidden name' (69.14). This is now identified with 'the Name of that Son of Man' from the original conclusion of the Similitude (69.26-29). The latter passage should follow chapter 71, in which Enoch is declared to be the Son of Man. His translation is described in an editorial conclusion (70). Charles's attempt to avoid the identification of Enoch with the Son of Man does not carry conviction, because it involves not only emendation but also the assumption that a crucial passage has been lost.

23. Cf. G.B. CAIRD, *The Glory of God in the Fourth Gospel: an Exercise in Biblical Semantics*, in *NTS* 15 (1968-69) 265-277.

process of his exaltation but also that it reveals his future glory. Jesus rejects the suggestion that he should try to evade the passion (verse 27). He will accept it for the sake of the glorifying of the Father's name (28). The Father's reply, by asserting that he has already glorified it, refers to the revelatory character of what Jesus has already done, and so, by going on to mention a future glorifying, ascribes the same character to the passion. The important thing is that God is himself the active agent of this glorifying of his name. The same thing is spelled out with greater solemnity in 13,31-32. In the act whereby the Son of Man is glorified (31a) God reveals his own glory in him (31b). Conversely, when God reveals his own glory in him (32a), he glorifies him in himself (32b), and does so immediatly (32c), without waiting for a further event. Since the act of crucifixion is not obviously an act of glorification, nor even an act in which God can be seen to be at work, John is desperately anxious that the point should not be missed. Evidently it is a matter of the utmost importance to him, and he knows how difficult it is for his readers to grasp it. So, in the Prayer of Jesus (17), Jesus prays on the brink of the passion: 'Glory thy Son, that the Son may glorify thee'. The supreme importance of what is at stake at this hour reverberates throughout the whole chapter. The same anxiety that the revelatory character of what Jesus is doing should not be missed can be detected also in 11,42; 12,35-36.

The glorification theme makes of the passion a revelatory act, comparable to the raising of Lazarus. The comparison must not be pressed too far, however, for with Lazarus the revelation is given in the act of resurrection, but with Jesus himself it is in his death. The resurrection of Jesus is not the revelatory act, but merely confirms the revelation that has already been given. The resurrection appearances are a concession for those whose faith is not fully fledged (20,29). Obviously no one can reach this quality of faith without discerning the glory in the passion. Seeing that John is so insistent on this point, it is necessary for the reader to try to discover in what sense it is true.

V

80 In the preceding section it has been shown that the passion can be regarded as glorification because of the mutual relationship between the Father and the Son which it expresses. The Son glorifies the Father's name (12,28; 13,31) and the Father glorifies the Son (13,32; 17,1.5). As there is no outward glory visible, and yet the passion is a revelatory act in this sense, it follows that the passion contains some

unmistakable indication of an inner meaning, which can only be detected by the eye of faith. For although John recognizes the attractive power of the passion (12,32), he is aware that spiritual discernment is necessary to perceive this. This is the reason for the juxtaposition of chapter 9, on the healing of the blind man, and the allegory of the shepherd in chapter 10. The reader's eyes must be opened: otherwise he may miss the crucial importance of the teaching that follows. For the allegory of the shepherd introduces another of John's passion themes, that of a voluntary laying down of one's life. Here it is said most emphatically that Jesus is in control of his destiny (10,17-18). The cross is not just forced upon him, for indeed he could have escaped it (12,27). But he accepts it of his own free will, because it is the will of the Father. He gives his life for the sheep, because he is the agent of the Father's love for them (10,29). Such is the moral accord between Jesus and the Father that Jesus can say, 'I and the Father are one' (10,30).

We have here the application to the passion of a theme that is common in the Fourth Gospel, that Jesus always acts in accordance with the Father's will. Not only does Jesus say so repeatedly, but he insists that his acts are the Father's works, so that they provide unmistakable testimony concerning his own identity (10,25). Thus it should already be possible for the discerning to perceive the unity that subsists between him and the Father (10,38), and the charge of blasphemy (verse 33) is simply an obdurate refusal to face the facts. There is, however, a difference between the acts which Jesus has already done and the passion which is about to take place. Those acts were works of divine power, so that they not only revealed God, and his own position in relation to God, through the quality of obedience to the Father's will which was inherent in them, but also had the quality of revelatory acts through the sheer display of divine power. It was thus always possible that they would be misinterpreted (cf. 6,26). But in the case of the passion there is no display of divine power at all. It is a revelatory act only because it is an expression of the perfect moral union between Jesus and the Father[24]. And precisely for this

24. John nowhere implies that the glory is revealed in the passion because divine truth reverses worldly values, so that earthly humiliation *is* divine glory. Such an idea might be deduced from the Sermon on the Mount and from such sayings as Mk 10,45, but is foreign to John's thought. It is equally mistaken to assert that the passion has no special significance as the supreme expression of Jesus' acceptance of the Father's will on the grounds that this is only a continuation of the basis of his entire ministry. For the passion is distinctive, not only as the ultimate test, but also as the one act in which there is no way of discovering its true meaning except by discernment of its moral quality. It thus remains opaque to all except those whose faith takes the form of personal moral

reason there is real danger that its quality as a revelatory act — indeed as the supreme revelatory act — will be missed altogether.

In the passion Jesus glorifies the Father's name (12,28) by laying down his life in voluntary obedience to him. The Father glorifies the Son (13,32; 17,1.5), not by any outward sign (such as the divine voice, 12,28b), but by his implicit approval of what the Son is doing. This is something that has to be deduced. The only hints are the comment of Jesus that God is in control of events (19,11) and the emphasis in the narrative that the scriptures, which are the word of God, are being fulfilled (19,24.28.30). The reader is expected to have learnt this lesson before he reaches this point. He should now understand that the unity of the Father and the Son is such that the glorifying of the Father by the Son and of the Son by the Father are fully mutual (5,23; 17,4-5.24). In spite of John's anxiety that this should be understood, he relies only on warnings of the need for understanding and on the total impact of his argument in the preceding chapters. The cyclic and repetitive character of the gospel is one facet of John's teaching method. His points come home to the reader gradually but inevitably, so that, when the climax is reached in the passion, the meaning is already in his grasp, and nothing further by way of interpretation has to be said.

The passion of Jesus anticipates the glory of his exaltation because it expresses in a supreme way the essence of that future glory, as John understands it. Obviously there is no anticipation of glory in the sense of regal splendour. The double meaning of 'lifted up', whereby Jesus' exaltation on the cross is symbolic of his exaltation to glory, depends on typology, but does not make the cross equivalent to the place at God's right hand. Even though the transition from death to glory is immediate in the Johannine scheme, without requiring the intermediate stage of the resurrection appearances, they are not identical, but remain successive. But the glory is anticipated in the passion because of what it is in itself. John follows the apocalyptic mythology in ascribing to the designated Son of Man honour equal to that of God himself (5,23). But he thinks of this equality not primarily in terms of equivalent splendour, but in terms of moral union. The glory of Christ is his union with the Father. His splendour consists, not in outward state, but in the perfect reflection of the Father which he displays[25].

response. It is thus at one and the same time the deepest truth of the gospel (and thereby the crucial item for faith) and also the most difficult to grasp.

25. For the idea of Jesus as the reflection of the Father's glory in the Johannine christology, cf. J.A.T. ROBINSON, *The Use of the Fourth Gospel for Christology Today*, in B. LINDARS and S.S. SMALLEY, *Christ and the Spirit in the New Testament*, Cambridge, 1973, pp. 61-78.

And because God is not to be visualised, but only to be described in terms of his moral attributes, this reflection appears in the moral perfection of Christ. But even this should not be conceived in an abstract way. Rather it is, as we have seen, the vital, dynamic union of wills that are in complete accord. It is only natural that John should refer to this from time to time in terms of love (3,35; 5,20; 10,17; 14,31; 15,9-10; 17,23-24.26) and mutual indwelling (6,57; 14,10-11.20; 17,21-22).

VI

John has taken from the primitive Christian tradition the apocalyptic mythology, according to which Jesus, who died on the cross, is the designated Son of Man, reserved in heaven for the End Time. In its simplest form the death of Jesus marks the transition from earthly to heavenly existence, and the resurrection proves that he did not go into hell but was translated by means of an ascension, like the righteous man Enoch[26]. But even before Paul at least two developments had taken place, which, as we have seen, are presupposed by John. One of these is the assertion of the pre-existence of Christ, which (whatever influences were at work) results from reflection on what is meant by the acknowledgement of Jesus as the exalted Lord. The other is the discovery of positive value in his death as an atonement sacrifice, which results from reflection on the death for what it is in itself. John does not follow Paul in bringing this into the centre of attention, which in Paul's case was rendered necessary by the exigencies of the critical situation of the Judaistic controversy. He thinks of it rather in terms of an anticipation of the eschatological cleansing. This brings us to a third development which John shares with Paul, the apocalyptic struggle with the forces of evil. Christ, in his obedience even to death, is the moral victor, and so in his person the final victory is anticipated.

The form of this mythology available to John thus already embodies an advance on its primitive form from several points of view. John, however, has his own special contribution to make. For him moral categories are primary, and the apocalyptic myth which he inherits is translated into terms of personal relationships. The pre-

---

26. John's scheme has no place for the 'harrowing of hell', which depends on further reflection on the details of Christ's death and resurrection, but is not certainly attested within the New Testament. 1 Peter 3,19 is taken by many recent commentators to refer to preaching during his passage from death to exaltation, cf. J.N.D. KELLY, *The Epistles of Peter and Jude* (Black's New Testament Commentaries), London, 1969, ad loc.

existent Son was *loved* by the Father before the foundation of the
world (17,24). The passion has positive value, because it is the
supreme expression of the moral union between the Father and the
Son, which is the essence of Jesus' heavenly glory. But it has this
quality because it is the result of a moral victory (12,27-28). The
cosmic struggle between good and evil has been already won (12,31;
14,30; 16,11). The cross is the arena for this struggle precisely because
it is a moral battle, rather than the phantasmagoric bloodbath of
apocalyptic fancy.

This, finally, brings us to the importance of the passion for the
believer. Its moral quality draws from him a moral response (12,32).
This response is usually spoken of as believing in (πιστεύειν εἰς)
Jesus, i.e. entrusting oneself to him as the giver of eternal life (3,16;
5,24; 6,40.47, etc.). It may be evoked by the various signs which Jesus
did in his ministry (2,13.23, etc.), but it will remain defective if it does
not take full account of what Jesus is (8,24), and that is only fully
manifested in the cross (8,28; 10,37-38). The believer accepts the cross
as the way of Jesus to the Father (7,33-36; 8,21; 13,33; 14,1-7.28; 16,28;
17,13), not because death as such has any value, but because the moral
victory which it entails most eloquently declares the union which
subsists between them, and in which he can share (14,2-3.6-7.18-23;
15,1-10; 16,25-28; 17,24-26). And seeing that this victory anticipates the
eternal life which belongs to the End Time, the believer has already
passed from death to life without coming into judgment (5,24; 6,37-
40.47-51.54-58; 16,33). It is in this way that, as the believer makes his
own the christological meaning of the cross, he actually partakes of the
benefits of the victory which it represents. But, just as the cross itself
is a moral victory, so the acceptance of it has moral consequences for
the believer. He must be ready to face persecution (15,18—16,4), he
must rely on the Spirit's guidance (16,12-15), and he needs to be kept
safe from evil (17,15). Above all, the disciples must make it their first
concern to show the mutual love which corresponds with the
relationship with God in Christ into which they have been brought
(13,34-35; 15,12-18; 17,21-23).

John's application of moral categories to the apocalyptic myth has
altered the perspective, but it has not demythologized it altogether.
The passion was essential to the apocalyptic myth from the beginning,
because it was necessary for Jesus to die before he could be raised to
the heavenly position for which he was designated, and the great
burden of the Christian kerygma was that God has raised him up in
this way. This could be taken, however, in terms, not of moral truth,
but of power. In refusing to be satisfied with such an interpretation,
and in bringing an acute moral sense to bear upon the apocalyptic

myth and its dualistic implications, John discovered greater depths in the tradition which he had received. But it may well be that he was not the first to do so. For his emphasis on moral realities in handling these traditions bears a remarkable resemblance to the genius of Jesus himself.

BETL 44, 1977, 107-124

7

TRADITIONS
BEHIND THE FOURTH GOSPEL

Many features of the Fourth Gospel are paradoxical, and not the least paradoxical among them is the evidence which it contains of sources and traditions used by the evangelist. The gospel has such a strong unity of purpose, such a well articulated and coherent theology, and such a consistency of style and diction, that it appears to be the product of a single creative mind. But there are strange breaks in continuity, even suggesting the displacement of certain passages. And closer inspection of the style shows variation at least between different types of material, not only between the simplicity and directness of the narrative portions and the poetic character and allusiveness of the discourses, but also between these and the editorial links and comments with which they are interspersed. Consequently the first impression that a single author has impressed his strong personality upon the whole gospel is contradicted by features which suggest the scissors-and-paste method of redaction of written sources. Four main types of theories have been advanced to account for this contradiction:

a) Traditional theories, which really deny that there is a problem here, on the grounds that ancient writers were not so careful to maintain continuity and consistency as we should expect today. This view is still found in critical commentaries[1].

b) Homiletic theories, which assume that the gospel is based on the evangelist's own sermons, which he has united to form the complete book. This view has been argued by R. E. Brown, and I have adopted it in my own commentary. The obvious objection — that an author is not likely to be the editor or redactor of his own work — can be answered on the same grounds as the traditional view[2].

---

1. E.g. L. MORRIS, *The Gospel of John* (The New London Commentary on the New Testament), London, 1972, pp. 53-58. A modified form of the traditional theory is that of accidental displacements, so as to preserve the integrity of the composition at the same time as accounting for the more glaring difficulties, e.g. J. H. BERNARD, *St. John* (The International Critical Commentary), 2 vols., Edinburgh, 1928, p. xvi-xxx.

2. The case for this theory was briefly, but excellently, sketched by C. K. BARRETT, *The Gospel according to St. John*, London, 1955, p. 20. Cf. R. E. BROWN, *The Gospel according to John* (The Anchor Bible), 2 vols., New York, 1966/70, p. XXXIV-LI.

c) School theories, which see the gospel as the product of the Johannine school or circle. In this theory the unity of purpose and style is traced to the dominating influence of the founder of the school, which has left its mark on all those who have contributed to the composite work. This theory has been freshly argued by Cullmann in his recently published *Der johanneische Kreis* [3].

d) Source and Redaction theories, which trace the observable differences to written sources, and the unity to the evangelist who edited them and adapted them for his purpose. This type of theory is especially associated with the work of Bultmann and his followers, and is probably the most widely held view today. [4]

Now it is not my purpose in this paper to decide between these theories. All of them are possible ways of accounting for the character of the gospel, and all of them have distinguished advocates. But, whichever theory we choose, we shall still have to consider the question of the underlying traditions, whether in written or oral [5] form, except in so far as we are prepared to admit some element of eye-witness reporting in the gospel. And what I want to do is to show how study of John's handling of traditions may help towards the determination of sources. For I believe, as I have argued elsewhere [6], that this is the right way to establish criteria for deciding the vexed question of sources in John and for assessing their historical value. Other methods are bound to produce questionable results. Bultmann's source criticism makes much use of Semitisms and of the forms of Semitic poetry in order to establish stylistic criteria, but in fact such phenomena are characteristic of the Synoptic tradition, especially the Q material, and the truly decisive factor for Bultmann is content rather than form, derived from his religio-historical approach. This method has been pursued to extreme lengths by some of his more recent followers, notably Luise Schottroff [7]. Another possible method is to apply strictly linguistic criteria based on variations of vocabulary and diction in the Greek text of the gospel, but a recent attempt along these lines by H. M. Teeple only succeeds in

---

3. O. CULLMANN, *Der johanneische Kreis*, Tübingen, 1975, p. 10.

4. Cf. D. M. SMITH, Jr., *The Sources of the Gospel of John: an Assessment of the Present State of the Problem*, in *NTS* 15 (1968-69) 336-51 ; R. D. KYSAR, *The Source Analysis of the Fourth Gospel: a Growing Consensus ?*, in *NT* 15 (1973) 134-52. A combination of (c) and (d) is to be found in J. BECKER, *Die Abschiedsreden Jesu im Johannesevangelum*, in *ZNW* 61 (1970) 215-46.

5. The use of oral tradition is stressed by B. NOACK, *Zur johanneischen Tradition*, Copenhagen, 1954.

6. *Behind the Fourth Gospel*, London, 1971.

7. L. SCHOTTROFF, *Der Glaubende und die feindliche Welt* (WMANT, 37), Neukirchen-Vluyn, 1970 ; *Heil als innerweltliche Entweltlichung*, in *NT* 11 (1969) 294-317.

demonstrating that the method is valueless, as the results do not even begin to appear plausible [8].

The method which I personally advocate starts with the finished product, and tries to understand the literary technique of the evangelist in the light of the effects which he produces. Looking at his work from this point of view, I am impressed by his skill in building up his material to a climax, often producing a powerful emotional impact. This seems to me to be the quality of a preacher rather than a writer, and it is for this reason that I favour the homiletic view of the composition of the gospel. The approach is comparable to that of redaction criticism, inasmuch as the final form of the material is studied first. It can be objected that it is a subjective approach and lacks sufficient control. It is possible, however, that more precision may be achieved by the application of the techniques of structural analysis, and a beginning along these lines has been made by B. Olsson [9]. But structuralism also has its dangers, because it rates the finished product too highly. Everything is explained in terms of the communication which the author seeks to make to his readers, and the fact that he may be adapting old material, and therefore to some extent may be limited by his material in communicating his message, is liable to be forgotten.

If, however, we work along the lines of redaction criticism to begin with, it may be possible to reach some conclusions with regard to John's handling of traditions and of the character of the traditions themselves, which may have a wider application in the gospel. For, although I do not believe that John writes with the Synoptic Gospels in front of him, there is sufficient overlap of material between John and the Synoptists for useful comparisons to be made.

Let us, then, take as an example the healing of the officer's son (Jn 4, 46-54). The advantage of this pericope is that it has parallels with both Matthew (8, 5-13) and Luke (7, 1-10), and also with a rabbinic healing story (B. Berakoth 34b). Obviously only a few salient points can be mentioned here. In the first place, the whole point of the story, and the reason why it has been remembered in the tradition, is that it is an example of healing at a distance [10]. This might, therefore, imply that the

8. H. M. TEEPLE, *The Literary Origin of the Gospel of John*, Evanston, 1974. The investigations of E. SCHWEIZER (*Ego eimi... Dei religionsgeschichtliche Herkunft und theologische Bedeutung der johanneischen Bildreden* [FRLANT, n.s. 38], Göttingen, 1939, ²1965) and E. RUCKSTUHL (*Die literarische Einheit des Johannesevangeliums*, Freiburg in der Schweiz, 1951) have shown that the linguistic unity of the gospel is too great to allow source criticism on these lines without other criteria.

9. B. OLSSON, *Structure and Meaning in the Fourth Gospel* (Coniectanea Biblica, N.T. Series, 6), Lund, 1974.

10. So Bultmann, Dibelius. Cf. also the rabbinic parallel (B. Berakoth 34b), and the story of the Syrophoenician woman (Mk 7.24-30).

chief point of interest is the miraculous power of Jesus, which appears all the more prominent in such an unusual situation. But this is not the case in the Synoptic parallels, which lay all the emphasis on the centurion's faith. It is thus reasonable to suppose that the story has been preserved in the primitive catechetical tradition as an object-lesson of faith, and this explains why it is a rare example of a miracle story within the Q tradition [11]. Now in John the story is also used in connection with faith, but it is precisely at this point that his version differs most significantly from the Synoptic versions [12]. For in the Synoptic story Jesus responds willingly to the centurion's request, but is hindered by the centurion himself, who then reveals that he believes that Jesus' word alone will be sufficient to achieve the cure. In John on the other hand Jesus refuses the officer's request on the grounds that he has not shown a deep enough quality of faith [13], and only after he has tested him in this way utters the word of healing. At this point the Synoptic story comes abruptly to an end, as nothing more needs to be said. John, however, expands the story, possibly making use of a motif from a separate tradition ("the fever left him", verse 52) [14], in order to show how the officer's faith, once evoked by Jesus, was justified, with the result that he and his household became believers in the sense of adherents to Jesus, like converts in the Christian mission [15]. Although at this stage we have not decided how much of John's version is to be attributed to his source, and how much is his own modification of it, comparison with the Synoptic parallels has shown that the motif of faith is common to all three versions. When we remember further that John has inserted the story at the conclusion of a discourse on Jesus as the giver of life (4, 14) and as the object of faith for the Christian mission (4, 27-42), we may well conclude that John's

11. T. W. MANSON *The Teaching of Jesus*, paperback edition, Cambridge, 1963, p. 29ff., argues that the narrative is secondary to the faith-dialogue, which alone stood in Q. The narrative, which differs considerably in Matthew and Luke, has then been added to provide a setting for it. But this theory, proposed in the interests of a rigid form of the Q hypothesis, is scarcely convincing.

12. See the analysis in R. SCHNACKENBURG, *Das Johannesevangelium* (Herders Kommentar), 2 vols., Freiburg im Breisgau, 1965/71, *ad loc.*; *Zur Traditionsgeschichte von Joh. 4,46-54*, in *BZ* n.s. 8 (1964) 58-88; R. T. FORTNA, *The Gospel of Signs* (SNTS Monogr. Ser., 11), Cambridge, 1970, pp. 38-48.

13. Verse 48 is widely held to be John's addition to his source, but the non-Johannine 'signs and wonders' and the somewhat proverbial character suggest that he has derived it from an independent tradition, cf. FORTNA, *op. cit.*, p. 41; *Source and Redaction in the Fourth Gospel's Portrayal of Jesus' Signs*, in *JBL* 89 (1970) 151-66.

14. On this phrase see further below.

15. The missionary vocabulary of verse 53 is not to be taken as evidence for source-material, as it is consistent with the theme of the Johannine context, cf. verses 27-42 (against Fortna).

different handling of the theme of faith in this pericope is dictated by his own evangelistic intentions. It thus becomes unnecessary to postulate a special tendency in the underlying form of the story, not attested by the Synoptic parallels, in which Jesus appeared as the *theios anēr* [16], which John is concerned to oppose with his own more spiritual understanding.

Secondly, a word must be said about the methods by which John has achieved his desired effects. (*a*) The primary method is the use of dialogue, which either replaces dialogue at a corresponding point in the Synoptic parallel or adds a new point which John wishes to introduce. It is instructive to observe how John has done both these things, not only here, but also in his account of the feeding of the multitude (6, 1-13), and with very similar intentions. For the dialogue on how the people's needs are to be met (verses 5-9) turns the conversation into a test of the disciples' faith, and the instruction to "gather up the fragments left over, that nothing may be lost" (verse 12) introduces the theme of the Christian mission [17]. (*b*) The test of faith in these two examples corresponds with a recurring feature of John's style in composing dialogue, i.e. the correction of a misunderstanding in order to move the thought to a deeper level [18]. As this is characteristic of the discourses as well as the narratives, it is unsafe to regard it as a feature of John's source, especially if it is supposed that John was dependent on such strongly differentiated sources as the postulated *Semeia*-Quelle and Offenbarungs-reden-Quelle. (*c*) The dialogue tends to use the vocabulary of its opening statement. Thus in 4, 47-49 the officer simply repeats his request that Jesus should "come down"; and in verses 51-53 the words of the servants, "his boy lives", echo Jesus' words, "Your son lives" (verse 50), which are repeated in verse 53. This stylistic feature is particularly

16. Such a tendency is commonly accepted by those who hold the Signs-source theory; cf., besides the works of Fortna, J. BECKER, *Wunder und Christologie: zum literarkritischen und christologischen Problem der Wunder im Johannesevangelium*, in *NTS* 16 (1969-70) 130-48. It must be pointed out, however, that both the concept and the title *theios anēr* are open to dispute in this connection. For in a Jewish circle it would have to mean a holy man or prophet, such as Moses, and it is doubtful if it could provide a bridge to a christology of the divinity of Jesus even if there were hellenistic influence at work in the formation of the tradition except in a thoroughly pagan setting (cf. Acts 14,8-18). Cf. H. KLEINKNECHT, *TDNT* III, p. 122; C. R. HOLLADAY, *Theios Anēr in Hellenistic Judaism: a Critique of the Use of this Category in New Testament Christology*, unpublished dissertation, Cambridge, 1974. For the pagan background, cf. Morton SMITH, *Prolegomena to a Discussion of Aretalogies, Divine Men, The Gospels, and Jesus*, in *JBL* 90 (1971) 174-99.

17. Cf. O. HOFIUS, *Die Sammlung der Heiden zur Herde Israels (Joh. 10,16; 11,51f)*, in *ZNW* 58 (1967) 289-91.

18. This feature is the subject of special study by H. LEROY, *Rätsel und Missverstandnis* (Bonner Bibl. Beitr., 30), Bonn, 1968. Cf. also D. W. WEAD, *The Literary Devices of John's Gospel*, Basel, 1970, p. 69f.

prominent in John's handling of the resurrection traditions in chapter 20 [19]. (d) Lastly we may note that John sometimes adopts a feature from a separate tradition in order to make his point. Here "the fever left him" (verse 52) specifies the sickness at too late a stage in the narrative to be regarded as part of the detail provided in the source. It may be derived from another healing which John has not used, and from this point of view it is significant that the precise phrase is used in the story which follows the Matthean version of this pericope in Mt 8, 15. The same words also occur in the rabbinic parallel. In a closely similar way John introduces the theme of the sabbath into the healing stories in 5,9 and 9, 14, and the healing in chapter 5 shows further signs of the fusion of traditions [20].

With these observations in mind we can hazard some cautious conclusions about the traditions behind John's narratives. First and foremost, the elements in the narrative which cannot be attributed to John's style are sufficiently similar to the kinds of tradition found in the Synoptic Gospels to suggest that he is drawing on a similar fund of oral or written material. These traditions are likely to have exactly the same degree of historical worth, and to have gone through exactly the same preliterary stages of development, as the traditions used by the other evangelists. What makes them different is John's highly individual way of handling them. John has integrated his source material far more closely into his theological design than the Synoptists [21]. It follows from this conclusion that very little can be said about the special character of the Signs source (if indeed it is correct to speak of a single source of this type). The widely held assumption that it was marked by a special tendency, which John sought to correct at the same time as reproducing its contents, has arisen from the attribution to the source of elements which are really part of John's style, as can be readily observed in Fortna's reconstruction of the source [22].

---

19. Cf. B. LINDARS, *The Composition of John xx*, in *NTS* 7 (1960-61) 142-7 ; G. HARTMANN, *Die Vorlage der Osterberichte in John 20*, in *ZNW* 55 (1964) 197-220.

20. The phrase, however, may be conventional, and therefore cannot be taken as a sure sign of the fusion of traditions in this case. Cf. FORTNA, *op. cit.*, p. 46, n. 2.

21. For Matthew's treatment of such traditions see H. J. HELD, *Matthew as Interpreter of the Miracle Stories*, in G. BORNKAMM, G. BARTH and H. J. HELD, *Tradition and Interpretation in Matthew*, London, 1963, pp. 165-299.

22. E.g. John's *omission* of the crucial Synoptic dialogue in the Healing of the Officer's Son is attributed to the source, but his additional dialogue (4,51-3) is *retained* ; the *fusion* of traditions in 5,2-9 is *retained in the Vorlage* ; so also in 6,1-14 the feeding takes place *immediately on the arrival of the people*, the question how to satisfy their hunger is put by *Jesus himself*, and the specification of Andrew is *retained* ; in the Man Born Blind the opening dialogue is *partially retained* (9,2f), and the possibility that it replaces a different opening is *not considered*. It is possible

So far we have been concerned with narrative traditions. We can also include under this heading the passion narrative, which clearly has the same general pattern as those of the Synoptic Gospels. As it seems not to be based directly on any of the three (though its relation to Mark is, in my opinion, rather closer than is often allowed), we must inevitably conclude that it is basically derived from established use in the church's worship as the Christian Passover *haggādāh*, whether in oral or literary form [23]. But this means once more that it is comparable to traditions used by the other evangelists. Moreover there are plenty of indications that John has reworked the material himself, producing striking dramatic effects in the trial scenes [24], and then an atmosphere of dignity and calm in the death of Jesus [25]. But this is a matter which we need not pursue further for our present purpose.

From what has been said so far it is evident that the traditions behind the Fourth Gospel are comparable to those used in the Synoptic Gospels. This is true, whether we think that John was drawing on a pool of traditions or reproducing already existing collections in the form of a Signs source and a passion account. For in the latter case we must assume that the documents available to him were composed of units comparable to those used by the Synoptists. The only question at issue is whether it is necessary to postulate such documents as an intermediate stage or not. But when we turn to the discourses of the Fourth Gospel, we are faced with more difficult issues, and we shall soon find ourselves caught up in endless controversy. Here we touch the nerve centre of Johannine studies. For there is no doubt that the discourses are John's chosen means of expressing his fundamental theological position. Here we have a strand in his gospel which is totally different from anything to be found in the Synoptic Gospels. The narratives are clearly subsidiary to the discourses, either closing a sequence (the marriage at Cana, 2, 1-12; the officer's son, 4, 46-54), or opening a sequence (the healing at

that these features belong to the source, of course, but incautious to assume that they do so. In fact the reconstruction tends to attribute too much to the source, and fails to allow sufficiently for omissions on the part of John. — FORTNA has now modified his contention that John wishes to *correct* his source. See his *Christology in the Fourth Gospel: Redaction-Critical Perspectives*, in *NTS* 21 (1974-75) 489-504

23. Or from the need to provide a relatively detailed account in connection with the primitive kerygma, cf. M. DIBELIUS, *From Tradition to Gospel*, London, 1934, pp. 22f, 178-215.

24. E.g. the Barabbas episode does not fit the Johannine scheme, and is left hanging in the air (18,39f); the mocking by the soldiers is built up into a major climax (19,1-16).

25. From 19,17 onwards all references to the sufferings of Jesus and the jeering of the crowd are suppressed, and the emphasis is placed on the fulfilment of scripture and the completion of Jesus' task.

Bethesda, 5, 1-16; the feeding of the multitude, 6, 1-21; the man born blind, 9, 1-7), or meshed in with it (Lazarus, 11, 1-44). The discourses are essential, and they are unique in the canonical gospels. Questions crowd in upon our minds. Are they entirely John's creation? Or has he taken over a source of a special type of religious writing, which he has incorporated into his presentation of the gospel? If so, is it to be regarded as a specifically Christian work? Or is it a speculative religious work which John has adapted in order to expound the meaning of Jesus for faith? And if this is the case, does it involve a radical alteration of the Christian religion? What did it look like before John adapted it for his purpose? What sort of traditions lie behind such a work? [26]

Before we attempt to find an answer to these questions, we must make a distinction between the discourses and collections of sayings of Jesus, which are found from time to time in the Fourth Gospel. Such passages as 4, 35-38; 12, 24-26; 13, 16-20 embody strings of sayings, often with very close Synoptic parallels, which certainly cannot be described as discourses [27]. The discourses are carefully constructed monologues or conversation pieces, with a definite progression of thought leading up to a climax. But these small collections of sayings need to be borne in mind, because they prove that John also had access to the sayings tradition. His Synoptic type of material is not confined to narrative traditions.

Moreover we should not forget the results of our study of John's use of narrative traditions, because they may help us in the search for criteria in order to deal with the discourses. For we found there that John's creative writing occurs frequently in the introduction of dialogue into his source, and that this feature of his work has certain distinct characteristics. It thus seems obvious that we should look for the same characteristics in the discourses, which are largely in dialogue form. One of these special marks of style is the correction of a misunderstanding on the part of Jesus' audience, and this may make a suitable point of departure for our study.

This feature first appears in a discourse in 3, 4, where Nicodemus takes Jesus' statement of the need for rebirth in a painfully literal way [28]. The

26. For a reconstruction and critique of Bultmann's proposed Offenbarungsreden-Quelle, see D. M. SMITH, Jr., The Composition and Order of the Fourth Gospel: Bultmann's Literary Theory, New Haven, 1965. For another reconstruction on similar principles, see H. BECKER, Die Reden des Johannesevangeliums und der Stil der gnostischen Offenbarungsrede (FRLANT, n.s. 50), Göttingen, 1956. Cf. also S. SCHULZ, Komposition und Herkunft der johanneischen Reden (BWANT, 81), Stuttgart, 1960.

27. Cf. C. H. DODD, Historical Tradition in the Fourth Gospel, Cambridge, 1963, especially pp. 388-405.

28. The misunderstanding does not depend on the two possible meanings of ἄνωθεν, but on a literal, as opposed to a metaphorical, idea of birth, cf. SCHNACKENBURG ad loc.

point to notice is that this not only opens the way for a better definition of the opening statement, but also draws attention to it as the foundation of the whole discourse. For the need for rebirth is stated afresh in verse 5, then further defined in verse 6, referred to once more in verse 7, with yet further explanation in verse 8. In fact it is possible to make a slight break after verse 6, which has completed Jesus' reply to the misunderstanding of verse 4. Then the new reference in verse 7 begins a fresh aspect of the discussion by referring back, not to the explanation in verses 5 and 6, but to the original form of the statement in verse 3. It is thus possible to describe this short sequence of verses 3-8 as an exegesis of the opening statement in two parts. Moreover this part of the discourse is clearly marked off from what follows by a brief transitional dialogue (verses 9 and 10), which leads to the introduction of a new theme at verse 11. This starts with the Amen formula, just like the opening statement in verse 3. It has been plausibly argued that this formula is not only a mark of Johannine style, taken over from the similar but much less frequent use of the formula in the Jesus-sayings tradition, but is actually a guarantee of the authenticity of the sayings which it introduces [29]. Although this is much less clear in verse 11, it does seem to apply to verse 3, which contains the non-Johannine " kingdom of God" and a general similarity to Mt 18, 3.

At this point we may suitably pause to ask what we can learn of the traditions behind the Fourth Gospel from the short sequence which we have considered. The first thing is that the discourse starts from what appears to be an adaptation of a genuine saying of Jesus. But this is not only the starting-point, for the rest of the sequence (verses 4-8) is a carefully structured exegesis, or midrash, of this saying in two parts, making a fresh beginning on the basis of it at verse 7, as has been already shown. Thus, whatever other sources were available to John, it should be recognised that it is possible, indeed probable, that he based some of his discourses on the Jesus-sayings tradition, and that his manner of using this material proceeds along the lines of targumic exegesis [30]. Secondly,

---

29. Cf. K. BERGER, *Die Amen-Worte Jesu : Eine Untersuchung zum Problem der Legitimation in apokalyptischer Rede* (BZNW, 39), Berlin, 1970 ; *Zur Geschichte der Einleitungsformel " Amen, ich sage euch "*, in *ZNW* 63 (1972) 47-75. The formula is comparable to several others in the NT and contemporary literature, which indicate that the speaker has personal authority for what he says, but the use of 'Amen' remains unparalleled ; cf. J. JEREMIAS, *Zum nicht-responsorischen Amen*, in *ZNW* 64 (1973) p. 122f.

30. John's use of such techniques in the composition of the Prologue and of the discourse of chapter 6 has been indicated by P. BORGEN, *Observations on the Targumic Character of the Prologue of John*, in *NTS* 16 (1969-70) 288-95 ; *Bread from Heaven* (Suppl. N.T., 10), Leiden, 1965, but I know of no systematic study of John's handling of the sayings of Jesus from this point of view.

however, we need to know whether he has used traditions of any other kind in the course of such exegesis. In the present passage such phrases as γεννηθῆναι ἄνωθεν (verses 3, 7), γεννηθῆναι ἐξ ὕδατος καὶ πνεύματος (verse 5), and the whole of verse 6, and the *pneuma* parable in verse 8, could all be regarded as derivative from other sources. As is well known, Bultmann traces them to a proto-Gnostic source [31], which is the basis of the Johannine discourses as a whole. From this point of view the " birth from above " is an expression of the Gnostic cosmology, in which the souls of men do not belong to the earthly order, but are pre-existent and heavenly. This, however, is not John's view, and it has to be presupposed that, in using this source as base, he has made a fundamental alteration to its meaning, so that the birth is " the attainment of authentic existence " (*der Gewinn seiner eigentlichen Existenz*). This explanation of John's use of the source suffers from precisely the same difficulty as the theory of the Signs source, that it presupposes that John took over a document at the same time as radically altering its meaning. But in this case the difficulty is much greater, because the source is taken to be the origin of the ideas which John has brought into relation with his Christian inheritance in order to produce a wholly new conception of the meaning of Christian faith. But it is not at all selfevident that John is using a single source in order to expound the Jesus-logion of verse 3. The theme of new birth is attested independently in the New Testament in connection with Christian initiation (cf. 1 Pet 2, 2, and of course Mt 18, 3 itself), the flesh/spirit contrast is already a feature of Paul's theology, and the *pneuma* parable has the appearance of being a proverbial saying, the origin of which is as impossible to discover as the wind itself [32]. Consequently, all that we can safely say about the special features of John's exegesis of the Jesus-saying is that they express John's own thought on the subject. They are part of his mental stock, and are to be traced ultimately to a variety of influences, but not to a single identifiable source.

Obviously it is unsafe to generalise from such a small sample as 3, 3-8. But the basis of the discourses in exegesis of the sayings tradition can be observed elsewhere. The discourse of chapter 5 is a particularly clear example. Here the Amen formula introduces the parable of the apprenticed son (verses 19-20a). The exegesis, which has already been anticipated in a transitional dialogue in 17f [33], starts at 20b, and proceeds to apply

---

31. Omitting ὕδατος καί (verse 5) as an insertion of the ecclesiastical redactor.

32. Cf. DODD, *Historical Tradition*, p. 364f.

33. For the parable of 5,19-20a, cf. C. H. DODD, *A Hidden Parable in the Fourth Gospel*, in *More New Testament Studies*, Manchester, 1968, pp. 30-40 ; P. GAECHTER, *Zur Form von Joh. 5.19-30*, in J. BLINZLER, O. KUSS, F. MUSSNER (eds.), *Neutestamentliche Aufsätze*, Regensburg, 1963, pp. 65-8. The parable may lie behind the saying of Jesus in Mt 11,27 = Lk 10,22, cf. J. JEREMIAS, *New Testament Theology*

the parable to the delegated authority of Jesus as the apocalyptic Son of Man. The ideas are well attested in Jewish apocalyptic literature, and do not require any other source than contemporary Jewish and Christian teachings. But in fact John expresses these ideas in words which are strongly reminiscent of sayings of Jesus in the Q tradition (i.e. verse 23 ; cf. Mt 10, 40; Lk 10, 16), and the two Amen sayings which follow in verses 24 and 25 have points of contact with the same and with other sayings [34].

Besides this example, we may point to the Bread of Life discourse in chapter 6, where two more Amen sayings point to contact with the Jesus-logia. In verse 26 such a saying occurs in a transitional dialogue, and it is clearly closely connected with Jesus' refusal to give a sign in Mk 8, 11f and parallels. In verse 32 the saying echoes the "daily bread" petition of the Lord's Prayer, which is more closely reproduced in verse 34. In this case, however, the Jesus-logion is not the text on which the discourse is based, as it is an exposition of the Manna miracle with actual citation of Exod 16, 4.15 [35].

A further example of exegesis of the sayings tradition occurs in 8, 35, the parable of the slave and the son, which sets out the terms of reference for the whole of the ensuing dialogue [36]. One more example may be adduced, the parable of the sheep and the shepherd in 10, 1-5, expounded in the following allegory [37].

I, London, 1971, pp. 56-61. For the anticipation of the parable in the transitional dialogue, cf. 8,31-4, anticipating the parable of verse 35 ; see B. LINDARS, *The Gospel of John* (The New Century Bible), London, 1972, *ad loc.*

34. The basic form of the first of these is not to be found in verse 24 itself, but in 23b, which is a variant of the Amen saying of 13,20, and has a number of Synoptic parallels (cf. DODD, *Historical Tradition*, pp. 343-7). The Amen formula goes with John's adaptation of this saying in 24a, because here the first person is used, whereas John has changed the underlying tradition of 23b to third person on account of the needs of his composition. The remainder of verse 24 may be influenced by another item from the sayings tradition, used by John in 8,51f (cf. Mt 16,28 and parallels). In verse 25 most of the vocabulary belongs to the range of consistent eschatology already used in verse 21f, but the phrase ἔρχεται ὥρα, which is a great favourite with John, corresponds with the authentic note of present crisis in Jesus' teaching. Consequently the Amen formula here serves to anchor conventional apocalyptic ideas in the authoritative framework of the preaching of Jesus and the apostolic kerygma.

35. See the analysis in P. BORGEN, *Bread from Heaven* (n. 30 above).

36. Cf. DODD, *Historical Tradition*, pp. 330-2, 379-82, and *Behind a Johannine Dialogue*, in *More New Testament Studies*, pp. 41-57. There is a further item from the sayings tradition in 8,51f (cf. n. 34).

37. The parable is drawn from life, with no sign of allegorization. It is reasonable to infer that John has taken it over from the tradition with very little change. As two themes can be distinguished (the one who has right of entry, verses 1-3a ; the rapport between shepherd and sheep, verses 3b-5), there may have been fusion of two parables, as suggested by J. A. T. ROBINSON, *The Parable of the Shepherd*

There is much which might be said about these examples of Johannine exegesis of Jesus-sayings, but we must content ourselves with a few brief observations. Firstly, the examples nearly all come from the beginning of a discourse. This implies that John intends his teaching to be an explication and extension of the tradition of the teaching of Jesus, and this explains why he has felt free to place so much of his creative writing upon the lips of Jesus. Secondly, it can be concluded that John is not modelling his discourses on an extraneous literary form. The description of his treatment of the Jesus-sayings as a targumizing procedure may be open to dispute, but it is more accurate than the description of the discourses as modelled on revelation discourses. For the revelation discourse, according to Bultmann's reconstruction, consists of three main constituents: the self-presentation of the Revealer, his invitation, and promised blessings or threats [38]. But this form can only be found in the Johannine discourses by carving them up and reassembling them with an *egō eimi* saying at the beginning. But *egō eimi* sayings are not found at the beginning of any discourse in chapters 1-12, except at 8, 12, which is a saying which has clear links with the Jesus-sayings tradition [39]. And, as Bultmann himself admits, the logical status of the formula varies in different contexts [40]. In fact it never operates as a self-presentation formula in the gospel as we have it.

A third and last observation must be made on the basis of our examples of John's exegesis. It is the fact that this procedure is much clearer in the earlier part of a discourse than in the later parts. It could thus be argued that, in starting with such exegesis, John is merely clearing the ground for what he wants to say, and that he is indebted to sources of another kind at this stage in his composition of a discourse. Our opening example was the discourse with Nicodemus in chapter 3, and the later parts of this discourse, especially verses 17-21 and 31-36, present considerable difficulties of analysis. It will be wise, therefore, to look at some more straightforward examples first.

The discourse with the woman of Samaria in chapter 4 does not start with an item from the Jesus-sayings tradition, but bears all the marks of

(John 10.1-5), in *Twelve New Testament Studies* (SBT, 34), London, 1962, pp. 67-75. For an elaborate study of the allegory, cf. A. J. SIMONIS, *Die Hirtenrede im Johannes-Evangelium* (Anal. Bibl., 29), Rome, 1967.

38. Cf. W. SCHMITHALS' introduction to the English edition of R. BULTMANN, *The Gospel of John*, Oxford, 1971, p. 7.

39. Mt 5,14 ; Mk 10,28f. There may also be influence of Isa 9,1[2] (cf. my commentary *ad loc.*), though this is not recognised by G. REIM, *Studien zum alttestamentlichen Hintergrund des Johannesevangeliums* (SNTS Monogr. Ser., 22), Cambridge, 1974.

40. BULTMANN (English edition), p. 225, n. 3. Thus, though an *egō eimi* saying is found at 15,1 in the supper discourses, it is not really a self-presentation formula, cf. my commentary *ad loc.*

Johannine style [41]. But the points at issue in the discourse are all closely related to the narrative background, i.e. Judaism, Samaritanism and Christianity. The patriarchal well, and the theme of the water of life which is based on it, can be interpreted in the light of Genesis and the Old Testament Wisdom tradition, notably Ecclus 24, 21. But, as the connection between wells and wisdom was already current in Judaism in connection with the spiritual value of the Law [42], it is not necessary to suppose that John has, if one may say so, done the spade-work for this discourse by digging up texts from the Old Testament. It is much more likely that he writes with contemporary discussions in mind, in which Christians claim for Jesus all the spiritual values which Jews claim for the Law [43]. Further points in the discourse distinguish Jewish and Samaritan claims in favour of the Jews, but only to show how both are superseded in Christ. The theme of the water of life can, of course, be connected with other religious literatures, and so can the theme of worship in spirit and truth. But there is no compelling reason to do so, as both themes are at home in the Jewish, Samaritan and Christian cultures which form the narrative background [44]. In any case the treatment of these two themes is not large enough to suggest an existing document which John has quoted at length at the same time as adapting it to his Christian interpretation.

From this example we can add to our stock of traditions behind the Fourth Gospel the issues in contemporary Jewish and Christian debate. First-hand experience, rather than written documents, is the most likely source of John's information. This appears very clearly in 5, 30-47, where the discourse on Jesus' future authority as the eschatological judge turns (after a fresh allusion to its opening statement in verse 30, according to John's usual midrashic style) to consideration of Jesus' credentials as the Father's delegate. This section shows not only knowledge of rabbinic discussion on the authentication of divine witness, but also familiarity with the rabbis' professional pride (verses 41-44). Again, the Bread of Life discourse of chapter 6 is not merely based on comparison of Jesus with the manna from heaven, but absolutely requires the Law as the middle term of the comparison, although this is not explicitly stated; otherwise the reference to divine teaching in 6, 45 is inexplicable. It may further be said in connection with this discourse that there is here

---

41. See the analysis in OLSSON, op. cit., pp. 115-257.

42. For the patriarchal wells in this sense, cf. CD 4,2 ; 6,2-11 ; Philo, de Fuga §§ 194-201.

43. Cf. C. H. DODD, The Interpretation of the Fourth Gospel, Cambridge, 1953, pp. 82-6.

44. For Samaritan ideas, cf. J. MacDONALD, The Theology of the Samaritans, London, 1964, especially chapter xii.

no real problem of material which does not seem to belong to the opening exegesis, for the close relation of the discourse to its opening theme is maintained until the end. If the final paragraph, verses 52-58, is accepted as a constituent part of the original composition, we have yet another example of exegesis of the sayings tradition, as the Amen saying which opens this paragraph is an adaptation of the eucharistic words of Jesus in the supper tradition of 1 Cor 11 and the Synoptic Gospels. Similarly, the discourse of 8, 31-58 maintains connection with its opening parable of the slave and the son all through, and introduces another Jesus-saying with Amen formula in verse 51 [45]. The argument in this discourse turns on the meaning of descent from Abraham, and thus has links with the issue of the Judaizing party which is so prominent in Galatians and Romans. It is true that it ends with the great affirmation of the pre-existence of Jesus in an Amen saying (verse 58), which, so far as I can see, has no links with the sayings tradition any more than it does with the Judaistic controversy [46]. Hence the climax of the discourse is a christological statement which represents John's own theology. It could be derived from the internal evolution of Christian thought in John's church without external influence, or it could be the result of contact with Hellenistic or proto-Gnostic groups, whose ideas have acted as a catalyst upon the unsophisticated tradition of early Christianity. But the actual verse, 8, 58, mentions Abraham and very little else. Hence the actual verse is not derived from an extraneous source.

It seems to me important to maintain this distinction which I have just made between influences of thought and literary traditions. When we turn back to the discourse of chapter 3, the later parts certainly owe their ideas to John's developed christology, which may have been influenced by a variety of intellectual currents in John's world, but it is by no means clear that John is reproducing a written source. The use in these verses of the light and darkness antithesis, and especially the contrast between "doing evil" and "doing the truth", remind the reader of Qumran, but cannot be pinned down to any particular system of thought. In fact Bultmann does not attempt to assign verses 19-21 to the source. But verses 31-36, which Bultmann takes to be very largely source-material, are closely linked to the earlier part of the discourse by subtle repetition of its leading words and ideas. Thus ὁ ἄνωθεν ἐρχόμενος

---

45. Cf. n. 34.

46. The suggestion that ἐγώ εἰμι in this verse is intended to allude to the tetragrammaton YHWH is impossible grammatically, and gives the wrong sense, cf. BULTMANN *ad loc*. A connection with the Judaistic controversy can be maintained, if the verse is taken to mean ' I am one of the pre-existent things ', which according to Jewish tradition, include the Law, as well as the name of the Messiah, cf. R. G. HAMERTON-KELLY, *Pre-existence, Wisdom and the Son of Man* (SNTS Monogr. Ser., 21), Cambridge, 1973, p. 20.

(verse 31) refers to the Son of Man, whose descent has been mentioned in verse 13, but uses the ἄνωθεν which is characteristic of verses 3-8 (cf. verse 2 ἀπὸ θεοῦ ἐλήλυθας). But then in the same verse it is repeated in a form which is closer to verse 13. The next verse, on the witness of the one who descends from heaven, reproduces the Amen saying of verse 11 [47]. In verse 34 the Father gives the Spirit to the Son, according to the most probable interpretation of the verse [48], and then in verse 35 we find that the Father loves the Son and has entrusted to him the means whereby men may have eternal life. These ideas reflect and elucidate the earlier propositions that Nicodemus needs to be born from the Spirit (verses 3-8) and that God so loved the world as to give his only Son (verse 16).

Once we have grasped the way in which John builds his discourses by successive expositions of his opening text, the case for John's creative composition in the discourses is stronger, and accordingly the case for extensive use of written sources in them is weaker. John's method of argument is like a spiral staircase, continually returning to its point of entry, but always a stage higher until the top is reached. Apparent inconsistencies of thought which have been detected in the discourses, such as the tension between consistent and realized eschatology, cannot be used as criteria for the separation of sources, because they belong to John's method of argument. John does not state conventional Christian ideas in order to refute them, but to take them to a deeper level of understanding. Frequently he starts from the Jesus-sayings tradition, because he has a reverent regard for this tradition. He regards his constructions upon the sayings as legitimate extensions and elucidations of their meaning, according to the promised guidance of the Paraclete [49]. Though he may quote from non-Christian sources, such quotations cannot be identified with certainty, because their resemblance to Hellenistic or Gnostic texts is only that of a general similarity of type, and the

47. The vocabulary of verse 11 is entirely Johannine, but the sudden change to first person plural (in this verse only) and the balanced clauses suggest that John is here reproducing a proverbial saying. There is a close parallel to this verse in 1 Jn 1,1-3, and of course the theme of witness is prominent throughout the Johannine literature. Hence the verse may well be a favourite maxim of the Johannine school, even if it is not to be traced back to Jesus himself.

48. Critical opinion is divided whether the unexpressed subject of δίδωσιν in 34b is the Father or the Son. Bultmann regards οὐ γὰρ ἐκ μέτρου δίδωσιν as an addition by the Evangelist, and τὸ πνεῦμα as a gloss. But the latter is to be accepted as an example of Johannine inclusion, as John brings the discourse to the christological conclusion which he has intended from the outset (hence 'shall not see life', verse 36, corresponds with 'see the kingdom of God' of verse 3).

49. 16,13. Cf. E. BAMMEL, Jesus und der Paraklet in Johannes 16, in B. LINDARS and S. S. SMALLEY (eds.), Christ and Spirit in the New Testament, Cambridge, 1973, pp. 199-217.

style and diction are not clearly differentiated from the rest of the gospel. Never do such possible quotations stand at the head of a discourse as the text to be expounded. The chief criterion for isolating them, apart from the theological content, is their form, which is the balanced couplet of Semitic poetry. But, according to Bultmann, not only can the Evangelist imitate this style, but even the Ecclesiastical Redactor (e.g. 6, 55)! Such a criterion offers no control.

The one place where the adaptation of an existing document in rhythmical poetic style really does look possible is, of course, the Prologue. I do not propose to consider this in detail, but will confine myself to a few brief remarks. Firstly, not only the form but also the content can be sufficiently accounted for on the supposition that it is consciously modelled on Jewish Wisdom poetry, notably Ecclus 24. There is no compelling reason to postulate a pre-Johannine Logos hymn as a necessary stage between such models and the Prologue as we now have it, in spite of the difficulties raised by the Baptist verses [50]. Secondly, the structure of the Prologue is comparable to that of the discourses, in which the opening statement is expounded in successive stages of interpretation [51]. Thirdly, the background of thought is once more the issues in the Jewish and Christian debate, as the incarnation of the Logos in the person of Jesus is compared and contrasted with the concrete self-expression of God in the Law [52]. Finally, it is a mistake to take the

50. Cf. J. A. T. ROBINSON, *The Relation of the Prologue to the Gospel of John*, in *NTS* 15 (1962-63) 120-9.

51. Cf. BORGEN, *art. cit.* (n. 30 above) ; B. LINDARS, *Behind the Fourth Gospel*, London, 1971, p. 73f. If the Baptist verses (6-8 and 15) be omitted, and also verse 9 (added to ease the transition after the addition of 6-8), as secondary to John's original composition, the structural similarity to the discourses can be easily discerned. Verses 1-5 are a midrash on Gen 1,1-5, interpreted with the aid of the Wisdom tradition, so as to express the cosmic position of the Logos at the creation and his function of enlightening men within the creation. This is comparable to John's use of a Jesus-logion, interpreted in the light of contemporary apocalyptic ideas, in 5,19-24. Verses 10-13 take up the thought of the Logos in the world and lead on to the nature of men's response to him. Notice that, if verse 9 is omitted, the natural subject of 10a is ὁ λόγος (cf. verse 4), so that this paragraph both reverts to the opening statement and explicates the thought with which the first paragraph closed. This is comparable to John's technique in 3,7f, as pointed out above. Finally verses 14-18 make a fresh statement concerning the Logos so as to introduce the christological climax, which is characteristically marked by inclusion in the final verse. This is comparable to 3,31-6, according to our analysis given above.

52. For the importance of this theme, cf. n. 43. Attempts to find a proto-Gnostic original behind the Prologue have failed to do justice to this highly important feature of it. There are no convincing grounds to exclude verse 17. Personal names (Moses, Jesus Christ) may be out of place in a Wisdom poem, but not in John's composition, for the use of the first person plural in verses 14 and 16 has already moved the thought into the actual experience of the contemporary church. But in any case the objection has no force, when due weight is given to the influence

Prologue as a sort of prototype of the discourses in their pre-Johannine form, in spite of the similarity of technique, because the structural similarity is with the discourses in their actual Johannine form as exegetical expositions of the sayings of Jesus. It is not possible to reconstruct earlier forms of the discourses on the basis of the Prologue, which, for all its clear Johannine styling, remains from a literary point of view without parallel in the rest of the gospel.

Our search for the traditions behind the Fourth Gospel has shown much that can be affirmed, but also much that must be left in uncertainty. It has been necessary to distinguish between the influences upon John's mind, which may embrace a wide spectrum, and the actual traditions, whether oral or written, which he has used in writing the gospel. These traditions include narratives, sayings, and an account of the passion, which are comparable to those which form the basis of the Synoptic Gospels. Study of John's methods of using these traditions does not support the theory that he was dependent upon a continuous document with a distinct tendency which he sought to correct. The discourses, which are a unique feature of the Fourth Gospel, show dependence on the sayings tradition, but other source material, as opposed to general influences, cannot be certainly disengaged from them. Whatever sources John had at his disposal, we must recognise that he was a writer of considerable originality and creative ability, who brought to his task a burning conviction and deep personal commitment. In the last analysis, however, the riddle of the Fourth Gospel remains unsolved. For the gospel has certainly undergone some degree of editing, but the work of the redactor cannot be shown to have different aims and presuppositions from those of the evangelist himself. These are expressed in the final verses of chapter 20, which are frequently cited to indicate the purpose of the gospel as a whole [53]. At this point it certainly looks as if redactor

of Ecclus 24, which is by far the most important of all the possible literary models available to John. In this poem (which may well be composite, cf. J. G. SNAITH, *Ecclesiasticus* [The Cambridge Bible Commentary on the New English Bible], Cambridge, 1974, pp. 119-26) Moses is mentioned as the giver of the Law, which is identified with Wisdom. In fact this poem has a structure remarkably similar to that of John's Prologue — first Wisdom's cosmic position (verses 1-7), then Wisdom's coming to her own people (verses 8-12), and finally her 'incarnation' in the Law (verses 23-9). The connection is strengthened by the possibility of a literary allusion to verses 8 and 10 in Jn 1,14 (ἐσκήνωσεν ; compare also verse 21 with Jn 6,35). Moreover the fact that John composes the Prologue in the light of Jewish speculations concerning the Law is indicated by the allusions to the Sinai theophany in Jn 1,14.18.

53. It is significant that these verses (with omission of the final clause of verse 31) are regularly held by proponents of the Signs-source theory to be the conclusion of that source as well as of the gospel itself, though it has to be assumed that *sēmeia* had a deeper theological meaning for the Evangelist than it had in the source.

and evangelist are at one. And the conclusion is not impossible that they are, in fact, one and the same person.

This view is reproduced without a qualm in so recent a commentary as that of S. SCHULZ, *Das Evangelium nach Johannes* (NTD, 4 ; 12. Auflage), Göttingen, 1972, p. 248. But if John really had to correct his source, it is hard to see how he could dare to leave such an ambiguity in his closing appeal to his readers.

8

JOHN AND THE SYNOPTIC GOSPELS:
A TEST CASE

The question whether John used one or more of the Synoptic Gospels continues to be hotly debated. It is obvious that John is indebted to other sources for much of his information. But where his material overlaps the Synoptic Gospels, it is more difficult to decide whether he is using independent traditions or not. In one case, however, it can be shown that he had a saying of Jesus which he received in a Greek form transmitted independently of the forms in Mark and Q. All go back to a common Aramaic original. The saying in question is Jn. 3. 3, 5. It will be convenient to set out the various forms in parallel columns:

Jn. 3. 3	Jn. 3. 5	Mt. 18. 3	Mk. 10. 15 = Lk. 18. 17
ἀμὴν ἀμὴν	ἀμὴν ἀμὴν	ἀμὴν	ἀμὴν
λέγω σοι,	λέγω σοι,	λέγω ὑμῖν,	λέγω ὑμῖν,
ἐὰν μή τις	ἐὰν μή τις	ἐὰν μὴ	ὃς ἂν μὴ
γεννηθῇ	γεννηθῇ	στραφῆτε	δέξηται τὴν
ἄνωθεν,	ἐξ ὕδατος	καὶ γένησθε	βασιλείαν τοῦ θεοῦ
	καὶ πνεύματος,	ὡς τὰ παιδία,	ὡς παιδίον,
οὐ δύναται	οὐ δύναται	οὐ μὴ	οὐ μὴ
ἰδεῖν	εἰσελθεῖν εἰς	εἰσέλθητε εἰς	εἰσέλθῃ εἰς
τὴν βασιλείαν	τὴν βασιλείαν	τὴν βασιλείαν	αὐτήν.
τοῦ θεοῦ.	τοῦ θεοῦ.	τῶν οὐρανῶν.	

(a) We may start with comparison of Matthew and Mark. Their versions occur in different, but closely similar, contexts. The relations between them are complex. Thus *Matthew* has the saying in the *dispute about greatness* (Mt. 18. 1-5 = Mk. 9. 33-37 = Lk. 9. 46-48). In this pericope he *omits* the saying on service (Mk. 9. 35), though he *retains* it in Mt. 20. 26 f. = Mk. 10. 43 f., and he *inserts* it into M material in the woes against the Pharisees (Mt. 23. 11). He also *omits* Mk. 9. 37b at the end of the pericope, though he uses that at Mt. 10. 40. Within the pericope he *inserts* not only the saying on becoming as children (Mt. 18. 3), but also a further saying on greatness, which has Q parallels (Mt. 18. 4, cf. Mt. 23. 12 = Lk. 14. 11; 18. 14).

Mark has the saying in the *blessing of the children* (Mt. 19. 13-15 = Mk. 10. 13-16 = Lk. 18. 15-17). Here Matthew *omits* the saying, and abbreviates Mark's conclusion (Mt. 19. 15 = Mk. 10. 16, 17a). It is easy to assume that Matthew has simply transferred the saying from this context to the earlier pericope, but the addition also of a Q saying in Mt. 18. 4 shows that this is too simple. This other saying has a further parallel in Lk. 9. 48c, which Luke has added to Mark, apparently independently. The interrelations between the three gospels can scarcely be explained by simple borrowing on the part of one evangelist from another. The number of similar, but probably independent, sayings involved suggests that each evangelist has drawn on his own stock of sayings on these themes, when writing his version of the two pericopae. Moreover, it is altogether probable that some of the sayings are independent versions of one original saying. It is thus reasonable to suppose that Mt. 18. 3 may be, not an adaptation of Mk. 10. 15, but rather an independent version of the same saying.

Matthew's omission of the saying from the blessing of the children was not simply due to his wish to use it elsewhere, for it is characteristic of his style to use the same saying twice, as already observed in connection with the saying on service. In this case, however, he decided not to use it, presumably in the interests of abbreviation. He was able to do so, because the pericope reads perfectly well without it. But if this is true of his understanding of the pericope, it is surely true also of the tradition behind Mark. The possibility lies open that the saying was not originally part of the pericope, but was inserted by Mark into his source. If so, we must reckon with another possibility, that Mark has to some extent adapted the saying in the process.

It thus follows that, even on the assumption of Markan priority,[1] the version of the saying in Mt. 18. 3 must be regarded as equally likely to represent the original as the version in Mk. 10. 15. In fact there are good reasons to conclude that Matthew's is the better version of the two. (i) The rhythm of Matthew's version is superior to Mark's. In Mt. 18. 3 both the conditional clause and the apodosis consist of verb(s) plus adverbial phrase (ὡς τὰ παιδία, εἰς τὴν βασιλείαν τῶν οὐρανῶν). In Mk. 10. 15 the full phrase of the apodosis has been taken into the protasis as object of the verb, thus destroying the balance. (ii) Mark's δέξηται is dictated by the context, and shows the influence of the earlier pericope (Mk. 9. 33-37). Jesus has just said that the kingdom belongs to such persons as children (τοιούτων, verse 14, cf. 9. 37), and so it has to be received as such.[2] But it is difficult to see any real distinction between receiving it and entering it, so that the saying is almost tautologous. On the other hand, Matthew retains Mark's δέξηται in Mt. 18. 5, so that it is unlikely that he has removed it from the saying in verse 3. (iii) Mark's version has singular παιδίον, although the plural would suit the context better in view of verse 14. Hence the singular has been carried over from the source. Matthew's version requires the plural τὰ παιδία, but if he were dependent upon Mark he would surely have retained the indefinite ὅς plus παιδίον, seeing that he has ὅστις . . . ὡς τὸ παιδίον τοῦτο in the very next verse (18. 4). Hence, whereas Mark has adapted his source, Matthew has left his intact. (iv) Finally, and most important for our argument, Matthew's στραφῆτε καὶ γένησθε is a Semitism = 'become again', as has been recognised long since by Jeremias.[3] Examples in the Septuagint show that the Hebrew idiom was not infrequently translated in this way, though it is not clear how far the translators understood the Hebrew in adopting it. But whether the translator of the saying in Mt. 18. 3 understood the idiom, or used στραφῆτε, as most commentators assume, to mean 'be converted',[4] it can scarcely be doubted that in this particular Matthew preserves the saying as it was translated from the underlying Aramaic untouched.

The original form of the saying is thus best preserved by Matthew. Naturally Mark's τοῦ θεοῦ is likely to be closer to the original than Matthew's τῶν οὐρανῶν. Apart from that, there is no need to decide whether the second person plural form with ἐάν (Matthew) or the third person singular form with ὃς ἄν (Mark) is to be preferred. They are alternative ways of expressing an indefinite subject. It is reasonable to suppose that the saying was current simultaneously in both forms.

(b) We now turn our attention to the forms of the saying in Jn. 3. 3, 5. There are two points of difference between them. (i) ἄνωθεν (verse 3) is more likely to be original, because ἐξ ὕδατος καὶ πνεύματος belongs to the progress of the argument as an explication of it. (ii) On the other hand εἰσελθεῖν εἰς in verse 5 is preferable to ἰδεῖν, because it accords with the Synoptic parallels. The weaker ἰδεῖν (= 'experience', perhaps due to Semitic influence on John's vocabulary)[5] is characteristic of Johannine diction: compare ἔχει and ὄψεται in 3. 36, and θεωρήσῃ and γεύσηται in 8. 51 f. In the latter case there is an exact parallel, because here we have another saying from the Jesus tradition, in which the original verb appears in the second version of the saying rather than the first (cf. Mk. 9. 1 and parallels: γευσῶνται).

When we compare John with the Synoptic Gospels, we can see at once that John's version has the same structure as Matthew's, and agrees with Mark's only in those details which have already been shown to belong to the Aramaic saying which underlies them both. Thus John is similar to Mark in using the third person singular form, although the idiom (ἐὰν μή τις) makes a third alternative method of representing the indefinite subject. John also agrees with Mark in having τοῦ θεοῦ. Moreover, John's οὐ δύναται for οὐ μή should not be regarded as a significant variation, as it probably does not represent a different underlying Aramaic text. There is a close parallel in the Beelzebul controversy, where Mk. 3. 23-26 repeatedly uses δύναμαι, while the Q version in Mt. 12. 25-26 = Lk. 11. 17-18 omits it altogether. Omission accords better with Semitic diction, so that insertion is likely to be for the sake of Greek idiom.

It is now clear that John's version of the saying presupposes an original identical with the form underlying Matthew, except for one feature, i.e. γεννηθῇ ἄνωθεν for στραφῆτε καὶ γένησθε ὡς τὰ παιδία. It will now be shown that the differences between these expressions provide the crucial evidence for the independence of the tradition used by John, and also illustrate his method of handling the tradition for the sake of his theology.

(c) There are really two differences here. In the first place John's ἄνωθεν can bear the meaning 'again', and so represents a more idiomatic translation of the Aramaic phrase which appears in Matthew's version as στραφῆτε καί. This is, indeed, how it is usually translated in Jn. 3. 3, 7. For the moment we may accept the fact, indicated by the Matthean parallel, that the Greek translator intended ἄνωθεν to mean 'again', whether John took it as such or not. This is the point which clinches the argument that John's is an independent version of the same Aramaic saying as we have in Mt. 18. 3. For it would not be possible for John (or his source) to derive ἄνωθεν from the Greek of Mt. 18. 3, unless he recognised the idiom behind the Greek and deliberately corrected it. This is scarcely likely. The conclusion that we have here independent translations of one Aramaic original appears inescapable.

Secondly, John's γεννηθῇ has to do duty for γένησθε ὡς τὰ παιδία. Here we can hardly suppose that John preserves an alternative rendering of a common original. The explanation must be sought in John's interpretative licence. (i) To 'become as children' does not mean to become childlike, but to become comparable to children, i.e. in the same situation as children (cf. Mt. 22. 30 and parallels: ὡς ἄγγελοι). Matthew's phrase (γένησθε ὡς) is yet another Semitism,[6] and the generic article with παιδία also betrays Semitic influence. So to become *again* comparable to children can easily be glossed with the phrase 'be born again'. Both represent the same metaphor, i.e. radical renewal.[7] (ii) γεννάω is very frequent in the Johannine literature. This verb can easily be confused with γίνομαι in the future and aorist forms. But it is not to be supposed that John's γεννηθῇ here is accidental, because his omission of ὡς τὰ παιδία shows that this is an intentional change. On the contrary, it can scarcely be doubted that he has been prompted by the similarity of the words to make an adjustment to the saying for the sake of the argument which follows in the rest of the chapter.

Taking all these considerations into account, the Greek form of the saying as it came to John can be reconstructed as follows: ἀμὴν λέγω ὑμῖν, ἐὰν μή τις γένηται ἄνωθεν ὡς παιδίον, οὐ δύναται εἰσελθεῖν εἰς τὴν βασιλείαν τοῦ θεοῦ. It is unlikely that John was working directly on an Aramaic tradition of the saying.

(d) John's γεννηθῇ is a deliberate change, but it is altogether probable that ἄνωθεν was found in the form which he received. The relationship with Mt. 18. 3 shows conclusively that it was intended to mean 'again'. We now have to ask whether John himself understood it in this sense, and intended it to mean 'again' when he wrote 3. 3; or whether he knew this, but intended the meaning 'from above' in 3. 3, thereby altering the meaning without verbal change; or whether he actually thought that it meant 'from above' in the original (not having access to the underlying Aramaic), so that he took it over with this meaning for the purpose of his discourse.

(i) In the New Testament ἄνωθεν has the following meanings: 'from the top', Mt. 27. 51 = Mk. 15. 38 = Jn. 19. 23; 'from above', Jn. 3. 31; 19. 11; Jas. 1. 17; 3. 15, 17; 'from the first', Lk. 1. 3; Acts 26. 5; 'again', Gal. 4. 9. The meaning in Jn. 3. 7 is determined by its meaning in 3. 3, but the explications of this in verse 5 (ἐξ ὕδατος καὶ πνεύματος) and in verse 8 (ἐκ πνεύματος) strongly point to the conclusion that it is intended to be 'from above'. It is also relevant that, in all the places where the meaning 'from above' is certain, it acts as a Semitic paraphrase for 'from God' (for the usage in James, cf. Jas. 1. 5).[8]

(ii) There are indications in the surrounding context that 'from above' is the intended meaning. This not only follows from the explications in verses 5 and 8, and from the various further elaborations in verses 6, 13, 27 and 31, but has *already* been indicated in the opening dialogue (ἀπὸ θεοῦ, verse 2). We may also compare 8. 23 (ἐγὼ ἐκ τῶν ἄνω εἰμί) for a similar expression. But it is also characteristic of John to use an expression denoting origination with γεννάω. We may note especially ἐκ θεοῦ ἐγεννήθησαν in the Prologue (1. 13, probably dependent upon this chapter), as well as several examples in I John.[9]

(iii) Although the meaning 'again' is not supported by John's usage elsewhere, and is contradicted by the considerations just mentioned, it is widely held that it is required in verse 3 to account for the misunderstanding of Nicodemus in verse 4. But this, as Schnackenburg has shown,[10] is not the case. Verse 4 certainly refers to a second birth, but this does not depend on the meaning of ἄνωθεν. There is nothing corresponding to it in Nicodemus' first question: πῶς δύναται ἄνθρωπος γεννηθῆναι γέρων ὤν;[11] The question is concerned with the *kind* of birth. In his second question Nicodemus reveals that he is thinking of childbirth literally: μὴ δύναται εἰς τὴν κοιλίαν τῆς μητρὸς αὐτοῦ δεύτερον εἰσελθεῖν καὶ γεννηθῆναι; It may be observed that δεύτερον qualifies εἰσελθεῖν rather than γεννηθῆναι. But if ἄνωθεν means 'again' there is no reason why he should not have used it in both questions to qualify γεννηθῆναι. There is no necessity to leave it out. On the other hand, if it refers to origination 'from above', the omission is necessary, for the birth is thought to be, not from above, but from the mother's womb. In fact the subject of the argument in these verses is the meaning of birth down to verse 6, and the implications of ἄνωθεν are not explored until verse 7.

There is thus good reason to assume that John intended the meaning 'from above' in verse 3, contrary to the required meaning of the underlying saying. So we have to ask what John himself thought that it meant in the saying. Here there are two possibilities, and it is hard to decide between them. He may have been well aware that it meant 'again', but, wishing to use it with the meaning 'from above', took advantage of the ambiguity of the Greek word, which allows both meanings. This possibility is supported by the omission of ὡς παιδίον, whereby the suggestion of repeating the natural process is reduced at the outset. Alternatively John may have assumed all along that ἄνωθεν meant 'from above', because the metaphor of becoming a child certainly refers to spiritual regeneration, and the source of regeneration is to be found, not in man as he is by nature, but in God. It is thus possible to maintain that John understood the saying (see reconstruction above) to mean, 'Unless one is made from above as a child . . .' It may be urged in favour of this alternative that, if John always *uses* ἄνωθεν with the meaning 'from above', he is likely to have *understood* it normally in the same sense.

(e) John has taken this saying of Jesus from the tradition in order to build up a christological discourse. It was not in the first instance a christo-logical saying, but a call on the part of Jesus for radical renewal in prep-aration for the coming kingdom. John clearly understands this, and the first part of his exposition is devoted to this theme (verses 4–8). But the point which interests him is the manner in which this renewal is achieved. It is done by cleansing ('water and Spirit', verse 5) and by heavenly instruc-tion (verses 9–13). These are both eschatological concepts, but Jewish spirituality would see them as available in the present through the Law. John, however, asserts that the true agent of this cleansing and this heavenly instruction is Jesus himself. It thus follows that, like the Law, Jesus has a heavenly origin. He cannot be the agent of the birth from God unless he himself comes from God. Thus, as often in John's discourses, the Law is the implied middle term between an accepted principle of spiritu-ality and the high christology of John, which claims that Jesus originates from God in a unique sense.[12] The idea of derivation 'from above' is the fundamental concept, which is applicable to the spiritual renewal of the believer, to the Law as the model of the means of this renewal (now super-seded), and to Jesus as the effective agent of renewal both now and in the coming age. The discourse ends by asserting that this estimate of Jesus is confirmed by experience (3. 36).

The saying is not in itself a christological statement. But, in John's under-standing of it, it lays down a principle which leads inevitably to a christo-logical conclusion. It may well be conjectured that John is under pressure to support his claims from the words of Jesus himself. It is as if John has had to answer the objection: 'But Jesus never claimed to be the Son of

God, as you Christians make out!' His answer is: 'Yes, but Jesus said, "Amen, amen I say to you, unless one is born from above he cannot enter the kingdom of God," and that cannot possibly be done unless Jesus is in fact the Son of God.' Thus the sayings tradition is pressed into service for the needs of a later time, resulting in the preservation and adaptation of authentic material.

(f) I have called John's use of this saying a test case. It is, in fact, a rare example of a saying, which obviously has links with the Synoptic tradition, where the interrelationships can be analysed with some degree of certainty. John adapted the saying for the purpose of his christological discourse, but his alterations are slight, and the underlying form can be reconstructed with reasonable confidence. John's form clearly presupposes the same Aramaic saying as lies behind Mt. 18. 3 and Mk. 10. 15. Mark's form cannot be reconstructed with assurance, because he has altered the conditional clause in such a way as to eliminate its significant features. On the other hand, it is possible that Mark depended on a form which was identical with that which lies behind John, except for minor details (ὃς ἂν μή for ἐὰν μή τις, and οὐ μή for οὐ δύναται), though it could equally well have been the same as Matthew's, apart from the second person plural. This last feature, however, suggests that Matthew is nearest the original, directly addressing the audience, whereas Mark and John have generalized forms. John and Matthew have derived the saying from variant translations of the Aramaic original, in which the idiom represented by Matthew's στραφῆτε is treated differently. It can thus be concluded that John did not derive the saying from Matthew, but received it from independent tradition.

NOTES

[1] Proponents of Matthean priority can reach this conclusion *a priori*, but will have to go through equally difficult contortions to explain why Mark has transferred the saying from the one context to the other.

[2] It is not clear whether Mark means 'receives the kingdom as one receives a child' or 'receives the kingdom as a child receives it'. The latter is supported by the parallels in Matthew and John. Many scholars argue that this verse is a Markan insertion into the source, e.g. Bultmann, A. Meyer, C. H. Turner, Nineham. R. Bultmann, *Die Geschichte der synoptischen Tradition* (Göttingen: Vandenhoek und Ruprecht³ 1967), p. 32; A. Meyer, 'Die Entstehung des Markusevangeliums', *Festgabe für A. Jülicher* (Tübingen: J. C. B. Mohr (Paul Siebeck), 1927), p. 45; C. H. Turner, in *A New Commentary on the Holy Scripture*, ed. C. Gore *et al.* (London: S.P.C.K., 1928), *ad loc.*; D. E. Nineham, *The Gospel of St. Mark*, The Pelican Gospel Commentaries (London: A. and C. Black, rev. 1963), *ad loc.*

[3] J. Jeremias, *New Testament Theology* I (London: SCM Press, 1971), p. 155.

[4] It is doubtful, however, if στρέφω can have this meaning. The only parallel in the New Testament is Jn. 12. 40, where it occurs in a non-LXX version of Isaiah 6. 10, and in fact represents the same Semitic idiom: wāšāb wᵉrāpā' lô' = 'and it be healed once more' (G. B. Gray, *Isaiah I-XXVII*, I.C.C. (Edinburgh: T. & T. Clark, 1912), p. 110). This is obscured in Jn. 12. 40, because the last phrase has been conformed to the LXX (καὶ ἰάσομαι αὐτούς). See my *New Testament Apologetic* (London: SCM Press, 1961), p. 161, for the suggestion that John's underlying text may have been closer to Mk. 4. 12, καὶ ἀφεθῇ αὐτοῖς (= MT).

[5] Cf. C. H. Dodd, *Historical Tradition in the Fourth Gospel* (Cambridge University Press, 1963), p. 359. On account of the Semitism, Dodd mistakenly took ἰδεῖν to be the original form of John's text, and used this as an argument for independence from the form in Mt. 18. 3, leaving the presence of εἰσελθεῖν in Jn. 3. 5 entirely unexplained.

[6] Cf. Jeremias (note 3 above).

[7] Almost all commentators assume that the saying is concerned with the excellence of child-like qualities, but this is a false impression, derived from Matthew's insertion of it into the Markan context. In Mk. 9. 33–37 Jesus uses the child to emphasize the reversal of values in the kingdom, in which the smallest becomes the greatest. In Mt. 18. 1–5 the point is changed, so that the pericope becomes a typical Matthaean exhortation to humility. This is achieved by the insertion of our saying in verse 3; but as this is not self-explanatory, Matthew has also inserted verse 4, in which the quality of humility is actually expressed. Without verse 4 and the surrounding context, the saying gives no indication of reference to moral qualities. In Mk. 10. 13–16 it is customary to see the child-like property as one of status, i.e. having no rights or grounds to claim a place in the kingdom, which must therefore be received as pure gift (cf. R. Bultmann, *Theology of the New Testament* I (London: SCM Press⁸, 1976), p. 14). Mark here seems to me to preserve the meaning of the saying better, in spite of the inferior form of his text.

[8] This is recognised for Jn. 3. 3, 7; 19. 11 by Jeremias, op. cit., p. 10, where he lists such features in the sayings of Jesus, but surely applies to James too, cf. 1. 17, where it is parallel to 'from the Father of lights'.

[9] Jn. 3. 5, 6, 8; 8. 41; I Jn. 2. 29; 3. 9; 4. 7; 5. 1, 4, 18.

[10] R. Schnackenburg, *Das Johannesevangelium*, Herders Theologischer Kommentar zum Neuen Testament (Freiburg-im-Br., 1965), I, *ad loc.*

[11] But ἄνωθεν is inserted in a few texts (H 28 aur e f sa bo), not always in the same place. This is clearly a harmonising addition.

[12] Cf. S. Pancaro, *The Law in the Fourth Gospel*, Supplements to Novum Testamentum 42 (Leiden: Brill, 1975), in which much of the relevant material is amassed. The essential place of the Law in the development of christology has been convincingly shown by W. D. Davies, *Paul and Rabbinic Judaism* (London: SPCK², 1955), pp. 147–76.

JSNT 13 (1981) 83-101

9

DISCOURSE AND TRADITION:
THE USE OF THE SAYINGS OF JESUS
IN THE DISCOURSES OF THE FOURTH GOSPEL

I

The Johannine discourses are a unique feature of the Fourth Gospel, but they include elements which have a close connection with the Synoptic sayings. These are not sufficiently numerous to warrant the suggestion that John had a discourse-source, comparable to the sayings-source Q[1]. If we have to suppose that the discourses are drawn from a previous source, it is better to stick to Bultmann's *Offenbarungsreden-Quelle*, and to assume that the evangelist has made use of items from the sayings tradition in reshaping the source as utterances of Jesus. But this would give to the sayings a very subordinate place in the composition of the discourses as a whole. In fact, though they are few in number, they occupy a crucial place in the construction of the discourses. For this reason it is much more likely that there never was a written source for the discourses. They are the free composition of the evangelist, building upon a careful selection of traditional sayings of Jesus. But although this means that the sayings tradition is the only source of the discourses in the strict sense, the meaning and purpose of the discourses are not dictated by the sayings, but relate closely to the conditions of Johannine Christianity at the time when the evangelist is writing, probably late in the first century. It may be said that John uses the sayings simply as a jumping-off place for what he really wants to say, in much the same way as many preachers use (or mis-use) a text of scripture. But John uses them much more purposefully than that. It is part of his intention in writing a gospel at all to uphold the claim that Johannine Christianity is directly related to Jesus himself. Thus the characteristic Johannine doctrines must be seen to be implied by the words of Jesus. This must be shown, in spite of the fact that the sayings tradition is extremely poor in christological material. So what John does is to select a saying in which he can perceive a principle suitable to his purpose. He draws out the principle

84

---

1. For a recent survey of theories concerning the sources of the discourses, cf. S.S. SMALLEY, *John: Evangelist and Interpreter*, Exeter, 1978, pp. 108-112.

98

in the typical cut and thrust of the argument of the discourses, and so leads up to his desired christological conclusion.

The point may be illustrated from Jn 8,28-29: "When you have lifted up the Son of Man, then you will know that I am he, and that I do nothing on my own authority but speak thus as the Father taught me. And he who sent me is with me; he has not left me alone, for I always do what is pleasing to him".

This is the climax of a very long and complex argument about the true identity of Jesus. The theme was enunciated in the parable of the apprenticed son in 5,19[2], after a carefully prepared introductory narrative and transitional dialogue in 5,1-18. The parable states that a son can do nothing on his own authority, but depends upon his father's instructions. If the parable is authentic, it would admirably suit Jesus' ironic style of self-defence, which can be seen so often in the synoptic gospels. Just as he defends his slackness about fasting by means of the parable of the bridegroom in Mk 2,18-19, so with this parable he defends his bringing of the gospel to the common people by pointing out that he is only copying the practice of "your Father who is in heaven, for he makes his sun rise on the evil and on the good, and sends rain on the just and on the unjust" (Mt 5,45). From this parable John has deduced the principle of Jesus' exact conformity to the will of God. He refers to it with reference to judgement in 5,30. He picks it up again with regard to teaching in 7,16-17. In 8,12-20 he shows that this conformity to the will of God is witness to Jesus' status as the Son of the Father. In the following verse there is a dark hint that this will become plain only in the cross (8,21). In 8,25 Jesus is directly challenged concerning his identity. Then comes the climax in 8,28, which not only picks up the phrases of 5,19.30 and 7,16-17, but relates the substance of the claim to the revelatory character of the cross, referring back to the lifting up of the Son of Man which had previously been enunciated in 3,14. But as that also depends upon the sayings tradition, it is fair to say that not only the opening of this great christological dispute comes from the tradition (5,19), but also the
85   conclusion (8,28, based on 3,14 and 5,19, etc.). The conclusion is that

---

2. The parable should not be taken to include 5,20a, as suggested in my commentary (*The Gospel of John*, The New Century Bible, London, 1972), following C.H. DODD (*A Hidden Parable in the Fourth Gospel*, in *More New Testament Studies*, Manchester, 1968, pp. 30-40) and P. GÄCHTER (*Zur Form von Joh. 5,19-30*, in *Neutestamentliche Aufsätze*, ed. J. BLINZLER, O. KUSS and F. MUSSNER, Regensburg, 1963, pp. 65-68). Verse 20a begins John's exposition of the parable, using words ("the Father loves the Son") almost identical with 3,35. It is possible that John intends to refer to the creation at this point (πάντα ... ἃ ... ποιεῖ, cf. verse 17 ἐργάζεται). Then the "greater things" of verse 20b prepare the way for the eschatological functions in verses 21-22.

Jesus is God's agent, and as such he has a special relationship with God, which corresponds with the father/son relationship commonly employed in the statements about Jesus. Thus the Christian claim that Jesus is the Son of God is here supported by an explanation of one aspect of the father/son relationship, based on a saying from the tradition from which the principle can be deduced.

It is not without significance that the saying in this case is unknown from the synoptic gospels. It has been suggested that a variant of the parable of the apprenticed son lies behind Mt 11,27 = Lk 10,22[3]. If so, we must think of more than one channel of tradition, and the saying has the warrant of double attestation. This also strengthens the contention that John had access to traditions comparable to those used by the synoptic writers, but not identical with them. John may have known and used one or more of the synoptic gospels. But he was not solely dependent upon them for his historical tradition.

The vexed question of the relationship between John and the synoptics is not our concern here. The point at issue is the place of traditional material in the composition of the discourses. What I want to emphasize is that recognition of this is essential to a correct understanding of the discourses themselves. This has already been indicated in connection with the unwieldly composition of chapter 5, and its continuation in 7,16—8,29. This will now be applied to the discourse with Nicodemus (chapter 3), the discourse on the bread of life (chapter 6), and the discourse on slave and son (8,31-58). The last case includes a new assessment of the nature of the underlying tradition which leads to a much more satisfactory analysis of the discourse than has previously been possible.

II

The discourse with Nicodemus begins with a saying from the tradition (Jn 3,3.5): "Amen, amen, I say to you, unless one is born ἄνωθεν (verse 5: from water and Spirit), he cannot see (verse 5: enter) the kingdom of God".

This saying is a variant of the synoptic saying on becoming a child, which is found in independent versions in Mt 18,3 and Mk 10,15. I have argued elsewhere that, when stripped of Johannisms, this saying can be seen to be an independent Greek translation of the same Ara- [86]

---

3. J. JEREMIAS, *New Testament Theology I*, London, 1971, p. 58.

maic saying which lies behind the other two versions[4]. There are thus three different Greek versions of the saying. The cardinal point is that Matthew's "turn and become as children" is a Semitic idiom, meaning "become again as children". This idiom is represented differently in Jn 3,3, if ἄνωθεν is understood to mean "again"[5]. It may be said in favour of this suggestion that it is most unlikely that John's text was the same as Matthew's, and he has deliberately expressed the idiom differently, because the same idiom occurs in a quotation at Jn 12,40, apparently unrecognized by John. On the other hand, even though John in all probability took ἄνωθεν to mean "from above", the fact that it is capable of being a rendering of the idiom preserved by Matthew can scarcely be mere coincidence.

John, however, has understood it to mean "from above" (cf. verse 2, "from God"), and this is the basic principle of the discourse which follows. Entry into the kingdom of God (= eternal life, verses 15, 16, 36) requires birth (i.e. renewal) from above (= from water and Spirit, verse 5; from the Spirit, verse 8). But the crucial point is that such renewal is possible only through belief in the one who is from above (= descended from heaven, verse 13; the one whom God gave, verse 16; the one whom God sent, verse 17; the one who comes ἄνωθεν, verse 31; the teacher from God, verse 2). Thus the whole point of the discourse is to prove that, just as salvation requires action from God, and cannot be obtained by human exertion, so the agent of salvation requires origination from God, and no earthly teacher can be a substitute for him (verse 13).

This is the main drift of the discourse. But there is another factor of the greatest importance to John, which is expressed with the aid of another saying of Jesus from the tradition (3,14-15): "And as Moses lifted up the serpent in the wilderness, so *must the Son of man be lifted up*, that whoever believes in him may have eternal life".

The motif of the serpent is peculiar to John, and the final clause follows his typical mode of expression. But the italicized words reflect the passion predictions of Mark, and are probably to be accepted as a variant of them. We may compare John's ὑψωθῆναι δεῖ τὸν υἱὸν τοῦ ἀνθρώπου with Mk 8,31, δεῖ τὸν υἱὸν τοῦ ἀνθρώπου πολλὰ

---

4. *John and the Synoptic Gospels: A Test Case*, in *NTS* 27 (1981) 287-294 [in this volume, pp. 105-112].

5. The meaning "again" occurs in Gal 4,9, but there it is in conjunction with πάλιν (= "all over again"). Thus it does not denote mere repetition, but renewal "from the start", so that it is an excellent translation of the Aramaic idiom. Comparable examples from the papyri are cited by MOULTON and MILLIGAN, *The Vocabulary of the Greek Testament*, s.v. ἄνωθεν.

παθεῖν. But if we also take into account that the verb παρα-   87
δοθῆναι is much better attested for the passion predictions (Mk 9,30;
10,33.33; cf. 14,21.41), it becomes possible to see that the variable verb
belongs to a pattern of interpretation which explains John's text here[6].
The underlying saying of Jesus (which cannot be reconstructed with
certainty) has been interpreted in the light of the passion prophecy of
Is 52,13-53,12. The verb παραδοθῆναι is an obvious link, because
this verb occurs three times in the Septuagint, including the crucial
verse 53,12. There is no need to doubt that John was aware of the
link. His variation of the verb can thus be explained as the deliberate
choice of a different verb from the same prophecy, i.e. 52,13, in order
to bring together the concepts of death by crucifixion and exaltation,
as suggested by the symbolism of the serpent (cf. Jn 12,33; 18,32). The
reason for this is a central position of John's theology. The cross to
John has revelatory significance, because it demonstrates the unity of
the Father and the Son. Acceptance of the fact that Jesus must die is
therefore indispensable to saving faith.

   It can now be seen that this verse (and the subsequent reflections
on it in Jn 3,16-21) plays a vital part in the argument of the discourse.
If Jesus is the agent of the birth from above, then belief in him as one
who originates from God is a matter of the first importance. But belief
in him will be defective, if it does not include acceptance of the necessity of his death on the cross. Thus the verse introduces a secondary,
but indispensable, element into the argument. And, like the opening
verses, it takes the form of an authentic saying of Jesus, which John
has exploited for his theology. This was not necessarily derived directly
from Mark, although Mark is our only source for the passion predictions as such. For they have clearly been subject to adaptation and
expansion on Mark's part, and their relation to primitive formulae
(e.g. 1 Cor 15,3) suggests that they go behind Mark to earlier tradition. Seeing that the Son of Man in this saying (both in Mark and in
John) operates only as a self-reference, and not as a title of honour,
it is to be accepted as an original feature. But what was its meaning
on the lips of Jesus in this connection is a question which lies outside
the scope of this article[7].

---

   6. I have analysed the passion predictions in an article on *The New Look on the Son
of Man*, in *BJRL* 63 (1980-81) 437-462, and more fully in *Jesus Son of Man*, ch. 4. "The
Passion Predictions"; see also ch. 9, "The Son of Man in the Theology of John" [in this
volume, pp. 153-166]. John's use of this material is given very full treatment in F.J.
MOLONEY, *The Johannine Son of Man*, Rome, [2]1978.
   7. The idiomatic *bar enasha*, which lies behind the Son of Man title, is neither an
exclusive self-reference (G. VERMES, *Jesus the Jew*, London, 1973, pp. 160-191) nor a
general statement (M. CASEY, *Son of Man. The Interpretation and Influence of Daniel 7*,
London, 1979, p. 232), but a generic usage denoting a class with which the speaker iden-

III

88   The discourse on the bread of life is primarily an exposition of the
miracle of the manna, introduced by the feeding of the five thousand
from the Jesus tradition. Hence it is not to be expected that sayings
of Jesus will play such an important part in the argument. On the
other hand two sayings from the tradition can be detected in the
discourse, and their function is quite similar to what we have seen in
the discourse with Nicodemus.

The discourse starts with the contrast between the gift of the
manna ("as it is written, He gave them bread from heaven to eat",
6,31) and the true bread from heaven which the Father gives. As 6,31
is an adapted quotation of Ex 16,15 or of Ps 78,24[8], it can be claimed
that the vocabulary of the discourse is derived from the quotation
material. So when the audience say "Lord, give us this bread always"
(6,34), it is unnecessary to look for any further allusions. On the other
hand there is a striking similarity between πάντοτε δὸς ἡμῖν τὸν
ἄρτον τοῦτον and the Lord's prayer, τὸν ἄρτον ἡμῶν τὸν
ἐπιούσιον δὸς ἡμῖν σήμερον (Mt 6,11). Seeing that John has
other probable allusions to the Lord's Prayer in the prayer of Jesus
before his arrest (πάτερ ... δόξασόν σου τὸν υἱόν, ἵνα ὁ υἱὸς
δοξάσῃ σε, 17,1; ἵνα τηρήσῃς αὐτοὺς ἐκ τοῦ πονηροῦ, 17,15),
it is likely that he was familiar with it, even though he does not
reproduce it formally. For John, the prayer of Christians for daily
bread (πάντοτε corresponding with ἐπιούσιον in his allusion to it)
is a prayer for Jesus himself, because Jesus is the bringer of the true
nourishment, which consists in belief in him as the agent of God
(6,40). If this discourse was composed originally as a homily at the
Christian eucharist it would very naturally include allusion to the
Lord's Prayer, which may have been recited in the course of the
liturgy[9]. The homily is based on the Jewish lections, taken over from
the synagogue. So it is an exposition of the *seder*, Ex 16, interpreted

tifies himself, in this case a man faced with betrayal or arrest (see the works mentioned
in the last note).
    8. The latter is to be preferred, because the psalm provides the means of linking the
expositions of *seder* and *haphtarah*, as explained below.
    9. Didache 8, the earliest reference to the Lord's Prayer outside the New Testament,
orders recital three times a day. The eucharistic thanksgiving immediately follows this
instruction. But the earliest witness to its actual use in the eucharist does not appear
until the fourth century (Cyril of Jerusalem).

in the light of the *haphtarah*, Is 54,9—55,5, quoted in Jn 6,45[10]. But John's Christian interpretation of the theme is already presupposed in the eucharist itself, in which fellowship with Jesus, the risen Lord and mediator of the new covenant, is experienced. Thus the petition for "daily bread", no doubt generally taken in the obvious practical way as a prayer for physical sustenance (cf. Mt 6,25-26), is applied to Jesus himself as the true spiritual food, for which he had instructed his followers to pray. The main principle of the discourse is that Jesus is the true bread, by contrast with the Jewish law, of which the manna was the symbol. John is able to anchor this principle in the words of Jesus by referring to the prayer which he gave to his followers.

The second allusion to the words of Jesus is also a liturgical reference in 6,53: "Amen, amen I say to you, unless you eat the flesh of the Son of Man and drink his blood, you have no life in you". The relationship with the eucharistic words is obvious. But its significance will be missed if it is not observed that the same tradition has already been referred to in verse 51c: "And the bread which I will give is my flesh for (ὑπέρ) the life of the world"[11]. John's ὑπέρ links up with 1 Cor 11,24 (τὸ σῶμα τὸ ὑπὲρ ὑμῶν) and Mk 14,24 (τὸ αἷμά μου ... ὑπὲρ πολλῶν). It establishes his intention to use this reference in order to bring in the notion of the sacrifice of Christ. This is confirmed by the Son of Man title in verse 53. As far as John is concerned, this is not a title of honour, but a self-designation used by Jesus in speaking of his sacrificial death. It refers to him specifically as the one whose cross reveals his true relationship with God, as we have already seen in connection with 3,14. The Son of Man title is derived from the passion predictions, and so properly belongs to the traditional material used there. It does not belong to the underlying words here, but has been introduced here by John, because he is using the eucharistic words to make the same point as he made in 3,14. Acceptance of Jesus as the true bread is defective unless it includes

10. This can be claimed only with due caution, because the reconstruction of the Jewish lectionary in the first century is far from secure. A. GUILDING (*The Fourth Gospel and Jewish Worship*, Oxford, 1960, p. 63) asserts that Is 54,9–54,3 (or 5) was the haphtarah to Genesis 6,9ff, but she includes both these and Ex 16 within the second half of Nisan, so that the connection between them was clearly recognized. All that can be said is that Jn 6 gives the appearance of being based on this connection of *seder* and *haphtarah*, and that no evidence has yet been produced which would make the supposition that they were used together in the synagogue in John's day impossible.

11. For the order of words, which varies in the manuscripts, cf. C.K. BARRETT, *The Gospel according to St. John*, London, ²1978, ad loc. The addition of ἣν ἐγὼ δώσω in some texts is comparable to the addition of διδόμενον to the text of 1 Cor 11,24 in Lk 22,19, and this fact enhances the fundamental similarity of the traditions.

acceptance of the necessity of the passion. If it is John's purpose to
persuade his readers that all the spiritual benefits, which Jews have
found through meditation upon the Law, can be gained through Christ,
then he must make it clear that this is possible only through his death.
That reveals his unique relationship with the Father, and acceptance
of it enables the believer to live within that relationship (6,57).

IV

Our last example is the discourse on slave and son in Jn 8,31-58[12].
This is more difficult to unravel than the other discourses, because it
does not appear to have a consistent theme. In the others which we
have considered the traditional saying employed by John at the outset
embodies a principle which is worked out in various ways in the
succeeding development of the discourse, and the concluding section
recalls the opening clearly enough to constitute a literary inclusion,
which enables the reader to think of the discourse as a whole. In the
present case the figure of Abraham provides an inclusion (verses 33
and 56-58), but his role is ancillary to the main argument. The
purpose of the discourse is very similar to that of chapter 3, where
John wished to prove the origination of Jesus from God, and did so
by pointing to the necessity of the divine initiative for salvation. If
God alone can give salvation, then the agent of salvation must come
from God. Here John wants to prove the pre-existence of Jesus. His
argument is that, if Jesus is the giver of eternal life, then he must
himself be the possessor of eternal life. He therefore has to prove that
Jesus does give eternal life, and only after that can he reach the
conclusion that Jesus is pre-existent.

The matter is complicated, because John writes against a
background of thought in which the means of gaining eternal life is
believed to be already available in the Jewish law. There is no appeal
to this belief in the course of the argument, but it is the unspoken
tertium comparationis in this discourse, just as much as it is in the
discourse on the bread of life. There is a reference to the
commandment not to kill in verses 37 and 40 (cf. 7,19), and Abraham
is invoked precisely because he is the founder of the covenant people

---

12. What follows is an abbreviated version of an article on *Slave and Son in John
8:31-36*, 1984 [in this volume, pp. 167-182]. A preliminary analysis on the same lines was
given in a lecture "Freedom in the Gospel according to St. John" given at the
Presbyterian Conference Centre, Massanetta Springs, VA, U.S.A.

who possess the law. It might be expected that John would argue on this basis that the law cannot give life. But John never repudiates the law. Like Paul, he regards the law as containing the revelation of God which reaches its true application in Christ (cf. 5,46-47). The rejection of Jesus is not, as one might suppose, a positive decision in favour of the law in preference to Jesus. John regards it as nothing less than transgression of the law, because it is in his eyes equivalent to killing Jesus. So Abraham and the law are on the side of Jesus, and the wish to kill him stems not from the law but from the devil. Even on the Jews' own terms of reference, then, belief in Jesus is essential for the obtaining of eternal life.

John's argument is thus more logical than appears at first sight, and it is conducted with exceptional verve and dramatic skill. But what has been said so far throws into relief a problem which is sure to trouble the attentive reader, that John starts off with a contrast between slave and son, but drops it after a few verses, and never refers 91 to it again. There are plenty of sharp contrasts in what follows, but the concepts of freedom and slavery play no part in it. In fact, John has confused the issue at the outset by making use of the idea of slave and son, because he is actually concerned only with sonship, and the contrast from verse 38 onwards is put in terms of different fathers. All are sons, whether they are sons of Abraham or sons of the devil or even the Son of God. There really seems to be no point in mentioning slaves at all.

This problem could be dismissed as carelessness on John's part. He has begun the discourse with the idea of slave and son in his mind, but then the issue of sonship claims all his attention, and he forgets to follow through his initial plan[13]. But closer observation of the text suggests a more cogent explanation. John very occasionally uses the concept of slavery (cf. 13,16; 15,15), but he never uses the concept of freedom outside this passage. The word ἐλεύθερος and its cognates occur only here in the Fourth Gospel. It is foreign to John's diction. It thus seems likely that John has used it here rather unwillingly, and abandons it as soon as he has established the terms of reference which he needs for the subsequent argument. If this is so, there must have been a certain constraint upon him to use it in the first place. Our previous observations of John's technique in constructing the discourses point to the conclusion that this constraint comes from his

---

13. Such changes are characteristic of Paul; see now the analysis of Paul's exegetical argument in 2 Cor 3 in M.D. HOOKER, *Beyond the Things that are Written? St. Paul's Use of Scripture*, in *NTS* 27 (1981) 295-309.

use of traditional material containing this word.

As before, John wishes to use an item from the sayings tradition which embodies the principle which is essential to his argument. But he must have found it no easy matter to hit upon one that was suitable to his purpose. If we were in John's position, with only Q before us, what would we have chosen? But John does not seem to have had access to Q, at any rate in the form used by Matthew and Luke. His saying on renewal in 3,3.5 has come through a separate channel. Similarly, the parable of the apprenticed son in 5,19 may be a variant of the Q saying in Mt 11,27 = Lk 10,22, but it is not derived from it. Now he is able to reproduce another parable, which could perhaps be taken from the same collection as 5,19. It is the parable of the slave and the son in 8,35: "A slave does not continue in a house for ever; a son continues for ever". In isolating this verse as a parable derived from the tradition, Dodd recognized that it was open to question, because the phrase μένει εἰς τὸν αἰῶνα is characteristic of John's diction[14]. But he found that these words occur just sufficiently often in the rest of the New Testament to persuade him that they could belong to the underlying material.

Our argument, however, suggests a different answer. If ἐλεύθερος is, by contrast, foreign to John's vocabulary, then it is likely to be the original word which John has replaced with his own phrase in reproducing the parable itself. Thus the underlying material can be reconstructed as follows: ὁ δοῦλος οὐκ ἐλεύθερός ἐστιν ἐν τῇ οἰκίᾳ· ὁ υἱὸς ἐλεύθερός ἐστιν.

Two things may be said in favour of this reconstruction. Firstly, it fits well into one side of the ethical teaching of Jesus, who not only recognized God as his Father, but also taught his disciples to regard themselves as God's sons, unenslaved by worldly possessions (cf. Mt 5,45; Lk 6,32-35). The motif occurs in the parable of the prodigal son (Lk 15,17-19). It is also a feature of Paul's cosmic understanding of the new status of those who acknowledge Jesus, who have been freed from the πνεῦμα δουλείας and have received the πνεῦμα υἱοθεσίας (Rom 8,15). This is the cosmic process, by which αὐτὴ ἡ κτίσις ἐλευθερωθήσεται ἀπὸ τῆς δουλείας τῆς φθορᾶς εἰς τὴν ἐλευθερίαν τῆς δόξης τῶν τέκνων τοῦ θεοῦ (Rom 8,21). Paul in this chapter is certainly building on a tradition of exposition of the Abba address, mentioned in Rom 8,15 and also Gal 4,6. Similar traditions lie behind John's exploitation of the father/son correlation

---

14. Cf. C.H. DODD, *Historical Tradition in the Fourth Gospel*, Cambridge, 1963, pp. 379-382.

in connection with his christology. It is thus not surprising to find that his resources include a saying on sonship as opposed to slavery, which belongs within this general range of teaching.

Secondly, the second, positive half of the saying as reconstructed actually occurs in plural form in Mt 17,26: ἄρα γε ἐλεύθεροί εἰσιν οἱ υἱοί[15]. It is the unique pericope of the temple tax (Mt 17,24-27). Critical opinion on the historical value of this pericope is much divided, but there seems to be no good reason to doubt the authenticity of the central core. The mention of Peter may be due to Matthew, and the question concerning payment of the tax may be an artificial setting for the saying, completed with a "fishing story" derived from a well known theme of folk-lore. But the saying itself is a parable, and has nothing to do with the temple tax: "From whom do kings of the earth take toll or tribute? From their sons or from others? (Do they not take it) from others? Then the sons are free". 93 If Jesus gave general teaching along these lines, it would be likely to belong to his teaching on the nature of the coming kingdom. The Q material in Lk 12,32-34 provides a good parallel.

Now, if this is the tradition which came to John, we can see why he uses ἐλεύθερος in the context, even though he has altered it in the saying itself. The alteration is, of course, a carefully chosen midrashic explanation. The singular ὁ υἱός in John's text was intended, like ὁ δοῦλος, to be generic. But John has picked out this saying precisely because it is capable of christological interpretation. The son in the parable is Jesus, and he it is who is free. But to be free in John's thought is to have eternal life, and it is essential for the subsequent argument that Jesus should actually say this concerning the son.

In order to understand this, it is necessary to analyse the sequence of verses more closely. John first sets out the form of the argument in verses 31-32, using the vocabulary of the saying: "If you continue (μείνητε) in my word, you are truly my disciples, and you will know the truth, and the truth will make you free". This establishes the principle of cause and effect, which is fundamental to the following argument. Here the principle is put in terms of truth and freedom. Jesus conveys the truth, and the truth effects freedom. John is going to drop the concept of freedom from the argument, but the concept of truth will be an essential ingredient (verses 39-47). In verse 33 the audience make the typically Johannine response of supposing that

---

15. Dodd drew attention to this parallel, but failed to observe its value for reconstruction of the actual text used by John.

Jesus is speaking of freedom in the political sense. This allows John
to introduce Abraham, who also will figure in the following argument.

It is tempting to suppose that John is here dealing with Stoic
concepts of truth and freedom. But this is completely foreign to John's
purpose. Truth has been introduced because it is one side in John's
essentially Jewish dualism, which comes to open expression in verses
44-46. This dualism is thus another basic feature of the argument,
along with the principle of cause and effect. John has deduced both
these features from the saying on slave and son. One of the values of
the saying from his point of view is that the contrast between slave
and son makes a splendid basis for his central position, in which
sonship to the devil is contrasted with Jesus' sonship to God. But the
94 principle of cause and effect is also contained in the parable because,
in John's view, the possession of freedom carries with it the right to
confer freedom.

This point is made clear in verses 34-36, which need to be
considered as an integrated whole, in spite of the fact that the core of
it is the parable from the tradition, which is both preceded and
followed by midrashic exposition:

> Amen, amen I say to you,
> every one who commits sin is a slave[16].
> A slave does not continue in a house for ever;
> a son continues for ever.
> So if the Son makes you free, you will be free indeed.

The contrast, then, is between the one who commits sin (identified
with the slave of the parable) and the Son (identified with, and indeed
incapable of being distinguished from, the son of the parable). The one
who commits sin does not continue for ever. In other words his
sinfulness leads to death, or exclusion from eternal life and the
authority to confer it. This double interpretation depends upon the
oscillation in the meaning of the parable, which at one level concerns
the sons of God in general, as intended by Jesus in the original saying,
but at another level can be applied to Jesus as the unique Son of God.
As such he is the agent of God for the salvation of God's people. In
this application of the parable it is essential that John should make it

---

16. Nearly all texts add τῆς ἁμαρτίας, but it is omitted by D b sy^s; Clem. This is
evidence that texts without it were current in the second century, and it is very likely that
we have here a genuine case of "western non-interpolation". Though the insertion does
not affect the sense, it introduces a personification of sin which is foreign to the context,
and breaks the artistic balance between slave (verse 34) and free (verse 36). But it was
an obvious addition to make, possibly under the influence of Rom 6,20.

unmistakably plain that what he is talking about is the capacity for eternal life, and this is why he has altered the parable. But he values the reference to freedom in the original, because it allows him to make the distinction between having freedom and conferring freedom, which he uses as the basis of verse 36. Here we have the principle of cause and effect, already laid out in verses 31-32, where the idea of freedom was used. But we can see now that freedom denotes eternal life as far as John is concerned, although eternal life is a phrase which is never actually used in this discourse.

After these preliminaries John can indicate the unique position of Jesus by following through the principle which he has enunciated, along with a rigorous application of the dualism suggested by the contrast of slave and son. The essential requirement for eternal life is to believe in Jesus. The refusal of the Jews to believe in him is identified with their intention to kill him. Their wish to kill him is the result of an attitude of falsehood, and falsehood comes from the devil. This represents one side of the contrast. On the other side there is Jesus who conveys truth which leads to life. Thus life is the result of truth, and truth comes from God. This argument is set out briefly in verse 38, and then worked out in detail in verses 39-47.

So far John has been concerned with the dualistic contrast and the sequence of cause and effect on either side. But he has still not reached the point which he really wished to make when he selected the saying on slave and son from his stock of traditional material. He has shown how the Son channels freedom, or life, but he has not explained what it means to possess it by right. This aspect of the argument is taken up in the remaining verses. To make the point, John introduces another saying from the tradition (verse 51): "Amen, amen I say to you, if any one keeps my word, he will never see (verse 52: taste) death". Here again it is possible to strip the text of Johannisms and relate it to a synoptic parallel (Mk 9,1):

Mk 9,1   Jn 8,51/52

ἀμὴν λέγω ὑμῖν   ἀμὴν ἀμὴν λέγω ὑμῖν
ὅτι εἰσίν τινες   ἐάν τις
ὧδε τῶν ἐστηκότων οἵτινες   τὸν ἐμὸν λόγον τηρήσῃ,
οὐ μὴ γεύσωνται θανάτου   οὐ μὴ γεύσηται θανάτου
ἕως ἂν ἴδωσιν τὴν βασιλείαν τοῦ θεοῦ   εἰς τὸν αἰῶνα.
ἐληλυθυῖαν ἐν δυνάμει.

John has two substantial differences from Mark. In the first place he has substituted for the subject of the verb "taste" a conditional clause based on the opening words of the discourse in verse 31 (ἐὰν ὑμεῖς μείνητε ἐν τῷ λόγῳ τῷ ἐμῷ). This, of course, did refer to "some of those standing here", as in Mark. Thus this change can be regarded as merely explanatory, elucidating the terms of the original in relation to the present discourse, without requiring an underlying text different from Mark[17]. In the second place, John has abandoned the reference to the coming of the kingdom of God, simply finishing the saying with εἰς τὸν αἰῶνα, which recalls the other saying in verse 35. It is easy to see that John would not wish to speak of the coming of the kingdom. The kingdom to John is a static concept, which can almost be identified with the truth (18,36-37). He has retained it in the traditional saying of 3,3.5, because it is there a state which can be entered. But the discourse of chapter 3 soon shows that the proper concept from John's point of view is eternal life. It thus seems necessary to suppose that οὐ μὴ ... εἰς τὸν αἰῶνα in the present verse is more than the idiomatic strong negative so frequently used by John, and refers to the coming age. On the other hand it is not followed up in this way, and all the emphasis goes on the idea of not dying. This is the point which John needs. In the past men have always died, including Abraham himself. But Jesus surpasses Abraham. He is not limited by the normal span of life, which ends in death. In the same way his life from the beginning cannot be measured in terms of years (verse 57). Therefore he can say, ἀμὴν ἀμὴν λέγω ὑμῖν, πρὶν Ἀβραὰμ γενέσθαι ἐγὼ εἰμί (verse 58).

The last stages of the argument are extremely tortuous. John has not found it easy to produce such a statement on the basis of the sayings of Jesus that are known to him. In particular, the background of verse 58 is not easily determined. Like the sayings from the tradition in verses (34) 35 and 51-52, it is solemnly introduced with the Amen formula, but it scarcely seems likely that John is indebted to the sayings tradition on this occasion. On the other hand the absolute ἐγὼ εἰμι has been used at the end of the preceding discourse in 8,24.28. Though the meaning was different there (I am he), it was almost certainly derived from scripture (cf. Is 43,10), and the same may apply in this case. Here we have to find parallels to the

---

17. It is not my intention to claim that the saying used by John was identical with Mk 9,1, though the argument shows that all the differences from it in Jn 8,51 can be explained from John's editorial work. There are several other instances of ἀμὴν λέγω ὑμῖν ... in both Mark and Q, cf. Mt 10,23b; 23,39; 24,34 (= Mk 13,30, which uses μέχρις); Mk 14,25; Lk 22,16.18; Lk 22,34 = Jn 13,38 (cf. Mt 26,34 = Mk 14,30); cf. also Lk 2,26. As all these sayings have a good claim to be considered authentic on other grounds, it would seem that we have here a stylistic feature of Jesus' speech. There is thus again no reason to assume that John was actually dependent on Mark here.

exceptional use of ἐγώ εἰμι to denote "I am in existence"[18]. The best parallel (noted by Bultmann) is Ps 90,2, though there it is in the second person (LXX Ps 89,2): πρὸ τοῦ ὄρη γενηθῆναι καὶ πλασθῆναι τὴν γῆν καὶ τὴν οἰκουμένην καὶ ἀπὸ τοῦ αἰῶνος ἕως τοῦ αἰῶνος σὺ εἶ[19]. The thought here is close to that of Wisdom in Sir 24,9: πρὸ τοῦ αἰῶνος ἀπ' ἀρχῆς ἔκτισέν με, καὶ ἕως αἰῶνος οὐ μὴ ἐκλίπω. There is a Hebrew parallel with the first person in Prov 8,27 (bhkynw šmym śm 'ny), but the Septuagint differs here. But we may note also Prov 8,23 and 25 (πρὸ τοῦ αἰῶνος ἐθεμελίωσέν με ἐν ἀρχῇ ... πρὸ τοῦ ὄρη ἑδρασθῆναι, πρὸ δὲ πάντων βουνῶν γεννᾷ με). The idea of the time span from aeon to aeon is a striking feature of these texts, and reminds us that the Son μένει εἰς τὸν αἰῶνα. Against this background the sleight of hand, whereby John changes from continuance into the future to continuance from the past, begins to seem less arbitrary. When he says "Before Abraham was", he is substituting Abraham for an expression of the creation (cf. πρὸ τοῦ ὄρη γενηθῆναι)[20].

The first saying from the tradition in this discourse (verse 35) gave a static view of Jesus as the possessor of eternal life, though the underlying saying itself provided the principle of cause and effect by using the concept of freedom (verse 36). The second saying (verses 51-52) concentrated attention on the effect, the capacity of Jesus to give eternal life. This enabled John to move his argument in such a way that he could finally adapt a Wisdom scripture to express the pre-existence of Jesus, which was what he had set out to demonstrate. Thus, unlike 3,14 and 6,53, the second saying does not introduce the theme of the passion, even though it is concerned with death. But it has helped John's purpose, because the opening saying on slave and

97

18. It is possible that ἐγώ εἰμι should be construed here as in 8,24.28, i.e. "Before Abraham came into existence, I am he", i.e. "I am the same" (cf. Is 43,10). In any case there seems to be no direct reference to the divine name of Ex 3,14 (ἐγώ εἰμι ὁ ὤν), except in so far as the notion of existence in a context dealing with origination from God (cf. verse 47) would easily bring it to mind. But the point of verse 58 is not to assert that Jesus is the abiding expression of God, but that he exists from before creation.

19. MT 'attah 'El. But LXX has read 'El as the negative 'al, and taken it with the next verse.

20. If 8,58 is modelled on the Wisdom sayings, with Abraham replacing the mountains as a symbol of antiquity, we may suspect that John's thought has been assisted by Is 51,1-2: ἐμβλέψατε εἰς τὴν στερεὰν πέτραν, ἣν ἐλατομήσατε ... ἐμβλέψατε εἰς Ἀβραὰμ τὸν πατέρα ὑμῶν ... For John's debt to Deutero-Isaiah (not, however, referring to this possible connection), see G. REIM, Studien zum alttestamentlichen Hintergrund des Johannesevangeliums, Cambridge, 1974, pp. 162-182.

son did not really contain the theme of eternal life at all, and it
needed to be supplemented by another traditional item in which this
theme was actually stated. This is what John has been able to do by
drawing on a saying comparable to Mk 9,1.

V

The four discourses with which we have been concerned in this article
do not exhaust the evidence for the use of traditional sayings in the
Johannine discourses. But they provide excellent examples of the
relationship of John to the common tradition. John values the
tradition, because he honestly believes that his christology is consistent
with it, and indeed is the truth which it contains. It is a great mistake
to suppose that John is at odds with the tradition on which he
depends. The disputes in John are against the unbelieving Jews, not
against fellow-Christians of differing views. John is not arguing against
an inferior christology, but against a high and sophisticated regard for
the Jewish law as the complete embodiment of the will of God. The
claim that the law has been superseded from this point of view by the
act of God in Christ had a profound effect upon the development of
christology. The beginnings of this effect can already be seen in the
writings of Paul. In John we see the same situation at a later stage.
Christian claims concerning Jesus have developed, and the breach
between church and synagogue has widened into an almost impassable
gulf. Meanwhile the corporate memory of Jesus has moved away from
the direct and vivid familiarity with his historic origins which can still
be seen in Mark, and which is so skilfully evoked by Luke. The idea
of Jesus as the Son of God has begun to take over from the memory
of him as a man. John wishes to bring his readers into vital relationship with Jesus, because this is the means of salvation. He is less
concerned with presenting Jesus as a model for moral example, and he
does not seek to expound the teaching of Jesus by means of a
commentary upon the tradition. Hence he is concerned to establish an
intellectual position, maintained in the mind by a deeply felt emotion.
It only confuses the issue to refer to this as mysticism. But, seeing that
the point of importance to John is the mental attitude of the believer,
it is inevitable that his position should appear to constitute a step in
the direction of gnosticism. It is thus not surprising that the opening
words of the Gospel of Thomas should be an adaptation of Jn 8,51-

52, which we have considered in this study[21].

In spite of these developments, which simply reflect the transition of Christianity from the apostolic age to the second century scene, John did make a notable effort to ground the beliefs of his time and milieu in the actual sayings of Jesus. The way in which he adapted them for his purpose may not seem strictly legitimate to us today. But he believed in the continuity of the faith which he had received, and he was not intentionally an innovator. The issues which he had to face in the debate with the synagogue could not be answered simply by quoting the tradition. John thus attempted to seize the essential meaning of the sayings of Jesus which were available to him, and adapted them to meet the actual situation which was pressing upon him. This is the reason for the historical tension of the Fourth Gospel[22], which appeals to the truth of the tradition, but at the same time treats it in a highly creative and original manner. One facet of this work is John's method of structuring the discourses, in which his theological positions are advanced, around the sayings of Jesus himself.

It is a pleasure to offer these thoughts in honour of Professor Anthony Hanson, who has laboured much to maintain the continuity of the faith in the many-sided scene of New Testament Christianity.

---

21. Thomas, Pref. and 1: "These are the secret words which the living Jesus spoke, and (which) Didymus Judas Thomas wrote. And he said: He who finds the explanation (ἑρμηνεία) of these words will not taste death" (cf. Pap Oxyrhynch. 654, ουτοι οι λογοι οι (...) λησεν Iης ο ζων κ (...) και Θωμα. και ειπεν (...) αν των λογων τουτ (...) ου μη γευσηται); Thomas 18 and 19: "... Blessed (μακάριος) is he who will stand at the beginning (ἀρχή), and he will know the end and will not taste death. Jesus said: Blessed (μακάριος) is he who was before he became. If you become my disciples (μαθητής) (and) hear my words, these stones will minister (διακονεῖν) to you ... He who will know them will not taste death". There seem to be allusions to Jn 8,31.51-52, and perhaps even 58, here.

22. See the essay on this subject in E.C. HOSKYNS and F.N. DAVEY, The Fourth Gospel, London, ²1947, pp. 58-85.

10

THE PERSECUTION OF CHRISTIANS
IN JOHN 15:18-16:4a

The nature of the Johannine community and its historical situation have been the subject of lively debate in recent years.[1] Information may be gleaned from both the Gospel and the Epistles of John, but the relationship between them is still an unsolved problem.[2] The persecution of Christians is one matter in which they presuppose completely different situations. In the Gospel the disciples are warned to expect persecution from the unbelieving Jews outside the Church. In the Epistles, on the other hand, the adversaries are dissident or heretical members within the Johannine community itself. A preliminary solution is to suppose that the persecution of which the Gospel speaks has ceased to be a factor by the time that the Epistles are written. On this showing the Epistles are the final product of the Johannine school, possibly overlapping the last stages of the editing of the Gospel. The Gospel itself, however, has a complex literary history behind it. The references to persecution may be fitted anywhere along that line of development. It will be the aim of this article to analyse John 15: 18 – 16: 4*a* in such a way as to show the connections between this passage and the literary history of the Gospel, and also to estimate its evidential value for persecution in the Johannine Church.

I

Apart from 15: 20 the verb διώκειν is used only once in the Gospel, and that is with Jesus as object in 5: 16. Thereafter, though the word is not used, the persecution of Jesus is a constant theme, reverberating through

---

[1] Cf. R. Kysar, *The Fourth Evangelist and his Gospel* (Minneapolis, 1975), pp. 83–172; O. Cullmann, *The Johannine Circle* (London, 1976); A. R. Culpepper, *The Johannine School* (Missoula, 1975); R. E. Brown, *The Community of the Beloved Disciple* (London, 1979).

[2] Cf. R. E. Brown, 'The Relationship to the Fourth Gospel shared by the author of I John and by his opponents', in *Text and Interpretation: Studies in the New Testament presented to Matthew Black*, ed. E. Best and R. McL. Wilson (Cambridge University Press, 1979), pp. 57–68.

the Gospel until the climax is reached in the Cross. The persecution of the disciples, however, is not referred to during the ministry of Jesus. But we find a first hint in chapter 9, where the man born blind is cross-examined by the authorities and ejected from the Synagogue (9: 34). J. Louis Martyn has argued that the account reflects conditions in John's milieu, where Jews were subjected to cross-examination if suspected of becoming converts to Christianity.[3] Once this connection is allowed, a great deal of the debate between Jesus and the Jews in the rest of the Gospel may be presumed to reflect the contemporary conflict between Church and Synagogue. In spite of efforts to date John early,[4] the picture that emerges from this interpretation suits best the Jamnia period, when the Pharisees were making strenuous efforts to preserve the purity of the people and the integrity of the Law.[5]

The crucial verse is 9: 22: 'The Jews had already agreed that if anyone should confess him to be the Christ, he was to be put out of the synagogue.' The same word (ἀποσυνάγωγος) occurs again at 12: 42; 16: 2, and is not found elsewhere in the New Testament. The word itself, of course, cannot decide the issue whether there is here a reference to the Birkat-ha-Minim.[6] For the possibility of exclusion from the Synagogue

---

[3] J. L. Martyn, History and Theology in the Fourth Gospel (New York and Evanston, 1968), p. 9.

[4] J. A. T. Robinson, Redating the New Testament (London, 1976), pp. 254–311.

[5] Cf. S. Pancaro, The Law in the Fourth Gospel, Supplements to Novum Testamentum 42 (Leiden, 1975), pp. 492–534.

[6] This is the addition to the Twelfth of the Eighteen Benedictions, which operated as a virtual form of exclusion of Christians and heretical Jews from the Synagogue, because it required them to curse the Nazarenes (ha-nōṣᵉrim) and the Minim (heretics), and was introduced towards the end of the first century precisely for this reason. A probable form of the Benediction is given by C. K. Barrett, The New Testament Background: Selected Documents (London, 1961), pp. 166f, as follows: 'For the renegades let there be no hope, and may the arrogant kingdom soon be rooted out in our days, and the Nazarenes and the Minim perish as in a moment and be blotted out from the book of life and with the righteous may they not be inscribed. Blessed art thou, O Lord, who humblest the arrogant.' The addition consists of 'and the Nazareans...inscribed.' For the Hebrew text and discussion of the problems, see W. D. Davies, The Setting of the Sermon on the Mount (Cambridge University Press, 1963), pp. 275f. Recent studies express doubt whether there was a direct policy of opposition to Christians in the Jamnia period, or that the addition to the Twelfth Benediction can be dated so early, but this is due to the inadequacy and inconclusive nature of the evidence, not to any fresh information, cf. E. Schürer, G. Vermes, F. Millar and M. Black, The History of the Jewish People in the Age of Jesus Christ, vol. II (Edinburgh, 1979), pp. 461–3; P. Schafer, 'Die sogenannte Synode von Jabne', Judaica 31 (1975), 54–64, 116–24. It must be pointed out, however, that the evidence of Justin, Dial. 16; 47; 93; 95; 96; 108; 117; 133 is misrepresented in the former (137 is not characteristic), and totally disregarded by the latter.

for particular offences was always present, and Jewish persecution of
Christians is attested already in 1 Thessalonians 2: 15. But the significant point is the *agreement* mentioned in John 9: 22. This suggests a
definite policy, rather than occasional *ad hoc* decisions. Moreover the
offence is the *confession of faith* in Jesus as the Messiah. This is the test
of membership of the sect of the Nazarenes, against which the *Birkat-
ha-Minim* was directed, and no one who confessed this faith could recite
it.

Similarly 12: 42 refers to leading Jews who were privately believers,
but 'did not confess (Jesus) on account of the Pharisees, lest they should
be put out of the synagogue'. Here again all the details fit the situation
implied by the addition to the Twelfth Benediction. The Pharisees are
the ruling party, the offence is the confession of faith, and the penalty is
exclusion from the Synagogue. This verse clearly has a strongly apologetic motive, and indicates that John has reason to believe that there are
indeed prominent men who are held back from throwing in their lot with
the Christians on account of their position in the Jewish community.
The Gospel itself includes two examples of such men in Nicodemus and
Joseph of Arimathea. Nicodemus came to Jesus 'by night' (3: 1), thus
avoiding public notice, but was accused of being a 'Galilean' when he
spoke up for Jesus in the Sanhedrin (7: 50–2). Eventually he assisted
Joseph with the burial of Jesus (19: 39). Joseph himself is expressly
stated to be a disciple, 'but secretly for fear of the Jews' (19: 38). In
calling Joseph a disciple, John is taking up a hint supplied by Matthew
(27: 52). But Matthew gives no indication that Joseph had anything to
fear from his fellow-countrymen. Thus the description of these two
leading Jews fits the situation presupposed by 12: 42. On the other hand
the verse cannot be regarded as intended to apply solely to them. It is a
general statement, and the bitter comment with which it ends (verse 43)
conveys a strong impression of active involvement. It is the way in which
John explains *to himself* this tragic failure of the Jews.

The reference to excommunication in 16: 2 will claim our attention below. Though it adds nothing further to what we have already
observed, the remainder of the verse goes further in suggesting that the
disciples will run the risk, not only of excommunication, but even of
death.

What conclusions can be drawn from this scanty evidence? In the first
place, it can be asserted that, if a late date is assigned to the Fourth
Gospel, a reference to the *Birkat-ha-Minim* is both possible and probable.
On the other hand it is unlikely that this happened suddenly, without
previous steps in the same direction. The Gospel of John gives evidence

only for the circumstances of the Johannine Church. A local decision of
the rabbinate is sufficient to account for what is said here. This could
have been taken some years earlier. This need not have been the addition of the *Birkat-ha-Minim* as such, and indeed may well have been
something more drastic. We have to allow for local variation in the
factors that led up to the Jamnia decision. But the persecution envisaged
by John appears to be more clearly defined and deliberately organised
than that which is implied by Matthew and Mark.[7] Matthew, indeed,
reveals a situation that has much in common with John: a Jewish Church
recognising the validity of the Gospel to the Gentiles, living in contact
with the Synagogue, and claiming to represent the true interpretation of
the Law against active hostility from the unbelieving Jews.[8] But in John
the struggle is intensified.

II

Though John probably belongs to the Jamnia period, there was certainly
persecution much earlier, and it appears in the Gospel traditions that
John received. John 15: 18 – 16: 4a is widely recognised to be dependent upon earlier traditions found also in the Synoptic Gospels. The most
important passages are the Mission Charge of Matthew 10: 17–25[9] and
the Little Apocalypse of Mark 13: 9–13. But these two passages do not
represent distinct sources, because most of the Matthaean passage is
derived from Mark. Consequently Matthew has reduced this material
in his own version of the Little Apocalypse at 24: 9. Luke similarly has
the material in both types of context, i.e. Luke 12: 11f and 21: 12–19.
In this case we may suspect that Q has contributed to one of the Lucan
versions, although the parallel passages cannot be convincingly separated
into a Marcan and a Q form.[10]

[7] D. R. A. Hare, *The Theme of Jewish Persecution of Christians in the Gospel
according to Matthew*, Society for New Testament Studies Monograph Series
6 (Cambridge University Press, 1967), p. 55, attempts to escape this conclusion by assuming that John's anti-semitic tendency has led him to say more
than was actually the case. The assumption is left unproved.

[8] Cf. Davies, *Sermon on the Mount*, pp. 256–315; D. Hill, *The Gospel of Matthew*,
The New Century Bible (London, 1972), pp. 48ff. H. B. Green, *The Gospel
according to Matthew*, The New Clarendon Bible (Oxford University Press,
1975), p. 33, places Matthew later than the *Birkat-ha-Minim*.

[9] See the table of correspondences in R. E. Brown, *The Gospel of John*, The
Anchor Bible, vol. II (Garden City, 1971), p. 694.

[10] Cf. I. H. Marshall, *The Gospel of Luke*, The New International Greek Testament Commentary (Exeter, 1978), p. 519. See also H. Schürmann, *Traditions-
geschichtliche Untersuchungen zu den synoptischen Evangelien* (Düsseldorf,
1968), pp. 150–5, who proposes a connection with Matthew 10: 23.

The question at once arises to which kind of context this material properly belongs. Even assuming the priority of Mark, it is less likely that Mark has the original setting, because his Little Apocalypse is an artificial compilation, including a number of items on discipleship. Indeed it may be conjectured that he has placed the teaching on persecution here because of the apparent remoteness of the circumstances with which the verses deal.[11] Mark 13 is notable for its ambiguity with regard to the time of the future events. Verse 32 ('no one knows') is 'out of harmony with the trend of 5–31'[12] (cf. verse 30: 'this generation'). At the time when Mark is writing, no actual fulfilment of Jesus' teachings on persecution has been reached. Matthew's transference of them to the Mission Charge is an indication that they have now become relevant to the actual situation of the Church. With his concept of a delay of the parousia, it is necessary for him to distinguish sharply between the contemporary struggle of the Church and the future tribulations. Luke 12 has the same material in a collection of general warnings concerning discipleship, which has parallels not only with the Mission Charge in Matthew, but with Q material elsewhere.[13] But Luke retains the same passage in its Marcan position in the Little Apocalypse (21: 12–17), though with considerable alterations. He does not need to remove it from this context, because he regards the apocalypse as already partially fulfilled, rather than wholly concerned with the future.[14] These con-

---

[11] This is not to deny the widely held view that Mark emphasises the suffering involved in discipleship because of a real threat of persecution; cf. B. M. F. van Iersel, 'The gospel according to St. Mark – written for a persecuted community?', *Nederlands Theologisch Tijdschrift* 34 (1980), 15–36. W. Marxsen, *Mark the Evangelist* (Nashville, 1969), pp. 171ff, has argued that Mark is applying persecution material to the situation facing the Church at the time of the Jewish War of A.D. 66–73. But he notes that Mark 13: 10 – an addition of the Evangelist to his source – changes the meaning of verse 9 from defence before a tribunal to preaching in general. If the 'abomination of desolation' refers to a fear of future action by an emperor, engendered by Caligula's attempt to place a statue of himself in the Temple in A.D. 40, and if the allusion to arraignment before the secular power in verse 9 refers to the reprisals of Nero against the Christians in Rome in A.D. 64, the mounting unrest in Judaea in this period would be sufficient to give rise to anxiety about the future even before the outbreak of war in A.D. 66. By placing this material within the Little Apocalypse, Mark expresses his conviction that the persecution is the prelude to the final woes, which now seem to be imminent. See also G. R. Beasley-Murray, *A Commentary on Mark 13* (London, 1957), pp. 40–53.

[12] V. Taylor, *The Gospel according to Saint Mark* (London, 1963), p. 523.

[13] Luke 12: 2–9 = Matthew 10: 26–33; Luke 12: 10 sides with Matthew 12: 32 against Mark 3: 28f; Luke 12: 22–31 = Matthew 6: 25–33; Luke 12: 33f = Matthew 6: 20f; Luke 12: 39–46 = Matthew 24: 43–51.

[14] In Luke 21: 20 a direct forecast of the destruction of Jerusalem is substituted for the obscure reference to the 'abomination of desolation' in Matthew and

siderations lead to the conclusion that the connection with discipleship
is primary.

It is generally agreed that this material goes back ultimately to Jesus
himself. Beasley-Murray has argued that it is to be seen in relation to
Jesus' teaching on his personal danger at the hands of the Jewish authorities. If so, the warning to the disciples is concerned in the first instance
neither with the Church's mission nor with the trials that precede the
end time, but with the danger that Jesus himself faces, in which the
disciples are necessarily involved.

The transition from discipleship to apocalyptic and back again, which
appears in the complex relationships of the Synoptic parallels, is only a
part of the tradition-history of this material. It also found its way into
the Fourth Gospel. It is not necessary to assume direct dependence on
Matthew and Mark, because the traces of a Q version are sufficient to
show that this material circulated in more than one form. But, like Matthew, John has used it in its traditional context of discipleship.

In composing the Fourth Gospel, John reserved the teaching on
discipleship for the setting of the Last Supper (John 13–17). Within
these chapters it is possible to distinguish two stages of composition,
inasmuch as 14: 31 should be followed by 18: 1.[15] Our passage on persecution in 15: 18 – 16: 4a thus belongs to a later redaction in connection
with the special reasons that led to the composition of chapters 15–17.

These new chapters are concerned with particular issues affecting the
life of the community. Chapter 17, the prayer of Jesus, shows grave
anxiety about the possibility of apostasy (verses 12–19) and the threat
of disunity in the Church (verses 20–3). John needs to give special
teaching on these matters, and he has done this by composing a fresh
discourse in chapters 15–16. For this purpose he has used materials,

Mark. Though the phrases used are drawn from Old Testament prophecy
(C. H. Dodd, *More New Testament Essays* (Manchester, 1968), pp. 69–83),
and so do not constitute a description of what actually happened (thus allowing for the possibility of an earlier date, Robinson, *Redating the NT*, p. 27), it
remains probable that the prophecy is a *vaticinium ex eventu*, and that the
reason for Luke's alteration of the tradition is his belief that the fall of Jerusalem is the proper meaning of this item in the Little Apocalypse, cf. Marshall,
Gospel of Luke, ad loc.

[15] This is not the only solution to this problematical verse, but the theory that
chapters 15–17 belong to a later stage of the composition of the Gospel has
much to commend it on other grounds; cf. B. Lindars, *Behind the Fourth
Gospel* (London, 1971), pp. 75ff; *idem, The Gospel of John*, The New Century
Bible (London, 1972), pp. 465ff; R. Schnackenburg, *Das Johannesevangelium*,
Herders Theologische Kommentar zum N.T., vol. III (Freiburg-im-Br.,
1975), p. 102; H. Thyen, 'Johannes 13 und die "Kirchliche Redaktion" des
vierten Evangeliums', in *Festgabe für K. G. Kuhn* (Göttingen, 1971), p. 356.

including the traditions on persecution, that were doubtless available to him all along, though not required previously. The fact that he now uses the persecution material, underlined by the fears expressed in 17: 12–19, suggests that the relationship between Church and Synagogue has deteriorated since the main part of the Gospel was written. The policy of exclusion from the Synagogue, already mentioned in chapter 9, is still operative, and John fears a more violent form of persecution (16: 2). There is a need to restore the morale of the Christians. We shall not be surprised to find that John's way of doing this is to point to the theological factors that are at stake.

III

We now turn to John 15: 18 – 16: 4a, and we shall expect it to be carefully composed to deal with the situation outlined above. From the point of view of literary structure the complete unit extends as far as 16: 15, embracing not only the persecution material but also the work of the Paraclete.[16] Persecution is referred to in 15: 18–25; 16: 1–4a, and the work of the Paraclete is dealt with in 15: 26f; 16: 8–16. The necessity for the departure of Jesus, in order that the Paraclete may take over his role through the disciples, is described in 16: 4b–7. These verses thus form a transition from the theme of persecution to the theme of the Paraclete. This throws into relief the anticipation of the latter theme, which has already appeared in 15: 26f. The conclusion follows that John has welded together materials that are distinct from a literary point of view, characteristically dovetailing them together by means of some measure of overlapping.[17] Nevertheless, at bottom the persecution material and the Paraclete material come from the same source. This can be seen in the parallel material of the Synoptic Gospels, in which the Holy Spirit inspires the disciples when they have to defend themselves on trial.

It thus comes about that we have here two developments from the persecution traditions, which nevertheless have had a separate history before being brought together again in their present form. This is due simply to John's method of taking up a point from the tradition and developing it into a discourse for a particular purpose. It does not necessarily mean that he was unmindful of the underlying relationship

[16] Cf. R. Bultmann, *The Gospel of John* (Oxford, 1971), p. 547.

[17] Similarly the theme of the disciples' sorrow in 16: 4b–7 anticipates the structurally separate section, 16: 16–22; cf. also the overlapping of material in chapter 10, where 10: 19–21 picks up the theme of chapter 9, and 10: 26–9 resumes the Shepherd allegory from 10: 1–18.

between them. In this case he has taken up the theme of persecution in order to expose its theological significance, and he has (presumably on some other occasion originally) taken up the theme of the witness of the Spirit so as to apply it more broadly to the teaching function of the Church.

With these facts borne in mind, it is tempting to seek for two self-contained homilies that have been welded together to form the present unit. Detailed analysis soon shows, however, that the truth is more complex. We shall see that the persecution material is closely integrated into the Gospel as a whole, so that very little underlying material can be extracted from it that might point to an earlier composition. The Paraclete material, however, does depend on previous work, although it is not possible to isolate a continuous discourse by putting together the relevant verses from chapters 14–16.[18] Thus the relationship between the finished result and the source-material is variable.

If we now try to imagine John at work in his study, we must assume that he composes 15: 18 – 16: 15 with the following materials in front of him. He has the Gospel, which he has already written, to which he will refer by means of a quotation in 15: 20. He has his various homilies, of which some have been used for the Gospel, and others are still available for his present task. These include something that he has written on the Paraclete. He also has collections of the sayings of Jesus and other Gospel traditions. We can leave the question open whether he has a copy of Mark, and how much of this traditional material is available to him in written form, and how much he simply carries in his head. With these materials to hand he incorporates into the Gospel an urgent message for the benefit of his fellow-Christians.

Having written 15: 1–17, which may well be one of the available homilies on his desk, he begins to compose his message on persecution. First, 15: 18–25 form an artistic unit specially composed for its present position:

15: 18 (a) If the world hates you,
       (b) know that it has hated me before it hated you.
   19 (a)   If you were of the world,
       (b)   the world would love its own;
       (c)   but because you are not of the world,

18 Bultmann postulates an underlying revelation–discourse, which had three sections, corresponding with 15: 18–20; 15: 21–5, 15. 26 – 16: 11. He omits 15: 27 – 16: 7 as an expansion of the Evangelist, and cuts out portions of the two preceding sections. H. Becker, *Die Reden des Johannesevangeliums und der Stil der gnostischen Offenbarungsrede* (Göttingen, 1956), is even more drastic in his excisions.

    (d)   but I chose you out of the world,
    (e)   therefore the world hates you.
20 (a) Remember the word that I said to you,
    (b) 'A servant is not greater than his master.'
    (c)   If they persecuted me,
    (d)   they will persecute you;
    (e)   if they kept my word,
    (f)   they will keep yours also.
21 (a) But all this they will do to you on my account,
    (b) because they do not know him who sent me.
22 (a)   If I had not come and spoken to them,
    (b)   they would not have sin;
    (c)   but now they have no excuse
    (d)   for their sin.
23 (a) He who hates me
    (b) hates my Father also.
24 (a)   If I had not done among them the works
    (b)   which no one else did,
    (c)   they would not have sin;
    (d)   but now they have seen and hated
    (e)   both me and my Father.
25 (a) It is to fulfil the word that is written in their law,
    (b) 'They hated me without a cause.'

The artistic balance is gained by alternating statements in prose (for the most part) with more rhythmical conditional sentences. Verse 25 makes an inclusion with verse 18 on account of the word 'hate'. The same word makes two lesser inclusions in such a way as to divide the material into well-defined stanzas. Thus verses 18 and 19 together make the first stanza, beginning and ending with 'the world hates you'. In the same way the final stanza before the conclusion consists of verses 23 and 24, bounded by the idea of hatred of both Jesus and the Father. In all there are four stanzas, each consisting of a prose verse and a rhythmical conditional sentence, plus a prose conclusion (verse 25). Furthermore, the first two stanzas are distinguished in form from the third and fourth, inasmuch as their conditional sentences (verses 19(a)(b)(c)(e), 20(c)–(f)) are in the form of well-balanced short couplets, whereas those of the third and fourth stanzas (verses 22, 24) are unreal past conditions followed by νῦν δέ. Finally the composition is bonded together by the recurrence of the hatred motif in verse 23, thus linking together the first stanza (18–19) and the fourth (23–4); and by the recurrence of the adversative particle ἀλλά in verse 25, thus linking together the opening of the third stanza in verse 21 ἀλλὰ ταῦτα πάντα ποιήσουσιν ...) with the conclusion to the whole piece (ἀλλ᾽ ἵνα πληρωθῇ...). It will be observed that this artistic connection implies that the contents of verse 21 are to be regarded as the suppressed main clause of verse 25.[19]

A quick glance shows that the argument is contained in the prose verses (18, 20(a)(b), 21, 23, 25), and the conditional sentences develop each point in turn. Thus verse 18 states the world's hatred (18(a)), expounded in verse 19. Verse 20(a)(b) resumes the point of 18(b), i.e. the relation of the world's hatred of the disciples to its hatred of Jesus, and this is expounded in verse 20(c)–(f). The third prose verse (21) introduces a new theme: the persecution of the disciples arises from the nature of Jesus' mission from the Father. Verse 22 describes the mission of Jesus and its effect, so that this verse forms the exposition of verse 21(a). Then, just as before, the point of 21(b) is resumed in the fourth prose verse (23), which briefly reintroduces the connection between Jesus and the Father, and this is expounded in verse 24. Verse 25 rounds off the whole argument by tracing these facts to what has been foretold in scripture.

This well-balanced composition is clearly artificial, and signs of adaptation can be easily detected. Verse 18 is not really prose; omission of 'know that' (γινώσκετε ὅτι) leaves a couplet in the form of a conditional sentence like verses 19 and 20(c)–(f). For this reason Bultmann takes verse 18 to be part of the underlying revelation-discourse. Verse 23 is also not really prose; it belongs to a type of proverbial statement that is common in the sayings-tradition, and indeed appears in the saying referred to in verse 20 (i.e. 13: 16–20). Conversely we also have to reckon with prose elements in the 'poetic' lines. Verse 19(d) is an addition to the original form of the couplet (so Bultmann). It is significant that this line is yet another quotation (cf. 15: 16). The poetical character of verses 22 and 24 is also not assured. They depend more on the repetition of the form of the sentence than on their rhythm for their overall poetic effect. In any case, even if verse 22 is regarded as a poetic fragment, verse 24 is overloaded. Omission of 24(b) helps (Bultmann), but still leaves the imbalance between the νῦν δέ clauses of the two verses.

Two conclusions already emerge from these observations. First, the

---

[19] Cf. C. F. D. Moule, *An Idiom Book of New Testament Greek* (Cambridge University Press, 1959), pp. 144f, for the view of Cadoux that ἵνα here is imperatival, so that the phrase means, 'the word...had to be fulfilled' (cf. NEB margin). BDF §448 (7) regards it as elliptical. The connection with verse 21 supports the translation 'it is to fulfil' (RSV, cf. AV, RV, against NEB text, JB).

additions to verses 18 and 19, and the lack of balance in verses 22 and 24, show that John is adapting miscellaneous material, which did not make a coherent sequence previously. Secondly, the prose lines, including 19(d), are remarkable for their allusions to other parts of the Gospel, and suggest that John has written this composition in full view of his work already contained in the Gospel. Hence this is a new composition, and it is legitimate to expect that it will provide information concerning the situation in which it was written.

We turn now to more detailed analysis.

Verse 18 has been adapted to form the opening of the whole piece, and so announces the theme of the hatred of the world. Two things need to be said about this, Firstly, verses 18 and 19, without the additions, make a well-rounded small unit, the first line being reproduced as the last line in chiastic order (εἰ ὁ κόσμος ὑμᾶς μισεῖ...διὰ τοῦτο μισεῖ ὑμᾶς ὁ κόσμος). It is true that the hatred of Jesus, referred to in 18(b), is not taken up in verse 19, but it is presupposed, seeing that the disciples belong to Jesus. John has felt it necessary to clarify this point by his insertion of 19(d). It thus seems probable that John is here using an item that was complete in itself, and it may be regarded as an example of the 'maxims' of the Johannine Church.[20] It is not necessary to assume that it is a fragment of a longer, sustained composition or revelation-discourse.

Secondly, the 'maxim' depends in the first instance on the tradition of the sayings of Jesus. Thus it echoes Matthew 10: 22//Mark 13: 13: 'You will be hated by all for my name's sake.' From this point of view verse 18(b) could be regarded as an explication of 'for my name's sake' in the underlying tradition. The hatred of the world is also a feature of the Sermon on the Plain (Luke 6: 22, 27; cf. Matthew 5: 11, 44).[21] This is a context of discipleship that has not been adapted for the apocalyptic discourse. Jeremias draws attention to this fact as an indication that this is a survival of tradition virtually unaltered.[22]

No reason is given for the world's hatred in verse 18, but this appears

[20] The Johannine writings contain certain statements of a proverbial type, which function in a similar way to the sayings of Jesus, but are not actually derived from the sayings-tradition, and these can be conveniently styled 'maxims of the Johannine Church'. Examples include the testimony-formula that lies behind John 3: 11; 19: 35; 21: 24; 1 John 1: 1–3; 3 John 12, and the invitation to drink in John 4: 14; 7: 37f; Revelation 21: 6; 22: 17. I hope to publish a study of these maxims on another occasion.

[21] For the originality of Luke's form against Matthew, cf. Marshall, *Gospel of Luke*, p. 253; H. Schürmann, *Das Lukasevangelium*, Herders Theologische Kommentar zum N.T., vol I (Freiburg-im-Br. 1969), pp. 345f.

[22] *New Testament Theology I* (London, 1971), p. 240.

in the remainder of the maxim in verse 19. It is because the disciples, as followers of Jesus (18(b)), are 'not of the world', i.e. do not belong to the world or derive their moral position from it.[23] The reason for this is that the proclamation of Jesus and the disciples has the effect of exposing the evil of the world (cf. 3: 20; 7: 7). This point (not stated here) will be taken up in verses 22 and 24, where the teaching and acts of Jesus himself expose the world's sin; and, because they are the works of God, the hatred accorded to Jesus is directed against him also. Similarly the disciples, who continue the work of Jesus, are his delegates to convey the divine judgement, and thereby incur the hatred of the world. It will be observed that the principles that lie behind John's maxim here agree with the implications of the Synoptic tradition with regard to the apostolic mission.

Before I leave the first stanza, it may be noted that the additional words in 19(d) refer not only to 15: 16, but behind this to 13: 18 (cf. also 6: 70). This is another indication that John is working on the basis of his Last Supper account in composing the present passage. When we add to this the underlying debt to the tradition in Matthew 10: 22, we begin to see that there is a kind of triangular relationship between the Mission Charge of Matthew 10, John's Last Supper account where sayings on discipleship are introduced (John 13: 16–20) and the present passage. This will appear more clearly in the next verse.

The second stanza (verse 20) begins with an acknowledged quotation of 13: 16(a). This is one of the clearest indications that we are here dealing with material that belongs to a later stage of redaction. But it is a necessary element in the argument. John wishes his readers to recall the whole of 13: 16, together with the context in which it is spoken. Moreover this is another instance of a saying that has its closest Synoptic parallel in the Mission Charge, Matthew 10: 24. John reminds his readers of this teaching because it is the foundation of the meaning of apostleship. John is fully aware of the principles of agency on which this is based.[24] As Jesus' accredited agents, the disciples will suffer the same treatment as Jesus himself. This was not mentioned in 13: 16–20. But it was present in the tradition, as we see from the continuation in Matthew 10: 25: 'It is enough for the disciple to be like his teacher, and the servant like his master. If they have called the master of the house

[23] For John's use of ἐκ, cf. R. Schnackenburg, *Die Johannesbriefe*, Herders Theologische Kommentar zum N.T. (1953), pp. 114f. The clearest example of the present usage occurs in John 18: 37, ὁ ὢν ἐκ τῆς ἀληθείας.

[24] Cf. P. Borgen, 'God's Agent in the Fourth Gospel', in *Religions in Antiquity: essays in memory of E. R. Goodenough*, ed. J. Neusner (Leiden, 1968), pp. 137–48; K. H. Rengstorf, *TDNT*, I, 398–447.

Beelzebul, how much more will they malign those of his household.' Here it is expressed in the couplet of verse 20(c)(d). As this and the following couplet (20(e)(f)), which refers explicitly to preaching, have the same rhythm as verse 19, it seems best to regard them as another Johannine maxim, used in the community in connection with the risks attaching to evangelistic work. Hence once more we have a maxim, expounded with the aid of the teaching already given in 13: 16–20 in the light of the pool of tradition that has come down to us in the Mission Charge of Matthew 10.

The principle of agency to which John has referred in verse 20 is important to him not only in connection with the position of the disciples, but also as one of the foundations of his christology. Jesus is the ἀπόστολος of the Father. By introducing this theme John can now show that the world's refusal of the teaching given by the disciples is nothing less than rejection of God himself.

This theme is worked out in verses 21–4, comprising the third and fourth stanzas of the composition. The opening words of verse 21 are resumptive, summarising the two preceding stanzas. The principle of agency is indicated by the phrase 'on my account' (διὰ τὸ ὄνομά μου). It is significant that this phrase belongs to the Synoptic saying on the hatred of the world, Matthew 10: 22 and parallels. Then in 21(b) this principle is referred back to the Father. Once more the phrase used, τὸν πέμψαντά με, is significant. It occurs in 13: 16(b), in the continuation of the quotation that we had in verse 20, and also in 13: 20, which again has a parallel in the Mission Charge at Matthew 10: 40. Verse 21 implies the opposite of 13: 20(b) ('he who receives me receives him who sent me'), and this could equally well be put in the form 'he who hates me hates him who sent me'. This is in fact what is said in verse 23, resuming 21(b), except that 'my Father' is substituted for 'him who sent me'. This change adds greater emotional force, but does not alter the point. It is artistically necessary to prepare for the climax in verse 24.

The failure of the world to respond to the disciples arises ultimately from their rejection of the Father. This rejection is due to lack of knowledge (21(b)). Knowledge in John's thought is inseparable from keeping the word (20(e)(f)). The preaching of the word brings the knowledge of God, and to keep the word is the practical expression of this knowledge (cf. 8: 55).

We can now turn to the two conditional sentences in verses 22 and 24. These are aimed at showing that the world's lack of knowledge of the Father is a culpable failure, because it has been given the revelation of the Father and has refused it. This point is first put in a straightforward way in verse 22. Then verse 24 makes the same point in a different way, by means of carefully chosen variations within the same formal structure. All are important for John's purpose, as he builds this short discourse to its climax. Hence it is a mistake to bracket 24(b) as a rather pointless addition (Bultmann), in the hope of recovering a saying from the under-lying revelation-discourse, parallel to verse 22. This verse is not a parallel to verse 22, but an adaptation of it. First, the *works* of Jesus replace his *speech*. This is not just a stylistic variation, but a step forward in the argument. The works of Jesus reveal not only his identity as the Father's agent, but also his unity with the Father. This point is put very strongly in 10: 22–39, which is the climax of the debates on the identity of Jesus (note especially 10: 25, 32, 37f). It is precisely because of the importance of Jesus' works from this point of view that John adds 24(b), 'which no one else did'. Jesus' works are unique in this respect, even though the disciples will perform works of a similar kind (14: 12).[25] For the works of Jesus comprise not only the miracles (signs) but also the Cross, in which his unity with the Father is supremely revealed. In fact, however, as John points out in his new version of the $\nu\hat{\upsilon}\nu$ $\delta\acute{\epsilon}$ clause (24(d)(e)), although the world has seen the works that lead inevitably to this con-clusion, it has responded with hatred (the refusal of belief being the sin that, thus exposed, produces hatred), and this is directed against the Father as well as Jesus, because it is the truth of the unity between them that is rejected.[26] The pairs of phrases ('seen and hated', 'both me and my Father') heighten the emotional effect in making this crucial point.

Finally verse 25 places the coping-stone on the argument. The phrase 'written in their law', with its distancing of Jesus to emphasise that the Law is an authority that the Jews themselves accept quite apart from the teaching of Jesus, occurs also with a psalm quotation in 10: 34, and performs the same function in the argument. In 10: 30 Jesus has made the fundamental christological statement, 'I and the Father are one.' When challenged by the Jewish authorities, he appeals first to scripture ('your law') and secondly to the evidence of his works. Thus the two corroborate one another, and the truth so confirmed cannot be denied by the Jews without rejecting the Law that they themselves accept as divine revelation (cf. 5: 36–47). Similarly in verse 24 John has explained

[25] In this verse $\mu\epsilon\acute{\iota}\zeta o\nu a$ means, not more impressive works, but works whereby the mission of Jesus is extended through the disciples, cf. Schnackenburg *Das Johannesevangelium, ad loc.* In 5: 20 the same expression is used to de-note the eschatological acts to which Jesus' works point forward.

[26] In verse 24(d) the implied object of $\dot{\epsilon}\omega\rho\acute{a}\kappa a\sigma\iota\nu$ is probably intended to be 'the works', and the following $\kappa a\acute{\iota}$ must be translated 'and yet' (BDF §444 (3)), as recommended by Barrett and Schnackenburg (cf. 6: 36).

the world's hatred from its reaction to Jesus' works, and here he affirms that this hatred also has the evidence of scripture. As the words quoted come from the Passion Psalms,[27] it is probable that John is building on previous work.

If we look back over the composition, it is striking how much of it alludes to earlier working. In verses 18–20 a triangular relationship was observed between the maxims of verses 18–19, 20(c)–(f), the sayings in John 13: 16–20, and the traditions used in Matthew 10.[28] These connections are also found in verses 21–4, but it does not seem safe to postulate a source for verse 22, which is the only verse that might claim to be taken from a revelation-discourse. The most impressive feature of this composition, however, is the debt that it owes to the central themes of the Johannine christology. It has been suggested earlier that one of John's objects in composing this piece was to restore the morale of the Church in the face of stronger hostility. We can now see that he has achieved this aim by taking up the persecution maxims, and by building around them a composition rooted in the christology of the Gospel and its scriptural evidence. The overall effect is to reassure the Christians that the increased pressure is only to be expected in the light of the Gospel tradition.

Next John inserts a fragment of his Paraclete material in verses 26f. If I was correct in claiming that he composed verses 18–25 for their present position in the discourse, we must also assume that his use of these verses here belongs to the same stage of redactional activity. We shall see that they make an excellent transition to the verses on persecution in 16: 1–4a.

15: 26 (a) But when the Counsellor comes,
     (b) whom I shall send to you from the Father,
     (c) even the Spirit of truth,
     (d) who proceeds from the Father,
     (e)   he will bear witness to me;
27 (a) And you also are witnesses,
     (b)   because you have been with me from the beginning.

The problems of the Paraclete material fall outside the scope of this

---

[27] The most likely source is Psalm 69: 5, as this psalm is much used in the Passion apologetic (cf. B. Lindars, *New Testament Apologetic* (London, 1961), pp. 99–108), but the identical phrase is found in Psalm 35: 19. Other possible sources are Psalm 109: 3; 119: 161; Ps. Sol. 7. 1, cf. E. D. Freed, *Old Testament Quotations in the Gospel of John*, Supplements to Novum Testamentum 11 (Leiden, 1965), pp. 94f.

[28] Both Brown and Schnackenburg stress that this relationship does not necessarily imply that John had these traditions in precisely the form in which we now have them in Matthew.

paper.[29] Suffice it to say that I think that John introduced the verses on the Paraclete in 14: 16f, 26 at the same time as he inserted the new discourse of chapters 15 and 16. A notable feature of these verses is the piling up of appositional phrases in order to explain who or what the Paraclete is. Hence John is aware that the title is not self-explanatory. Indeed, he feels the need to add explanatory phrases each time he uses Paraclete material. So the same is true of 15: 26(b)(c)(d). These phrases may be regarded as resumptive, reminding the reader of the descriptions already given in 14: 17 and 26. They are not, however, foreign to the intention of the underlying homily, but are derived from it. They correctly represent the character and origin of the Paraclete (cf. 16: 7, 13–15). Moreover these phrases serve a definite purpose in the present context. The Paraclete's assistance to the disciples when faced with persecution derives its validity from the fact that he is the Spirit of truth and originates from the Father himself. He is sent by Jesus as his agent (26(b)), but he comes from the Father (26(d)).[30] So he is an authentic agent of God, comparable to Jesus himself and available as his substitute.

Thus 26(b)(c)(d), though formally an addition to the saying that John is using here (so Bultmann, Becker), have been added deliberately for the sake of the present context. Omitting these phrases, we have in 26(a)(e) and 27 a pair of couplets in the form of a chiasmus ('Counsellor comes – witness – witnesses – from the beginning'). By this means John expresses the joint witness of the Paraclete and the disciples. The use of the word 'witness' suggests a forensic setting, in which the disciples give the message (cf. 20(e)(f)) when on trial. The knowledge that they have the assistance of the Paraclete at such a moment is calculated to reassure them. Thus this fragment of the Paraclete homily adds to the assurance already given in verses 18–25, and indicates the form that the coming persecution may be expected to take.

It is universally recognised that these verses are based on the promise of the Spirit's aid to the disciples (Matthew 10: 19f; Luke 12: 11f and all three Synoptic versions of the Little Apocalypse; on these see Prof. Lampe, pp. 129–31 below). In fact it is very likely that this tradition is the starting-point of John's Paraclete homily, and that he has broadened the idea in the process (so Brown). But the fact that he has brought this

---

[29] See the excursuses in the commentaries of Brown and Schnackenburg; also G. Johnston, *The Spirit-Paraclete in the Fourth Gospel*, Society of New Testament Studies Monograph Series 12 (Cambridge University Press, 1970).

[30] For the synonymous parallelism of these two lines, cf. Schnackenburg, *Das Johannesevangelium, ad loc.* It is evident on this showing that ἐκπορεύεται is equivalent to the sending by Jesus, and is not really concerned with trinitarian relationships.

particular feature into the present context of persecution shows yet again that he has not forgotten the starting-point in the traditions of Matthew 10 and parallels.

It has now been shown that John has organised his material in such a way as to bring assurance to his readers during their time of testing and to restore their morale. This accounts, at least in part, for the unexpected feature of the use of a Paraclete fragment apparently out of context. After giving these assurances, John is ready to speak openly concerning the persecution. This is the subject of 16: 1–4*a*.

16: 1 (a) I have said all this to you
    (b)   to keep you from falling away.
  2 (a) They will put you out of the synagogues;
    (b) indeed the hour is coming
    (c)   when whoever kills you
    (d)   will think he is offering service to God.
  3 (a) And they will do this
    (b)   because they have not known the Father, nor me.
 4*a* (a) But I have said these things to you,
    (b)   that when their hour comes
    (c)   you may remember
    (d)   that I told you of them.

These verses make a suitable climax and conclusion to John's composition concerning the coming persecution. They cannot be analysed along the lines of source and redaction, and lack the rhythmical character that would suggest a debt to previous material. On the other hand the structure is not unlike that of 15: 18–25. These verses are thus best regarded as belonging to the same literary process.

The most obvious structural feature is the inclusion provided by ταῦτα λελάληκα ὑμῖν in verses 1 and 4*a*. This feature not only agrees well with the style of 15: 18–25, but also provides further proof that the composition of these verses has been undertaken in the course of the redactional work of chapters 15–16 as a whole. For the phrase ταῦτα λελάληκα ὑμῖν, with slight variations, is a special characteristic of John's editorial style in these chapters. In chapter 14 it occurs only at 14: 25, introducing the Paraclete verse 26. As we have seen, this is likely to be an insertion, made at the same time as the addition of chapters 15–16. Within these chapters it occurs at 15: 11; 16: 1, 4, 25, 33. Generally it marks a transition of thought, bringing the subject back to the present situation in order to point up by contrast the future conditions following the Passion. But 16: 4*a* is exceptional, as it does not open a fresh topic, and it is distinguished from the rest by the particle ἀλλά. This makes the phrase resumptive of verse 1.

The contents also of verses 1 and 4a are virtually equivalent, and betray John's great anxiety concerning the steadfastness of the Christians in his own day. In verse 1 he shows contact with the Gospel traditions by his use of σκανδαλισθῆτε, which is a feature of Jesus' warning about the flight of the disciples (Matthew 26: 31//Mark 14: 27). He will allude again to this tradition later at 16: 32. He had previously quarried from it in his Last Supper account, where the forecast of Peter's denials in 13: 38 is extremely close to Mark 14: 30, but the previous verses have been replaced by characteristic Johannine themes. In verse 4a the motif of forewarning also has precedents in the earlier tradition, being a feature of the Little Apocalypse (Matthew 24: 25//Mark 13: 23).

Within the inclusion of verses 1 and 4a there is another inclusion in verses 2 and 3, achieving a formal balance by the repetition of ποιήσουσιν (2(a), 3(a)). Thus the whole paragraph forms a chiasmus: λελάληκα – ποιήσουσιν – ποιήσουσιν – λελάληκα. The nodal point in the structure is thus 2(c)(d), which thereby receives particular emphasis. The ground is prepared in 2(b), which points to the future, using a phrase that denotes a climactic moment.[31] Hence this marks a stage beyond what is described in 2(a), and therefore still future at the time of writing. In 3(a) the future verb, which is repeated from 2(a), is now laden with the extra meaning provided by 2(b)–(d). But in 3(b) the tension is reduced, as John briefly recalls the theological explanation already furnished in 15: 21–4.

It thus appears that verse 2(c)(d) comprises John's most serious warning to his readers. It is a real fear that a violent persecution is about to begin. We cannot tell how far John's fears were realised. But violent attacks on Christians, causing death, are known to have taken place in the time of Bar Cochba's rebellion, and are referred to in a number of passages in Justin's *Dialogue with Trypho*.[32] John correctly points out that this action will be carried out with a genuinely religious motive.[33] The expression is compressed, and should be understood to mean 'will

---

[31] The phrase ἔρχεται ὥρα is used in various connections, but always with this sense, cf. 2: 6; 4: 21, 23; 5: 25, 28; 7: 30; 8: 20; 12: 23, 27; 13: 1; 16: 21, 32; 17: 1.

[32] Justin, *Dial.* 16; 95; 110; 122; 133. *Dial.* 16 also attests the application of the *Birkat-ha-Minim* in the Synagogue; cf. Davies, *Sermon on the Mount*, p. 278. For other references in Justin, cf. p. 49, n. 6.

[33] For the 'holy zeal' that fired Jewish movements from Maccabaean times onwards, cf. M. Hengel, *Die Zeloten* (Leiden, 1961), pp. 151–234.

think that he makes an act of worship equivalent to the offering of a sacrifice'.[34] John does not intend to justify the action by these words. It is much more likely that there is an ironical intention behind them. For of course the martyrdom of Christians is indeed an acceptable sacrifice (cf. 17: 19). Thus, in the very act of placing before his readers this alarming possibility, he provides the means of seeing it positively within the framework of Jesus' own sacrifice.

IV

In the preceding pages I have attempted to show that John 15: 18 – 16: 4a was penned as part of the process of the composition of chapters 15–16. These chapters, along with chapter 17, were added to the Gospel at a later stage. The passage that we have studied owes a small debt to previously written work on the part of the Evangelist, consisting of the 'maxims' in 15: 18–20 and the Paraclete material. But in the main it is a new composition, and the contributions from previous work are subordinated to the argument of the pièce as a whole. It therefore follows that this passage is concerned with conditions at the actual time of writing, comparatively late in the redactional history of the Fourth Gospel. In composing this piece, the Evangelist has made use of his own previous work within the Gospel, and has also drawn afresh on the traditions, known to us from Matthew 10 and other Synoptic references, which were fundamental to his theological presentation of the Gospel. He is at pains to show the vital relevance of this theology to the urgent situation with which he now has to deal. His object is not to provide information on the persecution. Nor is it an attempt to give authoritative guidance by the literary device of an address by the Master.[35] It is rather an attempt to interpret the present situation in the light of the truth of the Gospel. He wishes to show how it is to be understood within the divine ordering of events, which has been revealed for all time in the person of Jesus, and supremely in his Passion. It is thus significant that John does not make any exemplary use of the sufferings of Jesus, as is done, for instance, by 1 Peter. Jesus is not held up as the model of patience, but as the declaration of the Father. The disciples are fore-

---

[34] The verb προσφέρειν should properly specify the thing offered, either gifts or sacrifices, whereas λατρεία denotes an act of worship, which may include such offerings. The use of τῷ θεῷ in this verse, rather than τῷ πατρί, indicates that John is employing conventional religious language. The idea expressed in this verse is echoed in Num. R. 21.4 (cf. Barrett, *NT Background, ad loc.*).

[35] This kind of motive is probably the best explanation of the pseudepigraphic books of the New Testament, especially the Pastorals.

warned of sufferings, so that, aided by the Paraclete, they may stand firm in their confession of faith and not fall away.

The situation that has evoked these reflections is a time of sharp conflict between the Church and Synagogue in John's circle. The Gospel in its earlier state included hints that there were secret Christians among the Jews who were hesitating to declare themselves for fear of reprisals. Some sort of ban from the Synagogue is implied, and this must be taken seriously, however difficult it is to correlate with information derived from Jewish sources.[36] When John writes 15: 18 – 16: 4a the situation, though not fundamentally altered, is becoming critical. There is a real risk of violent, even fanatical, conflict.

We know from various sources[37] that Jewish persecution of Christians continued in the early part of the second century. But the success of the policy represented by the *Birkat-ha-Minim* must have changed the situation radically. The Johannine Church ceased to be in an uneasy relationship with the Synagogue, but became totally separate from it. It thus comes about that the Epistles of John contain no certain allusion to persecution by the Jews. Instead, the Church has become a closed society, jealously guarding its traditions and keeping a close watch on its members.

In this situation the use that is made of the Johannine teaching on persecution is not without interest. The opponents are dissident members of the Church itself, whose identity has never been satisfactorily decided.[38] They can be referred to as 'the world', because their beliefs and behaviour put them on the side of the godless world over against the true members of the Church. Thus in 1 John 3: 1 'the world' fails to recognise the true members as the children of God because it does not know God. We are at once reminded of John 15: 21. The difference between 'the world' and the true members is fundamental, for 'the world' are children of the devil and the true members are children of God (1 John 3: 10). But they are not easily distinguished. The only ways

[36] See the discussion in Hare, *Persecution*, pp. 54ff.

[37] Cf. p. 49, n. 6 above, and Hare, *ibid.* pp. 76f; J. W. Parkes, *The Conflict of the Church and the Synagogue* (London, 1934), p. 132. There are even indications of a Jewish counter-mission to Christians in later strands of the New Testament and the Apostolic Fathers, cf. G. W. H. Lampe, '"Grievous Wolves" (Acts 20: 29)', in *Christ and Spirit in the New Testament: Studies in Honour of C. F. D. Moule*, ed. B. Lindars and S. S. Smalley (Cambridge University Press, 1973), pp. 253–68.

[38] R. E. Brown (cf. p. 48, n. 2 above) asserts that, in spite of showing similar tendencies, they cannot be certainly identified with any of the known heretical groups of the second century. Schnackenburg compares them with the opponents of Ignatius.

in which the children of the devil can be detected are by their failure to do right and by their lack of love for the brethren.

At this point the argument of 1 John 3 has two items that link up with our study. First, the author gives the example of Cain, a brother who proved himself a son of the evil one because he murdered his brother instead of loving him. 'And why did he murder him? Because his own deeds were evil and his brother's righteous' (verse 12). Here we have the same explanation of persecution as we found in connection with John 15: 19. It is the exposure of the world's sin that arouses the world's hostility.[39] This provides the explanation for our second item, which follows immediately in verse 13: 'Do not wonder, brethren, that the world hates you.' This appears to be a direct quotation either of John 15: 18 or of the underlying 'maxim'. Moreover there is a clear allusion to John 15: 13 in verse 16 ('he laid down his life for us'). Whether these passages depend directly on the Gospel as we have it, or on earlier forms of its materials, they are certainly secondary from the point of view of its thought. For here the author has taken up the themes of love and hatred, which are not directly correlated by John in chapter 15, and worked out a comprehensive scheme, whereby sonship of the devil and all forms of wrongdoing, especially hatred, are opposed to sonship of God, righteousness, and the love of the brethren. The result of this scheme is that 'the world' can be used to denote anyone who belongs to the former class, including an individual who fails to respond to the claims of charity (verse 17).[40] There is thus a single category, which applies equally to the 'antichrists' (2: 18–22) and 'false prophets' (4: 1–3) who have separated themselves from the congregation, and also to Diotrephes and his kind, who refuse hospitality to 'the brethren' (3 John 9f). This category cuts across the formal distinction between members of the Church and those outside, for there are those within the Church who do not truly belong to it (1 John 2: 19;[41] 4: 5f). Evidently

[39] M. Wilcox, 'On investigating the use of the Old Testament in the New Testament', in *Text and Interpretation* (cf. p. 48, n. 2), p. 240, has drawn attention to the parallel between this verse and Pal. Tg. Gen. 4.8, suggesting that the writer is dependent upon a Jewish exegetical tradition. The parallel is illuminating, but omits the essential point at issue here, i.e. the reason *why* Cain should have murdered his brother.

[40] 'The love of God' in this verse probably denotes the love that comes from God (genitive of origin), cf. R. Bultmann, *The Johannine Epistles*, Hermeneia (Philadelphia, 1973), *ad loc.* Schnackenburg, however, treats it as genitive of quality, i.e. 'divine love'.

[41] The Greek (ἀλλ' ἵνα φανερωθῶσιν ὅτι οὐκ εἰσὶν πάντες ἐξ ἡμῶν) is ambiguous. Bultmann takes the ὅτι clause to mean, 'not all (who so claim) belong to us'. Schnackenburg translates, 'they do not belong to us – all of them', citing BDF §275(5). The former seems best (so NEB, RV margin).

John's anxiety for the unity of the Church in John 17: 20–3 has been sadly justified.

Finally, the real test of the false brethren is the confession of faith (1 John 2: 22f; 4: 2f, 15; 5: 10; 2 John 9). This again could well owe a debt to John 15: 21–4. But once more the terms of reference are really quite different. In the Gospel it is a matter of faith in Jesus as such. In the Epistles it is a perverted form of this faith, held by those who claim to be true Christians (Brown would say, true followers of the Gospel of John), but are not. Failure to show love to the brethren is proof that they are false (1 John 4: 20). It is obvious that, in these circumstances of internal strife, the categories of love and righteousness have become constricted in their application, and so to some extent debased. Consequently the great Johannine themes of the Gospel can be seen to be losing their freshness. They are degenerating into stereotypes. The life of the Johannine Church does not match the greatness of John's vision, and his call to courageous discipleship. For that we have to return to the Gospel itself.

Jesus Son of Man, 1983, 145-157

11

THE SON OF MAN IN THE THEOLOGY OF JOHN

In the Fourth Gospel the Son of Man is more than a literary feature. The title has become the vehicle for a definite theological idea. This is sufficiently consistent and coherent to permit a general treatment of the Johannine sayings, instead of a complete analysis. But it will also be necessary to attempt to ascertain the literary sources of John's use of the phrase, and to decide whether it was a current title for Jesus in the Johannine community[1].

I. THE LIFTING-UP OF THE SON OF MAN

In the first place, the Gospel of John contains no sayings which can be taken directly back to Jesus as examples of the *bar enasha* idiom[1a]. The nearest that we get to this is Jn 3,14, "... So must *a man* be lifted up". It is universally recognized that this is modelled on the passion predictions, especially Mk 8,31, which does go back ultimately to an authentic saying, as has been argued above[1b]. But John shows no awareness of the idiom, which is in any case impossible in the verse which immediately precedes this one, where reference is made to the Son of Man (3,13), "No one has ascended into heaven, but he who descended from heaven, the Son of Man"[2]. Here the context requires a specific personality, and the same is true of all the other Son of Man sayings in the Fourth Gospel.

---

1. The most recent extended treatment is by F.J. MOLONEY, *The Johannine Son of Man*, Rome, [2]1978. The conclusions reached in the present chapter agree largely with those of Moloney, and differ to some extent from my essay, *The Son of Man in the Johannine Christology*, 1973 [in this volume, pp. 33-50].
    1a. [By this Lindars is referring to his theory, argued earlier in his book from which this chapter is extracted, that *bar enasha* in Aramaic is an idiomatic way of a speaker referring to a limited group of people, including himself. Hence it is perhaps to be translated as something like "a man like me", or "someone in my position". Ed.]
    1b. [See *Jesus Son of Man*, chapter 4, "The Passion Predictions", pp. 60-84. Ed.]
    2. "The Son of Man" stands awkwardly in apposition to the participial phrase, but thereby a chiastic structure is produced, which emphasizes the contrast between "no one" and the Son of Man, and so introduces him as the sole revealer. Verse 14 then proceeds to explain the manner in which he makes his revelation. The idea of a descent apparently following ascent in verse 13 caused much trouble to the ancient interpreters, so that many manuscripts have additional words to try to ease the sense ("who is in heaven" or "who is from heaven").

The connection between 3,14 and the passion saying is important, because it provides the link between John's use of the title and earlier tradition. The passion predictions were developed in relation to the primitive kerygma, so that in Mark they include not only the death of Jesus but also his resurrection. It was also noted that the various forms of the prediction have been influenced by the prophecy of the suffering servant in Is 53, whether Jesus himself made allusion to this prophecy or not. These two features of the synoptic forms of the prediction are combined in Jn 3,14. Here the Son of Man is not said to be delivered up or to die, but to be lifted up (ὑψωθῆναι). The natural interpretation of the word is exaltation. But John has begun by referring to the brazen serpent which Moses set on a stake in the course of the journey of the Israelites through the Wilderness (Num 21,8-9). Thus the point of comparison is lifting up on a stake, and the application can only be to the crucifixion. This, then, is the *primary* meaning here, even if it is not the most obvious meaning of the word. Just as the serpent was raised so that "everyone who saw it might live" (Num 21,8 LXX), so the crucifixion of Jesus will have the result that "whoever believes in him may have eternal life" (Jn 3,15). There is thus inevitably a double meaning in the verb "lifted up", and this may be confidently traced to the suffering servant prophecy, where the servant of the Lord "will be lifted up and glorified" (Is 52,13 LXX: ὑψωθήσεται καὶ δοξασθήσεται).

These facts are well known, but the importance of them is not always sufficiently realized. John is certainly indebted here to what one may justly claim is the mainstream of early Christian thought. The process of the transformation of the passion sayings into passion and resurrection predictions in the light of the kerygma, and the further work upon them in relation to the passion prophecy, lie behind Jn 3,14. But John continues the process in his own unique and brilliant way. First, he adduces a further Old Testament text (Num 21,9), which had not been used in this connection before. Secondly, he adopts an unusual word for "lifted up", which normally refers to exaltation in an honorific sense, and thereby contrives to combine the two notions of crucifixion and exaltation in a single ambiguous word. This word, as we have seen, is probably drawn from the passion prophecy. Thirdly, his new contribution to the biblical typology of the crucifixion includes also the idea of the healing effect of the passion, even supplying the notion of giving life, which is John's chief way of expressing it. Finally, just as the passion sayings in Mark spawned further sayings, so also John has a series of sayings which depend upon this one, and reveal the central importance of it for John's theology.

Put in a nutshell, John's point is that the crucifixion, which is the actual method of execution, is an outward sign of Jesus' exaltation. This is because the exaltation of Jesus denotes his special relationship 147 with God, which is visible already in the passion to those who under-stand its true meaning. For Jesus accepts death as an act of union with the Father's will.

This point is clarified and pressed home in further Son of Man sayings. The "lifting up" theme reappears in 8,28 and 12,32-34. The latter passage includes the information that, for the saving purpose of Jesus' death to be achieved, death had to be by a specific means. Obviously this means crucifixion (cf. 18,32).

In two places John varies the verb by using "glorified" (δοξασ-θῆναι), 12,23 and 13,31. The context in the first case suggests that John is thinking of the crucifixion in terms of the cosmic moral victory over the power of evil (cf. 12,31). But this is also true of the other, as it immediately follows the entry of Satan into the heart of Judas Iscariot at the Last Supper, and his departure to betray Jesus. That we have here a variant of "lifted up" is suggested by the juxtaposition of both these verbs in Is 52,13. But the use of δοξάζω allows John to draw out the meaning further. For the exaltation of the Son of Man is an act which redounds to the honour both of Jesus himself and of God for whose glory it is undertaken. This agrees with the theological use of δοξάζω elsewhere in John.

The two themes of the lifting up and the glorifying of the Son of Man account for six out of the thirteen occurrences of the title in John. Behind them all stands the passion prediction, shaped in the light of the kerygma of the death and resurrection of Jesus, but ultimately stemming from a saying of Jesus himself. Obviously John has derived the title from this tradition, so that there can be no doubt that he understood it as an exclusive self-designation of Jesus, like the other evangelists. But it is also inevitable that his creative use of the passion prediction should colour his idea of the Son of Man. On the strength of these Johannine sayings we can conclude that the Son of Man is to John the earthly revealer of a divine and saving relationship. This relationship is available to all through faith (3,15).

II. THE SON OF MAN AND REVELATION: JOHN 1,51

This preliminary conclusion must now be tested by comparison with the other seven Son of Man sayings. The first saying in the order of the gospel is 1,51, "Amen, amen, I say to you, you will see the heaven 148 opened, and the angels of God ascending and descending upon the Son of Man". The Amen-formula is a feature of Jesus' style in the sayings tradition[3]. Very frequently in John it is an indication that John is drawing on this tradition, but this does not prevent him from freely adapting his sources at the same time[4]. The closest parallel to the present verse is the baptism of Jesus in Mk 1,10, "and immediately, *ascending* from the water, he *saw the heavens opened* and the Spirit *descending on him* like a dove"[5]. John is clearly aware of the baptism story, though it is not described directly in Jn 1,29-34, and he has referred to this very verse obliquely in verse 33, "Upon whomsoever you see the Spirit descending ...". There is thus good reason to suspect that John has modelled the saying of verse 51 upon this tradition. On the other hand, the similarity to Stephen's words in Acts 7,56 may be no more than coincidence.

Of course John is not actually referring to the baptism in this verse. He is concerned with something that is to take place in the future. But it may be surmised that the baptismal experience of Jesus is not irrelevant to this future event. For John agrees with Matthew that the experience was not confined to Jesus alone, but was perceived by John the Baptist too. Indeed, it was the sign to him of the identity of Jesus as the coming one of whom he had preached. Thus it was an earthly act which revealed the true status of Jesus, in much the same way as the lifting up of the Son of Man is a revelatory act on earth. It may thus be concluded that verse 51, modelled upon the baptism but referring to the future, is also intended to indicate a future act which will reveal something about Jesus. In the light of 3,14 it is likely that this event is the cross, which at this stage John does not wish to mention directly.

The meaning of 1,51 in its context must be deduced from the remaining words about the angels. There is widespread agreement

3. Cf. J. JEREMIAS, *Characteristics of the* ipsissima vox Jesu, in *The Prayers of Jesus*, London, 1967, pp. 112-115; ID., *Zum nicht-responsorischen Amen*, in *ZNW* 64 (1973) 122-123. As it is confined to the sayings of Jesus it is unlikely to have arisen only in the post-Easter community, as argued by V. HASLER, *Amen. Redaktionsgeschichtliche Untersuchung zur Einführungsformel der Herrenworte "Wahrlich, ich sage euch"*, Zürich and Stuttgart, 1969, pp. 181ff., and by K. BERGER, *Die Amen-Worte Jesu. Eine Untersuchung zum Problem der Legitimation in apokalyptischer Rede* (BZNW, 39), Berlin, 1970, pp. 147ff.

4. Thus Jn 13,16.20.38, are all very close to their synoptic parallels. On the other hand careful and deliberate adaptation can be seen in John 3,3.5; 8,51-52; cf. B. LINDARS, *Discourse and Tradition: The Use of the Sayings of Jesus in the Discourses of the Fourth Gospel*, 1981 [in this volume, pp. 113-129]; ID., *John and the Synoptics. A Test Case*, 1981 [in this volume, pp. 105-112].

5. Matt 3,16 stands a little closer to John in some respects: the verb for "open" (ἀνοίγω), "Spirit *of God*", and preposition ἐπί ("on him"), for Mark's εἰς. For the interpretation of Jn 1,51 adopted here, cf. MOLONEY, pp. 39-40.

today that John has composed the saying in such a way as to recall Jacob's dream (Gen 28,12), "And he dreamed that there was a ladder set up on the earth, and the top of it reached to heaven; and behold, *the angels of God were ascending and descending on it*". It is also recognized that the movement of the angels "upon the Son of Man" has a parallel in rabbinic exegesis, in which "on it" (the ladder) is taken to mean "on him" (Jacob). This is possible in the Hebrew, but not in the Greek. In the rabbinic exegesis the angels are familiar with the heavenly archetype of the righteous man, and are now delighted to discover the earthly reality in Jacob[6]. It may be conjectured that the "greater things" (Jn 1,50) which Jesus' audience will see are something that belongs to a similar line of exegesis. They will see an act in which the Son of Man on earth reflects a heavenly reality. There is a sense in which this is true of all the acts of Jesus in the Fourth Gospel. But it is especially true of the passion, in which death and glorification are two sides of a single reality. Thus, just as the baptism of Jesus was an earthly act which revealed his heavenly identity, so the cross will be a supremely revelatory act.

This interpretation of 1,51 makes full allowance for its contextual position[7]. It confirms the connection between it and the reference to the baptism of Jesus earlier in the chapter. This connection is indicated in the actual words with which the saying begins, but extends to the theme which they have in common. There is thus a literary inclusion which encapsulates the paragraphs concerning the call of the disciples, with their preliminary confessions of faith, and so suggests that the disclosure of the full meaning of the confession of faith must wait until a further revelatory act has taken place. Thus 1,51 is a programmatic statement, pointing to the significance of the story that is to be unfolded.

Two further points should be observed. First, the saying shows no influence from Dan 7,13-14, or such sayings as Mk 14,62 which are related to it. This is not to say that John is unaware of the connection, but only that it is not operative here, and therefore is not a

---

6. Cf. Targum Neofiti at Gen 28,12; Genesis Rabba 68,18.

7. R. BULTMANN (*The Gospel of John*, Oxford, 1971, p. 98) has rightly seen that the climax of the section on the first disciples is reached in 1,49, and the section should stop here (he assumes a pre-Johannine source, whereas I would argue for a homily by John himself as the earlier state of this material). The addition of 1,50-51 relates this section to the larger plan of the Gospel, and is no longer concerned with confessions of faith; cf. B. LINDARS, *The Gospel of John*, London, 1972, pp. 119-120.

controlling factor for the interpretation of the saying[8]. The scene is not
the heavenly court, and there is no reference to the coming of the Son
of Man. Secondly, John's choice of the Son of Man title is not dictated
by the contents of the saying, which, as we have seen, have different
literary affinities. Moreover it is not clear that he intends it to be an
additional form of the confession of faith, surpassing the confession
just made by Nathanael in verse 49. What Nathanael and the others
will see is an act which surpasses the display of insight on the part of
Jesus which evoked Nathanael's confession, and that act will evoke
confession not of the Son of Man, but of "the Christ, the Son of God"
(20,31; cf. 20,28). Thus the Son of Man is not here a title in the same
series as the rest. It appears to be no more than the third-person self-
reference of Jesus, with which we are familiar from the synoptic
150 sayings. But our study of the "lifting up" and "glorification" sayings
entitles us to see a functional use of the Son of Man in John. This
saying agrees with them in denoting Jesus as the earthly revealer of a
divine and saving relationship. But for the present the nature of the
act by which Jesus fulfils this function is not specified. It is merely
alluded to as something more significant than the baptism, and more
significant than the act of recognition which evoked Nathanael's
confession of faith. The reader has to wait until 3,14 to discover that
in fact it is the cross.

These two observations show that the Son of Man in John is not
a title which he has adopted already laden with meaning apart from
the tradition of the sayings of Jesus. The function of the Son of Man
in 1,51 is no different from the function in 3,14, and there it is derived
from the passion predictions, as developed in the light of the kerygma
and incorporated into Mark.

III. THE SON OF MAN AND REVELATION: OTHER TEXTS

a. The next occurence of the Son of Man title is in 3,13; "No one
has ascended into heaven but he who descended from heaven, the Son
of Man". This can be quickly dealt with. The phrase is carefully placed
at the end of the verse to prepare the way for the important statement
on the lifting up of the Son of Man which immediately follows. In
view of what has just been said above about the function of the Son

8. Contrary to what I have written elsewhere, in which I have assumed that John
worked on the basis of the identification of the Son of Man with the Danielic figure; cf.,
besides the above-mentioned works, *The Passion in the Fourth Gospel*, 1977 [in this
volume, pp. 67-85].

of Man in John, it can suitably be paraphrased "the revealer" (not, of course, implying Bultmann's mythological use of this idea)[9]. John has asserted that salvation requires birth "from above", i.e., from the Spirit[10], and now he is going to prove the christological consequence of this, that the bringer of salvation comes from above too (3,11-13). So the revealer comes from heaven, and he will reveal on earth the heavenly truth by means of the exaltation described in 3,14. Because John uses the Son of Man in this functional way, there is no question here whether the Son of Man was thought to be pre-existent or not[11]. John does believe that Jesus is pre-existent, in the sense that he has divine origination, and therefore the Son of Man is pre-existent, because the Son of man is none other than Jesus. But John has no concept of the Son of Man apart from Jesus, and so the theoretical question of the pre-existence of the Son of Man, which has often been raised on the basis of this verse, simply does not arise.

b. This seems to be the best place to mention 9,35, where the Son   151
of Man is used in connection with what appears to be a confession of faith: "Jesus heard that they had cast him out, and having found him he said, 'Do you believe in the Son of Man?'"[12] The person addressed is the man born blind. So the theme is the removal of the blindness which prevents perception of revelation. According to our functional understanding of the Son of Man the question can be paraphrased, "Do you believe in the revealer?", i.e., that there is one who "makes manifest the works of God" (9,3). On the other hand this cannot be reduced to a mere substitute for the first person ("Do you believe in me?"), because the man does not realize that the Son of Man is to be

9. In Bultmann's presentation the Revealer denotes Jesus as one who embodies the postulated redeemer-myth of early Gnosticism, cf. W. SCHMITHALS, Introduction to English edition of BULTMANN, *The Gospel of John*, pp. 7ff.

10. For the interpretation of ἄνωθεν in this chapter, cf. B. LINDARS, *John and the Synoptic Gospels: A Test Case* (n. 4 above).

11. The question presupposes the common, but erroneous, view that there was a Son of Man figure in the thought of Judaism apart from the Jesus tradition. For discussion of the issue, cf. R. SCHNACKENBURG, *Der Menschensohn im Johannesevangelium*, in *NTS* 11 (1964-65) 123-137 (English version in ID., *The Gospel according to St John* I, London, 1968, pp. 529-542).

12. The majority text, reading "the Son of God", is probably influenced by liturgical use in connection with the baptismal confession, but "the Son of Man" is well supported: P[66] P[75] Sin B D W sy[s] co (verse 38-39a should perhaps also be considered a liturgical addition, being omitted by P[75] Sin* W b (l)). As will be seen in what follows, to interpret this verse correctly it is important to free the mind from the whole idea of the confession of faith in the formal sense, and to try to see it strictly in terms of the Johannine theology.

identified with Jesus himself (verse 36). We may well ask what the man thought the title meant. No indication of its content is given. It seems, then, that it must be regarded as having a meaning that can be taken for granted. Naturally, scholars have assumed that the meaning was provided by the current apocalyptic title, which was held to be a feature of the background to the New Testament. This solution is no longer open to us. Hence the meaning must be derived from John's use of the title elsewhere in the gospel, rather than from external sources. If John 9 is taken to be historical reporting, it is, of course, difficult to think of the man as capable of understanding the Son of Man in the specifically Johannine sense. As the chapter has much more probably been artificially constructed on the basis of a much simpler tradition, this difficulty ought not to be pressed. The functional meaning of the Son of Man as the revealer of God is sufficient to justify the form of the dialogue in verses 35-37, and admirably suits the theological purpose of the chapter as a whole.

c. The discourse on the bread of life in John 6 mentions the Son of Man three times (6,27.53.62). In the dialogue which leads into the discourse proper, Jesus says (6,27), "Do not labour for the food which perishes, but for the food which endures to eternal life, which the Son of Man will give to you; for on him has God the Father set his seal". It is natural to interpret this saying in relation to the Jewish expectation of the renewal of the manna miracle in the eschatological age[13]. This has led to the conclusion that the Son of Man is the apocalyptic title of the future Messiah, who here includes the provision of the bread as one of his eschatological functions. The study of the Son of Man in John which we have so far undertaken suggests, however, that this may be a false track. The interpretation turns on the question *when* the bread will be given. It transpires in the course of what follows that the bread is the true teaching from God (verse 45). From this point of view the bread is available already (hence the timeless present participles in verses 35, 40, 47 and indefinite clauses in 50b, 51b). Finally, the bread metaphor is explained by the fact that the teaching from God is not so much what Jesus teaches verbally as what he is in himself, the one who gives his life for the world (51c). It then comes as no surprise to discover that consumption of the bread in this sense is identified with eating and drinking the flesh and blood

152

13. The idea is referred to in 2 Baruch 29,8; Mekilta to Exod 16,25; Ecclesiastes Rabba 1,9.28. Of course there is no concept of the Son of Man as the giver of this bread.

of the Son of Man (6,53), "Amen, amen, I say to you, unless you eat the flesh of the Son of Man and drink his blood, you have no life in you". The language is eucharistic, but the reference is certainly to the passion as the essential factor in Christology which must not be missed. The faith required to gain the bread (verse 28) is inadequate unless it includes the necessity of Jesus' sacrificial death. The revealer must die (or, as John said in 3,14, be lifted up), and this *fact* is "the food which endures to eternal life, which the Son of Man will give you" (verse 27).

These two Son of Man sayings belong together, and enclose the whole discourse. The climax in verses 53-58 has been prepared for from the very beginning. The connection between verses 27 and 53 shows that the Son of Man has the same functional purpose here as in the other passages. The title stems from the passion predictions, and the passion is the supreme moment of revelation. The Son of Man will give the imperishable food when he is lifted up on the cross.

We still have to ask why John adds in verse 27, "for on him has God the Father set his seal". Here Moloney, following Barrett, is right in suggesting that the sentence refers to the exclusive position of Jesus as the authentic revelation of God. God's plan to reveal himself through the act of the Son of Man is like a document signed and sealed. This detail thus confirms the interpretation which we have already reached. It suits the exclusive character of the discourse, which emphasizes several times the unique position of Jesus as the agent of salvation (verses 37, 40, 44-45, 49-50, 53).

The third of these three Son of Man sayings stands outside the discourse as such, and belongs to the record of the reactions of the audience (6,62), "Do you take offence at this? Then what if you were to see the Son of Man ascending where he was before?" (verses 61-62). It is not clear whether this would remove the offence or make it even worse[14]. The former seems best, because it accords with the spiritual understanding required by the next verse. To see the ascension of Jesus would be to have proof that, contrary to outward appearance, the death of Jesus is the truly saving act. But the spiritual

153

---

14. It is important to realize that the offence is not just the sacramentalism of 6,53-58 (C.H. DODD, *The Interpretation of the Fourth Gospel*, Cambridge, 1953, pp. 341-342), nor the incarnation as such (MOLONEY, p. 122), nor even that here is a man who claims to be the revealer of God (BULTMANN, *John*, p. 445), but the revelation itself which Jesus brings. It has already been indicated in verse 53 that it is the cross that is the revelatory act. This is the fact which causes offence (cf. 1 Cor 1,23). This offence cannot be removed by seeing a fresh act. It can be removed only by grasping the real meaning of the cross itself, i.e., that it is not only a "lifting up" in the sense of being nailed to a stake (3,14), but also a "lifting up" in the sense of exaltation to the Father.

220

person (6,63) should be able to perceive this without actually seeing the ascension (cf. 20,29). Once more, as in 3,13, it is implied that the Son of Man has descended first. As before, it is necessary to stress that pre-existence is not ascribed to Jesus as Son of Man, as if there were a ready-made concept of the pre-existent Son of Man. But it is essential to John's position that Jesus could not achieve his saving work without origination from God, and so in this sense the revealer has descended from God, and in accomplishing his appointed task by way of the cross he reaches his destination in God. Thus the whole plan, sealed by God (verse 27), is brought to its conclusion. John uses the notion of ascension rather than "lifting up" precisely because he is not speaking of the cross in its outward aspect, but in terms of a demonstration of its inner meaning[15]. The death and exaltation of Jesus are for John the reverse sides of a single coin. But John is careful to keep them separate conceptually. We have already observed a similar distinction in the use of ὑψοῦν and δοξάζειν.

d. John has one more Son of Man saying, and this appears to break the pattern which has held together so well up to this point. All the references to the Son of Man hitherto have been amenable to interpretation in the light of John's use of the passion predictions in 3,14. In his death on the cross Jesus reveals God, and it is in this capacity, and in relation to this act, that he is referred to as the Son of Man. But when we turn to 5,26-27 we find a different picture, "For as the Father has life in himself, so he has granted the Son also to have life in himself, and has given him authority to execute judgement,

15. John has no concept of the ascension as a separate event, as in the Lucan scheme, nor does he make use of the descent-ascent motif of the Hellenistic redeemer myth. He normally thinks of Jesus as coming from God and going to God (by way of the cross), cf. 13,3; 16,28. The metaphors of descent and ascent are, in fact, never fully correlated in the Fourth Gospel. In 1,51 it is the angels who ascend and descend, as in Gen 28,12, and this denotes the conjunction between heaven and earth which will be achieved in the cross of the Son of Man as the supreme revelatory act. In 3,13 ascent is mentioned first, probably alluding to Enoch and other seers who, according to Jewish tradition, penetrated heaven. By contrast the Son of Man is said to have descended, and nothing is said of ascent apart from the cross. In the discourse on the bread of life descent is a leading motif, referring to the incarnation (the verb καταβαίνω, to come down, suits the imagery of the manna miracle, and is actually used in connection with it in Num 11,9). The descent is to provide the saving revelation, and this is achieved in the cross (verse 53). Again, nothing is said of ascension in the discourse. The concept is used in verse 62, however, so as to maintain the terms of reference established in the discourse (which may originally have been an independent homily by John). It is not stated when this ascent might take place. The only clue is provided by the use of the Son of Man title. This suggests that the ascent belongs to the characteristic function of the Son of Man, and that is the cross.

because he is the Son of Man (ὅτι υἱὸς ἀνθρώπου ἐστίν)".

As far as the Greek text goes, this verse has a unique feature. This is the only place in the gospels where the Son of Man is mentioned without the definite article (υἱὸς ἀνθρώπου)[16]. This brings it into line with the places outside the sayings tradition where the phrase is used (Heb 2,6, in a quotation of Ps 8,4; Rev 1,13; 14,14, both alluding to Dan 7,13). This difference from the rest of the sayings has never been satisfactorily explained. A considerable number of scholars trace it to direct influence from Dan 7,13-14 on account of further allusions to Daniel in the immediate context[17]. Thus verses 28-29 seem to be inspired by Dan 12,2. In verse 27 itself the words "has given him authority" (subject: God) may well be an allusion to Dan 7,14, "and to him was given dominion ..." This is strenuously denied by P.M. Casey, who insists that John means that the Son will have this authority "because he is a son of man", i.e. a human being[18]. But this interpretation is open to the objection that John certainly means υἱὸς ἀνθρώπου to be definite, in spite of the omission of the definite articles, because this is always the case in comparable passages (cf. 1,1;

154

16. In spite of the absence of the definite articles, it is correct to translate the phrase as if they were present, because the definite articles may properly be omitted from the predicate of a noun-sentence when the predicate *precedes* the copula, cf. C.F.D. MOULE, *An Idiom Book of New Testament Greek*, Cambridge, ²1959, pp. 115-116, referring to E.C. COLWELL, *A Definite Rule for the Use of the Article in the Greek New Testament*, in *JBL* 52 (1933) 12-21. But because Greek has no indefinite article, it is always possible that the anarthrous phrase is intended to be indefinite rather than definite, hence the difference of opinion about "Son of God" in Mk 15,39 (cf. my *Jesus Son of Man*, ch. 4, n. 25 [p. 205]); cf. P.B. HARNER, *Qualitative Anarthrous Predicate Nouns: Mark 15,39 and John 1,1*, in *JBL* 92 (1973) 75-87. As the title of the latter article shows, this order of words is adopted when the noun, or nominal phrase, which forms the predicate is intended to be qualitative, rather than denoting identification. For instance, 8,12, "I am the light of the world" (ἐγώ εἰμι τὸ φῶς τοῦ κόσμου) denotes identification, but 9,5, "As long as I am in the world, I am the light of the world" (φῶς εἰμι τοῦ κόσμου) is qualitative.

17. This opinion was favoured in my article (see n. 1 above). See MOLONEY, p. 81, for a list of recent scholars who take this view.

18. P.M. CASEY, pp. 198-199, following R. LEIVESTAD, *Exit the Apocalyptic Son of Man*, in *NTS* 18 (1971-72) 243-267, p. 252. Leivestad objects that the second article would normally be retained by John, but the evidence shows variation: it is retained in 1,49; 8,34.39; 9,5; (10,36); 12,31; 19,21; it is omitted in 5,27; 8,33.37; (10,36). In 10,36 the majority of MSS include the second article, but it is omitted by P⁶⁶* Sin D W 28 1424. The evidence for the omission of the first article in such phrases is overwhelming, and this of course applies to cases where the predicate consists of a single noun (cf. 1,1; 3,29; 4,19; 8,42.54). The criterion with regard to the second noun appears to be the closeness of the two nouns in the genitive relationship. If the genitival phrase forms a conventional unit, it is natural to drop *both* articles, e.g. the seed of Abraham, the Son of God (cf. 19,7).

221

8,33; 10,36).

The really significant feature is that the Son of Man is the predicate of a simple noun-sentence. This is what makes this verse different from all the other Son of Man passages, and demands explanation, whether it means "because he is a man" or "because he is the Son of Man". The word order, with predicate *before* the copula, places the emphasis on υἱὸς ἀνθρώπου. It is because the Son (verse 26) is υἱὸς ἀνθρώπου that the Father has given him authority to execute judgement. Grammar and syntax cannot tell us why this should be so. The question has to be decided from the context as a whole.

The discourse of John 5 is based upon the nature of the relationship between father and son. As a son learns his craft from his father (verse 19), so Jesus' acts are done under the instruction and at the bidding of God. Two functions have been specified in verses 21 and 22, giving life and executing judgement. These are both eschatological acts. Jesus has asserted that they have been delegated to the Son by the Father, and that those who believe in him can experience them now (verse 24). Then in verse 25 there is a change of perspective. The present moment is not merely an anticipation of the general resurrection and judgement. It is in fact the beginning of the whole process, which ultimately includes all men (verse 28). The entire eschatological action will be performed by the Son, not mere antic-ipations of it, because the Father has granted him the power and au-thority to do it. Why, then, has the Father delegated his prerogatives to the Son in this way? It is because he is the proper person to receive them. But what makes him the proper person? Surely not the

155 bare fact that he is a man! He is not simply interchangeable with any other human being. It is because he is who he is, the revealer of God to mankind. The reader can be expected to know this, even when expressed so very briefly in the three words υἱὸς ἀνθρώπου ἐστίν, because the function of the Son of Man has already been introduced in 3,14-15, and it has already been shown that his coming inevitably leads to judgement (3,16-21).

On this view, which is substantially that of Moloney[19], the Son of Man in 5,27 has to be accepted as titular, in spite of the syntactical position which requires the omission of the articles. A connection with Dan 7,13-14 may be allowed, because the apocalyptic picture derived from that passage is the source of the scenario of these verses. John need not be supposed to be ignorant of Daniel. But this does not alter the fact that he uses the Son of Man title in his own way. To

19. MOLONEY, pp. 83-86.

him it refers to the one whose crucifixion reveals God's glory. Precisely because the cross is the vital factor for faith, it is the judgement, the criterion, for all time. The lifting up of the Son of Man brings into operation faith in Jesus as the new criterion for salvation. This not only applies now (verse 24), but to the whole subsequent history of humanity, culminating in the general resurrection and final judgement (verses 25-27).

IV. CONCLUSION

The saying of 5,27 does not break the pattern after all. When John says that the Son has authority to execute judgement because he is the Son of Man, he means that he has it because he is the one who must "be lifted up, that whoever believes in him may have eternal life". The Son of Man in this verse is consistent with the functional idea which we have already noted. *The Son of Man in John is the agent of the revelation which is disclosed in the cross.* In this way the expression is almost a technical term. It is not intended to refer specifically to the humanity of Jesus, though the act of revelation is the climax of his human life. But the Son of Man sayings in John never occur in discussions of the human-ness of Jesus. From this point of view it may be considered a rather misleading phrase to use. One might feel that John could have found a better and more precise expression for the agent of revelation.

This takes us to the question of the source of John's use of the title. The reason why he used this title is that it came to him in the sayings tradition. It is not possible to be sure how far his familiarity with the sayings tradition extended. It cannot be proved that he had direct access to any of the Synoptic Gospels. But it is certain that he was in a position to use material which is also contained in them[20]. On the whole he uses a surprisingly small number of traditional sayings of Jesus in constructing the discourses. Hence we have no means of telling the range of Son of Man sayings available to him. But there can be no doubt that he had a form of the passion prediction, which he exploited in his own unique way in 3,14. None of the other Son of Man sayings in John relate to any other Son of Man sayings known from the Synoptic Gospels. Moreover, it has transpired that 3,14 is fundamental to all the rest. It is the basis of John's use of the Son of Man in a functional way, as a sort of technical term. It thus becomes

156

---

20. Cf. C.H. DODD, *Historical Tradition in the Fourth Gospel*, Cambridge, 1963.

unnecessary to look for any other source for the sayings in John, because all relate to the one saying which is derived from the passion prediction.

It thus comes about that, whether John was familiar with other Son of Man sayings or not, it can be safely asserted that he has derived his own use of the title from the passion prediction. The reason for this is obvious. It made an admirable base for one of his central theological themes. John is selective in his use of material, because he has a burning sense of purpose. There is no point in using what is not suitable to promote his argument. Having found what he wants, he makes good use of it.

What, then, of the Son of Man in the Johannine church[21]? The above argument suggests that, however distinct this church may have been in the spectrum of early Christianity, it possessed or had access to traditions of the sayings of Jesus, and these included at least the passion prediction, and perhaps other Son of Man sayings too. The fact that John uses the title fairly frequently argues that he is familiar with it as style-feature of the Jesus tradition, just like the other evangelists. But we can scarcely impose upon the Johannine community the quasi-technical sense which John has derived from the passion prediction. That belongs to the creative, theological thought of the gospel, but it is not a distinctive feature of Johannine Christianity. Hence it is not found in the Johannine epistles. It follows that the Son of Man is unlikely to have been a title in current use in the Johannine church at all. There was no Son of Man Christology there any more than in any of the other early Christian communities. The Son of Man remains a feature of the sayings tradition. Like the other evangelists, John has exploited it in his literary work. In fact his whole presentation of the gospel is done by building on the Jesus tradition, repeating and refining the same words and themes until his purpose is achieved. The Son of Man in John begins in a promise of revelation (1,51) and ends at the moment when it is fulfilled (13,31).

157

21. Recent work on the Johannine church includes W.A. MEEKS, *The Man from Heaven in Johannine Sectarianism*, in *JBL* 91 (1972) 44-72; O. CULLMANN, *The Johannine Circle*, London, 1976; A.R. CULPEPPER, *The Johannine School*, Missoula, MT, 1975; R.E. BROWN, *The Community of the Beloved Disciple*, London, 1979.

12

SLAVE AND SON IN JOHN 8,31-36

Recent treatment of the parable of the slave and the son in Jn 8,35 exhibits the great change that has occurred in Johannine studies. Formerly this verse was felt to be an intruder in its context. The first part, asserting that the slave does not remain in the house forever, could be accepted as a comment on the preceding verse. Bernard complains that it alters the metaphor, which was concerned with slavery to sin[1]. He says that it "seems to be meant as a warning to the Jews, who are really slaves because of their sins, that they have no fixed tenure in the household of God"[2]. The second part, that the son remains for ever, then has to be regarded as a way of reinforcing this point by introducing the contrasting status of the son in a household. But this is immediately followed in the next verse by ὁ υἱός used absolutely which cannot be taken as a continuation of the metaphor in v. 35 because here the Jews are addressed directly in the second person. Hence it must mean "the Son" as a self-reference on the part of Jesus, who has the power to free the Jews on account of his relationship to the Father. Realising this, the reader is likely to revise his ideas about v. 35b and assume that there also "the Son" is intended[3]. Verse 35b then hangs awkwardly as a christological statement unrelated to the flow of the argument. Bernard claims that this is the reason why it is omitted by several important manuscripts and by Clement of Alexandria[4]. He himself is inclined to dismiss the entire verse as a gloss. 272

---

1. J.H. BERNARD, *A Critical and Exegetical Commentary on the Gospel According to St. John* (ICC, 29), 2 vols., Edinburgh, T. & T. Clark, 1928, II, p. 307. But in v. 34 τῆς ἁμαρτίας, omitted by D b sy[s] and Clement of Alexandria, should be regarded as a gloss (so Rudolf BULTMANN, *The Gospel of John: A Commentary*, Oxford, Blackwell, 1971, p. 438, n. 1; C.H. DODD, *The Interpretation of the Fourth Gospel*, Cambridge, University Press, 1953, p. 177, n. 2).

2. BERNARD, *John*, II, p. 308.

3. Moreover such an interpretation is supported by 12,34: ὁ Χριστὸς μένει εἰς τὸν αἰῶνα. Cf. also 6,27.

4. BERNARD, *John*, II, p. 308. It is omitted by ℵ W X Γ 0141; 33 124 *al*, but the omission is probably due to homoioteleuton. The omission in Clem. Alex., *Strom.* 2.5, on the other hand, appears to arise from simplification of the paragraph as a whole for the purpose of Clement's argument.

More recent studies of the traditions behind the Fourth Gospel have rescued the verse from this banishment and given it a new status[5]. It is now seen to be a parable in its own right[6]. The articles with δοῦλος and υἱός are generic[7]. From this point of view the verse can stand alone as an item of previous tradition which John has incorporated into his argument. It will thus repay careful study for what it is in itself. At the same time its relationship to the actual context can be seen in a new light. It no longer appears as an illustration arising in a short paragraph about slavery and freedom, but it provides the point of departure for the paragraph and dictates its terms of reference.

(a) Once the parable of v. 35 has been isolated, the question of its provenance naturally arises. Dodd held that it was derived from the tradition of the sayings of Jesus[8]. This may be disputed, but it is altogether probable that John introduced it into his argument in the belief that it was a genuine logion. Hence there is at least the possibility that the parable can be added to the meagre stock of sayings of Jesus which have been preserved outside the synoptic gospels.

(b) As an item of earlier tradition which John has taken over, the parable may be significant as one of the source of the Johannine christology[9]. It can take place alongside the parable of the apprenticed

273   son (5,19)[10] as a logion on the meaning of sonship which John has

---

5. The reassessment began with the work of Bent NOACK, *Zur johanneischen Tradition: Beiträge zur Kritik an der literarkritischen Analyse des vierten Evangeliums*, Copenhagen, Rosenkilde, 1954, and culminated in that of C.H. DODD, *Historical Tradition in the Fourth Gospel*, Cambridge, University Press, 1963. Cf. also Barnabas LINDARS, *Behind the Fourth Gospel* (Studies in Creative Criticism, 3), London, SPCK, 1971; and ID., *Traditions behind the Fourth Gospel*, in M. DE JONGE (ed.), *L'Évangile de Jean. Sources, rédaction, théologie*, Gembloux, Duculot, 1977, pp. 107-124 [in this volume, pp. 87-104].

6. DODD, *Historical Tradition*, pp. 379-382.

7. As is also the article with οἰκία. Cf. BULTMANN, *John*, p. 440, n. 1.

8. DODD, *Historical Tradition*, pp. 382, 331.

9. Cf. J.A.T. ROBINSON, *The Use of the Fourth Gospel for Christology Today*, in B. LINDARS and S.S. SMALLEY (eds.), *Christ and Spirit in the New Testament: in Honour of Charles Francis Digby Moule*, Cambridge, University Press, 1973, p. 72.

10. Jn 5,19-20a (αὐτὸς ποιεῖ) was recognized as a parable from pre-Johannine tradition independently by C.H. Dodd (*A Hidden Parable in the Fourth Gospel*, in *More New Testament Studies*, Grand Rapids, MI, Eerdmans; Manchester, University Press, 1968, pp. 30-40) and by Paul GÄCHTER (*Zur Form von Joh 5,19-30*, in J. BLINZLER, O. KUSS and F. MUSSNER (eds.), *Neutestamentliche Aufsätze: Festschrift für Professor Josef Schmid*

taken from the teaching of Jesus and applied to the special relationship between Jesus and God. It may be objected that John has radically altered the meaning of these parables in order to press them into service for his christology. But a similar process can be observed within the synoptic tradition in Mt 11,25-27[11]. Moreover, it will be shown below that it is at least possible that the parable of the slave and the son in v. 35 had already been interpreted in a christological sense before it was employed by John in its present context. Thus there may be a greater degree of continuity between John and Christian origins than is often supposed.

(c) The parable is the logical starting point of the short paragraph in which it stands (vv. 31-36), and indeed of the whole argument which comes to its climax in the electrifying assertion of Jesus' preexistence in v. 58. For reasons which will become clear later, John begins with the application of the parable in vv. 31-34 before actually quoting the parable itself. In these opening verses the disciples who hold fast by (literally "remain in", μείνητε ἐν) the word of Jesus correspond with the son of the parable (v. 31). Those who commit sin correspond with the slave (v. 34). Thus, though the parable appears to be closely joined only to this latter verse about the slave, it does in fact summarize the whole of the preceding verses. But it deals with the son and the slave

274

---

zum 70. Geburtstag, Regensburg, Pustet, 1963, pp. 65-68). I have accepted this in my commentary (*The Gospel of John* [The New Century Bible], London, Oliphants, 1972, p. 221), but I now think that v. 20a belongs to John's exposition of the parable, which did not extend beyond v. 19. This means that v. 20a is to be regarded as a Johannine reformulation of the logion, adapted for a specific purpose. "The Father" now means God, as is clearly the case in v. 21. It follows the "the Son" is also a definite person, though not necessarily identified with Jesus himself at this stage of the argument. He may, then, be regarded simply as God's offspring. When we add to this the Father's love (φιλεῖ, cf. 3,35; Gächter takes this as a sign of pre-Johannine tradition on the dubious supposition that John himself would have written ἀγαπᾷ), and the general reference to what the Father does (or makes), we are entitled to conclude that this half verse refers to the *creation*. Hence the relationship between the Father and the Son is drawn from the Wisdom tradition (cf. especially Prov 8,30). This reference back to the beginning paves the way for the eschatological reference of the second half of the verse, which is then specified in vv. 21-22. As the functions there described are undeniably divine prerogatives, the Son is demonstrated to be the Father's delegate. Thus the conclusion is reached that the Son is the proper object of the honor which is normally held to belong to God alone (v. 23a). The works of Jesus in his ministry both show continuity with the creation and anticipate the future resurrection and judgment. We shall see a similar combination of beginning and end in the argument of 8,31-58.

11. Cf. Joachim JEREMIAS, *New Testament Theology*. Vol. I: *The Proclamation of Jesus*, New York: Scribner's; London, SCM, 1971, I, pp. 56-61.

in reverse order, so that the son comes second. This allows John to introduce a fresh interpretation of the son in v. 36. This time the son is Jesus himself, and the point is that he has the power to give freedom. This makes an inclusion with the opening verse, and the whole paragraph can thus be seen to have a chiastic structure:

a   those to whom freedom is given (31b.32)
ba   question on slavery and freedom (33)
b   those who are slaves (34)
ba' parable of the slave and the son (35)
a'   the Son gives freedom (36)

This preliminary glance at the context is enough to show that the parable is the source of the leading ideas of vv. 31-36, and that the whole purpose of these verses is to present Jesus as the giver of freedom, in contrast with the Jews, who have no power to do so. This is the basis of the argument which follows in the rest of the chapter. The metaphor of the slave, however, is dropped. In vv. 37-47 the identity of the son in the parable is discussed in terms of paternity, and the contrast between Jesus and the Jews is worked out. It transpires that, whereas the Jews are spiritually sons of the devil, Jesus is the Son of God. Then vv. 48-58 take up the thought that Jesus can confer freedom, though here expressed by the idea of immortality ("will never see death", v. 51). The conclusion is drawn that, if he has such a capacity, Jesus must himself be preexistent (v. 58).

The parable of the slave and the son thus has greater importance than has been commonly recognised. It is a logion on sonship which may perhaps go back to the teaching of Jesus himself. It forms part of the groundwork of the Father/Son christology in John. It also provides the starting point for his argument on the preexistence of Jesus[12].
275 These three points must now be considered in detail.

---

12. *Pace* BULTMANN (*John*, pp. 327-328), John is not arguing for a timeless notion of eternity in opposition to the Jews' linear view of salvation, which would include a literal idea of preexistence. The point at issue is not the distinction between two world views, and it makes no difference to John's argument whether his words are understood in a temporal or a timeless sense. The real issue is whether the language of preexistence, involving a quasi-divine claim, can be properly applied to Jesus. This is why the Jews attempt to stone Jesus (v. 59, cf. 5,18; 10,33).

I. REDISCOVERING THE ORIGINAL PARABLE

Dodd supposed that the parable had survived in v. 35 without any significant alteration on the part of John, and paraphrased it as follows: "A slave is not a permanent member of the household: a son is a permanent member"[13]. He noted that the contrast between the status of a son and the status of a slave has several parallels in the synoptic tradition. For the status of a son he adduced Lk 15,31 and Mt 17,25-26, and he compared Mt 5,9.45; Lk 6,35; 20,36. He illustrated the insecurity of the position of a slave from Mt 18,25; 24,50-51; 25,30; Lk 12,46; 16,1-8[14]. It could thus be maintained that the parable would be at home in the teaching of Jesus.

The only difficulty was the obviously Johannine phrase μένει εἰς τὸν αἰῶνα. Dodd acknowledged that this phrase, with ὁ υἱός as subject, must have been intended by the evangelist himself as a christological statement in view of the use of the same phrase in 12,34[15]. But in fact it occurs outside John with a different subject in quotations from the LXX (2 Cor 9,9; 1 Pet 1,25; cf. Heb 7,24), and of course εἰς τὸν αἰῶνα without μένειν is common. It is thus not impossible that the phrase here should go behind John.

But it still remains improbable, if the saying is attributed to Jesus. In the words of Jesus, εἰς τὸν αἰῶνα occurs with a negative particle as an expression for "never" on rare occasions (Mk 3,29; 11,14; Mt 21,19), but elsewhere αἰών always refers to the present or the coming age. Here, however, we have the one case in the whole of the New Testament where εἰς τὸν αἰῶνα following a negative does *not* mean "never", but the negative applies to the whole of the following verbal expression. V. 35a is in fact ambiguous, as it could be understood to mean "a slave never remains" (implying that slaves always have the misfortune of being turned out by their masters), and this is not the same thing as Dodd's interpretation in terms of status. It is only when we reach 35b that it becomes clear that μένει εἰς τὸν αἰῶνα is to be taken as a semantic unit. It thus appears probable that these words replace some other phrase in the underlying tradition.

276

13. DODD, *Historical Tradition*, pp. 380-381. Thus BERNARD (*John*, II, p. 307) comments: "The slave has no tenure". But it is hazardous to offer this as a translation of the Greek, as if μένει εἰς τὰ αἰῶνα were a normal and idiomatic expression for security of tenure or permanence of position in domestic service.
14. DODD, *Historical Tradition*, pp. 381-382.
15. DODD, *Historical Tradition*, p. 380.

If it is accepted that John has himself adapted the form of the parable, the conclusion follows that he has altered it in order to make it suitable for his christological application. This seems inescapable in the light of the connection between 35b and 12,34. In making this change John breaks the flow of the argument in vv. 31-36, but at the same time he bends the parable into the argument of the discourse as a whole by subtle connections of vocabulary. Thus μένει has been anticipated by μείνητε in v. 31, where it is the disciples who correspond with the son of the parable. And εἰς τὸν αἰῶνα occurs, with its normal meaning of "never" following a strong negative, in vv. 51-52, where the whole expression "will never see (taste) death" is equivalent to "continues for ever" in the parable.

Within the rest of vv. 31-36, however, the contrast is not between continuing and not continuing for ever, but between freedom and slavery. These ideas at once claim our attention, because they are extremely rare in John. "Slave" as a metaphor is used twice elsewhere in the Fourth Gospel, but then the contrast is with the master (13,16) and with friends (15,15). But ἐλεύθερος and its cognates never occur anywhere else in the gospel. Moreover, neither freedom nor slavery are necessary to the argument which follows in the rest of the discourse. As has already been pointed out, the slave is not mentioned any more. Instead of the contrast between slave and son, vv. 37-47 are concerned with the contrast between sonship of the devil and sonship of God. Similarly, whereas in vv. 31.36 Jesus confers freedom, in vv. 51.52 where this point is taken up again, he conveys the capacity to escape death.

In the light of these facts it is fair to say that the idea of slavery would never have been brought into the discourse at all, if it had not been already present in the parable which John wished to use as his point of departure. But then the same can surely be said of the idea of freedom. Not only is the idea unnecessary for the following argument (for the concept of continuing for ever suits John's purpose better), but the very word ἐλεύθερος is not a normal item of John's vocabulary. This word also, therefore, is likely to come from the parable. It may thus be deduced that the pre-Johannine form of the parable had ἐλεύθερός ἐστιν in place of μένει εἰς τὸν αἰῶνα. The concept of freedom is then derived from the parable in exactly the same way as the concept of slavery. The parable may thus be tentatively reconstructed as follows: ὁ δοῦλος οὐκ ἐλεύθερός ἐστιν ἐν τῇ οἰκίᾳ· ὁ υἱὸς ἐλεύθερός ἐστιν.

277

If this reconstruction is approximately correct, the question arises why John altered the logion. This will be considered below. For the moment it may be useful to try to see the logion (which seems better described as a proverb than as a parable) in relation to the teaching of Jesus. The contrast between slave and son is unusual in the New Testament. Normally the contrast is either with the master or with a free man. Slave and free man occur together in 1 Cor 7,21-24; Gal 3,28; Eph 6,8; Col 3,11; Rev 6,15; 13,16; 19,18. The contrast between master and slave is more frequent, occurring in the *Haustafeln* (Eph 6,5-9; Col 3,22—4,1; 1 Tim 6,1-2; Titus 2,9-10; Phlm 16; 1 Pet 2,18), and quite often in the parables of Jesus[16].But direct contrast between slave and son occurs only in Paul's celebrated argument in Gal 4,1—5,1[17]. It is often claimed that there is a connection between this passage and Jn 8,31-36, and this impression is enhanced by the fact that descent from Abraham figures in both. But the point at issue is quite different. Paul is concerned with liberation from bondage to the Law, whereby Christians gain the status of sons, and so the right of inheritance. The Law plays no part in John's argument, and descent from Abraham is applied only to the unbelieving Jews as a foil to an argument on descent of another kind, as will be shown later. None of these issues are present in the logion itself.   278

There is, however, one item in the Jesus tradition which may have a bearing on our estimate of the logion. This is the story of the temple tax (Mt 17,24-27). Though the historical value of this story is hard to assess[18], and it has clearly been subject to legendary

16. Mt 10,24-25; 18,23-34; 20,27; 21,33-41; 24,45-50; 25,14-30; Mk 10,44; 13,34-36; Lk 12,36-38.41-47; 17,7-10; 19,13-27.

17. BERNARD (*John*, II, p. 308) cites Heb 3,5, but this is not a true parallel, because the contrast between Moses as a θεράπων and Jesus as a son is part of a larger typological comparison, in which Jesus is superior to Moses at each point. The point of the comparison is that both Moses and Jesus are "faithful" in their different situations. But Jesus, as son, is virtually the master (ἐπί) of the house. There is no direct contrast between slavery and sonship as such (θεράπων, only here in the New Testament, is derived from Num 12,7 [LXX], where it properly means "worshipper").

18. The story presupposes that payment is still to be made to the temple funds, so that the tax has not yet been converted to the *fiscus Iudaicus*. Hence a date before A.D. 70 is required for the formation of the pericope (cf. Hugh W. MONTEFIORE, *Jesus and the Temple Tax*, in *NTS* 11 [1964-65] 60-71; J.D.M. DERRETT, *The Law in the New Testament*, London, Darton, Longman and Todd, 1970, pp. 245-265). For an opposite view, cf. David HILL, *The Gospel of Matthew* (The New Century Bible), London, Oliphants, 1972, p. 270. If v. 27 is excluded as an addition (warranting payment of the tax by Christians, and incorporating a folklore motif), then the question concerns only

embellishment, it is possible that the core of the pericope is a genuine saying of Jesus. In the story as it stands, Peter is asked whether his master pays the temple tax. Peter says yes, but subsequently Jesus makes it clear that he does so only as a concession to avoid scandal. He regards himself as exempt, on the analogy of kings' sons, who do not pay taxes as the subjects do: "Then the sons are free" (ἄρα γε ἐλεύθεροί εἰσιν οἱ υἱοί). The contrast is thus between sons and subjects, not between sons and slaves. But the words are very close to our reconstruction of the logion. Moreover there is a considerable similarity of meaning. If we may detach Mt 17,25-26 from the context of the temple tax, we have a general statement of the condition of those who rank as kings' sons. It is natural to refer this to the condition of those who have responded to the gospel, the people whom Jesus calls μακάριοι in the Beatitudes. They might well be referred to as "the sons of the kingdom", though this phrase is not actually used of the followers of Jesus in the gospels (but cf. Mt 5,45). Unlike subjects who have to pay taxes, they already enjoy "the glorious liberty of the children of God" (Rom 8,21)[19]. So also, according to our logion, those who respond to Jesus' message have the freedom which belongs to sons but is not available for slaves. If this is correct, then the original parable behind Jn 8,35 belongs to Jesus' ethical teaching and may be compared to such developments of it as Rom 8,12-17, where the πνεῦμα δουλείας is contrasted with the πνεῦμα υἱοθεσίας[20].

279

Jesus himself. It is also probable that Matthew has added Peter into the context, because the setting of the pericope corresponds with the redactional verse Mk 9,33 and includes reminiscences of its actual phrases (cf. G.D. KILPATRICK, *The Origins of the Gospel according to St. Matthew*, Oxford, Clarendon, 1946, pp. 41-42).

19. For the relation of Paul's cosmic eschatology to the teaching of Jesus see James D.G. DUNN, *Jesus and the Spirit: A Study of the Religious and Charismatic Experience of Jesus and the First Christians as Reflected in the New Testament*, Philadelphia, PA, Westminster; London, SCM, 1975, pp. 308-342.

20. The use of υἱοθεσία in Rom 8,15.23 strikingly illustrates the tension between the present and the future, which is characteristic alike of the teaching of Jesus and the teaching of Paul (DUNN, *Jesus and the Spirit*, p. 310). Jesus' personal experience of sonship was taken up into Christian spirituality through the *Abba* address to God (Rom 8,15) (cf. JEREMIAS, *Theology*, I, pp. 56-68).

II. THE CHRISTOLOGICAL APPLICATION

John has taken over the parable from previous tradition for use in connection with a complex christological argument. He appears, however, to be aware of the ethical interpretation of it in connection with response to the message of Jesus, which may well have been its original meaning. This is suggested at the outset in v. 31, where response to the word of Jesus is the condition of freedom.

On the other hand, the parable did not require alteration in order to be understood in a christological sense. This certainly seems to have been the case in the parallel passage in Mt 17,26[21]. For here the pericope of the temple tax makes a distinction between Jesus himself and Peter. The question is not whether both Jesus and Peter must pay the tax. It is taken for granted that Peter should pay. The question is whether Jesus is exempt. And the reason given is that he is in the position of a king's son. Naturally, Jesus, as the Son of God, does not expect to pay the tax for the house of God.

Similarly it is likely that the parable was remembered not only for its ethical meaning but also for its value in connection with christology. It is obvious that the singular υἱός with the generic article invites application to Jesus as the Son of God in suitable contexts. We cannot, of course, tell whether John received it as a christological saying or not, but clearly he has understood it as such. This applies to the parable in its original form. John's adaptation of the parable does not introduce the christological application, but uses it as the basis. For if μένει εἰς τὸν αἰῶνα replaces ἐλεύθερός ἐστιν, it concentrates attention on one aspect of freedom, but it remains a static quality, a condition which attaches to a person on account of his sonship. But it is essential for John's argument that Jesus not only has this condition, but is able to confer it on others. This is expressed in v. 36 in the vocabulary of the underlying logion (ἐὰν οὖν ὁ υἱός ὑμᾶς ἐλευθερώσῃ). It may be said that this capacity is a normal consequence of sonship. Any son is not only free in a house, but also has the capacity to free slaves. But, insofar as this is true at all, it is not because the son is free (or has a permanent place in the household). The only person who can free a slave is the owner, and

280

---

21. H. Benedict GREEN, *The Gospel according to Matthew in the Revised Standard Version: Introduction and Commentary* (The New Clarendon Bible: New Testament), Oxford, University Press, 1975, p. 158.

the son can only do so if he acts on his father's behalf. Thus, if it is claimed that the son can confer freedom, it is because of his sonship rather than his own freedom. The christological understanding of the logion, and also of John's adaptation of it, presupposes that he who has freedom can give freedom, and this is because it is Christ, and not any son, who is in mind.

It now becomes clear that the christological interpretation depends upon a certain ambiguity in the logion. Superficially the meaning is so obvious that it appears to be nothing more than a truism. But if it is found in a collection of logia with no more indication of context than the opening "Jesus said" (like so many of the logia in the Gospel of Thomas), it compels the reader to search for a deeper meaning. If the son is taken to mean any Christian, it refers to the freedom of the disciple in the kingdom of God. But if the son is Jesus himself, his freedom is a quality which he has for the sake of others, and so implies the capacity to give freedom. John has realised the potentiality of the text to suggest both these possibilities in his comment on the logion in v. 36. The first half of the verse takes up the thought of Jesus' capacity to give freedom, the second half the freedom of all disciples. John sees a causal connection between these interpretations. Jesus is the Son of God, therefore he is free, and therefore he can give the freedom which belongs to God alone.

III. THE ARGUMENT

It is now time to consider the question why John felt it necessary to alter the logion. The answer to this question will provide the clue to understanding the relationship between the parable and the argument of the discourse as a whole.

It has already been pointed out that freedom is not a normal word 281 in John's theological vocabulary and occurs nowhere in the gospel outside these verses. John's usual concept for salvation is life, or eternal life. Thus John takes the parable to mean that Jesus, as the Son of God, has life in himself and also the power to give life (cf. 5,26). But this is not the purpose of his argument. His purpose must be deduced from the conclusion in v. 58. It is to prove the preexistence of Jesus as the Son of God. Thus the capacity of Jesus to give life is only one step in the argument which leads to this conclusion. John wishes to say that the *experience* of eternal life as a result of belief in the teaching of Jesus proves that Jesus is the

preexistent Son of God. This appeal to experience is apparent at the
very beginning of the discourse, where Jesus addresses the disciples: "If
you continue in my word, you are truly my disciples, and you will
know the truth, and the truth will make you free" (vv. 31-32). John
returns to this point at vv. 51-52, but first he has to draw attention to
the consequence of accepting the truth of Jesus' words. The fact that
Jesus speaks the truth proves that he has been sent by God (v. 42).
John makes it quite clear that he means not merely that Jesus has
been commissioned by God as a prophet, but that he actually
originates from God, who is the source of the truth which he conveys
(vv. 38.40.42). The argument thus presupposes an inevitable sequence
of effects: God is the source of truth, and truth gives life. Jesus,
however, is the mediator of God's truth. His words give life (v. 51).
But because such an effect can only be produced by one who has life
in himself, it follows that Jesus — in contrast with all other men (v.
53) — is not subject to the limitations of human life. He is eternal,
and therefore he is preexistent.

This argument is accentuated throughout by being set over against
its opposite. There is another equally inevitable sequence of effects.
The Jews plot to put Jesus to death (vv. 37.40). Such an intention can
only proceed from falsehood, and the father of lies is the devil (v. 44).
Thus, though the Jews claim to be sons of Abraham (vv. 33.37.39),
their actions prove a different and far more sinister spiritual affiliation.
In the construction of the argument the idea of affiliation to Abraham
is used to build up suspense, so that the exposure of their real
affiliation comes with all the more telling effect.

It is now clear that, though the starting point of the argument is
the Christian experience of life through belief in Jesus, the cogency of
the argument depends upon a dualistic understanding of spiritual
relationships, comparable to the two spirits doctrine at Qumran. As   282
John sees it, there can only be two alternatives. On the one side there
is God, whose Son conveys the truth, which enables the hearer to
avoid death. On the other side there is the devil, who conveys
falsehood, and who "was a murderer from the beginning" (v. 44). On
each side there is an inevitable sequence of effects — divinity, truth,
life, and devilry, lies, death. The connections between them are to
John's mind so certain that he can argue from the Christian experience
of life to the preexistence of Jesus as the Son of God.

In order to anchor the argument in the teaching of Jesus, John has
selected the parable of v. 35 from such logia as were available to him.
The choice is not perfect, because the parable does not mention life

and death. On the other hand, it has features which render it peculiarly apt for John's purpose. In the first place, the contrast between the slave and the son suits the dualism which is essential to his argument. In the second place, the fact that the interpretation of the parable easily oscillates between the christological meaning, in which Jesus is the giver of freedom, and the ethical meaning, in which the disciple has freedom through response to the message of the kingdom, suggests the sequence of effects which is worked out in the course of the argument.

The parable thus suits John's purpose, provided that he can translate the concept of freedom, which is a given feature of it, into his own terminology of eternal life. So he begins by setting out the main lines of the argument, but using the vocabulary of the parable[22]. It has already been shown that this applies to the whole of vv. 31-36, with the exception of the parable itself. But here we must note another feature of John's technique. He frequently uses the "Amen" formula in relation to traditional logia (cf. 3,3.5; 5,19; 8,51; 13,16.20.21). Here the formula occurs at the beginning of v. 34, although the logion does not appear until the next verse. This suggests that the three verses which follow the formula and contain the logion in the middle should be treated as a unit. It has already been pointed out that vv. 31-36 form a chiasmus. The same is true of vv. 34-36 within this frame:

283   Amen, amen I say to you
    a every one who commits sin is a slave
    a' A slave does not continue in a house for ever;
    b' a son continues for ever.
    b So if the Son makes you free, you will be free indeed.

The contrast, then, is between *a a'* and *b' b*. The Jews who are intent on sin (by seeking to kill Jesus, v. 37) are spiritually slaves, and slavery is a condition which excludes eternal life. Sonship, on the other hand, is a condition which implies eternal life, so that, when the messianic Son gives freedom, it is the true freedom (i.e. eternal life). Thus the three verses unpack the meaning of the parable in such a way as to enunciate the basis of the following argument. The fact that John introduces an interpretative change into the parable itself is to be

22. Consequently it is a complete misunderstanding of John's aim and method of composition to see in these verses reference to the Stoic ideas of the liberating effect of truth (Cicero, *Parad.* 5; Seneca, *Ep.* 78.2) or of enslavement to sin (Epictetus, 2.1.23).

attributed to his overriding care to set out the main lines of the argument correctly[23].

Nevertheless, John does not actually use the expression "have eternal life" as the substitute for "is free" in the parable. Nor does he use it later on. His preference for alternative expressions is dictated by the form of the argument. Eternal life can denote both continuance from the past and continuance into the future. In the parable μένει εἰς τὸν αἰῶνα implies the future. The phrase is capable of being understood strictly within the terms of reference of the parable (= permanent), but it also prepares the way for the christological application which follows in v. 36. It also recalls the μείνητε of v. 31, as we have seen, referring to the condition of those who are capable of receiving eternal life. After v. 36 the idea does not occur again until v. 51. Here it is expressed in the long and emphatic phrase θάνατον οὐ μὴ θεωρήσῃ (οὐ μὴ γεύσηται θανάτου, v. 52) εἰς τὸν αἰῶνα. The connection with the wording of the parable is clear. But the "Amen" formula again suggests that John is also indebted to another logion from the Jesus tradition[24]. It seems at first sight that the reference is still to the future. But the introduction of the idea of death enables John to turn attention to the other side of eternity, continuance from the past. In the past men have always died, including Abraham, whom the Jews claim as their father in order to assert their freedom (v. 33). But Jesus has a capacity greater than that of

284

23. This is not unparalleled in John. In 3,3.5 γεννηθῇ ἄνωθεν replaces στραφῆτε καὶ γένησθε ὡς τὰ παιδία in the parallel at Mt 18,3, in order to apply the logion to the issue discussed with Nicodemus. Matthew's version is independent of Mk 10,15 (which he omits) and nearer to the Aramaic original. Seeing that "turn and become" is a Semitism for "become again" (JEREMIAS, *Theology*, I, p. 155), it can be deduced that Matthew and John represent variant Greek versions of the same Aramaic. Thus John had before him γένηται ἄνωθεν ὡς παιδίον, but changed "become as a child" to "be born" and interpreted ἄνωθεν to mean "from above". It will be observed that it has to be presupposed that John was working from Greek versions of the traditional logia, rather than directly from the original Aramaic.

24. Here again it must be assumed that John has adapted the logion for his purpose, without necessarily altering the meaning radically. The nearest synoptic equivalent is Mk 9,1, also an "Amen" saying, which includes the words οὐ μὴ γεύσωνται θανάτου. John's εἰς τὸν αἰῶνα is not *merely* the completion of the negative after οὐ μή, as the connection with the parable shows, and may well correspond with Mark's ἕως ἂν ἴδωσιν τὴν βασιλείαν τοῦ θεοῦ (hence the variant θεωρήσῃ in v. 51). It is only at 3,3.5 that John has retained "the kingdom of God" from an underlying logion, but he then proceeds to interpret it in terms of his own concept of eternal life in the course of the argument (3,15-16.35-36).

Abraham, which places him outside the limitations of a normal span of life which ends in death. By the same token his life from the beginning cannot be measured in terms of years (v. 57). This is asserted finally in v. 58, in words which seem to be explicable only from the Wisdom tradition (Sir 24,9)[25].

IV. CONCLUSIONS

The parable of the slave and the son has been adapted from a logion which may have been spoken by Jesus as a vivid way of indicating the freedom of the sons of the kingdom of God. John has given it a christological interpretation and used it as the basis of an argument for the preexistence of Jesus as God's Son. This has importance both for understanding John's purpose and for determining his approach to christology.

However the purpose of the Fourth Gospel is defined[26], the disputes with the Jews certainly reflect the debate between church and synagogue. From this point of view John's use of a logion as a basis of argument has an apologetic purpose. The discourse is aimed at proving that Jesus is the preexistent Son of God. It would be easy to object that this idea is an invention of the church with no foundation in the teaching of Jesus himself. Consequently John makes use of an item from the sayings attributed to Jesus which appears to support his case. It has been argued above that it is not necessary to suppose that John was the first to understand the logion in a christological sense. It is even possible — though the point cannot be proved — that John genuinely believed that Jesus intended to make a christological statement when he spoke these words.

Though John has used the parable as the point of departure for his argument, it cannot be maintained that his argument is derived from it. This is obvious from the fact that he has found it necessary to

285

----

25. The statement is introduced by the "Amen" formula, but there is nothing comparable to it in the traditional logia. The nearest Wisdom parallel is Sir 24,9, cf. Prov 8,22-25 and especially 8,27 (MT) where the pronoun אני corresponds with the idiomatic use of absolute ἐγώ εἰμι here (BULTMANN, *John*, p. 327, n. 4, compares Ps 89,2 for the idiom). The influence of Isa 43,10, widely recognized as lying behind Jn 8,28, may also be suspected, though there the idiom is different.

26. Cf. Robert KYSAR, *The Fourth Evangelist and His Gospel: An Examination of Contemporary Scholarship*, Minneapolis, MN, Augsburg, 1975, pp. 147-172.

adapt it for his purpose. He has not reached the conviction of Jesus' preexistence as a result of reflection on the logion[27]. But he has picked it out of such logia as he had at his disposal because it fitted the needs of his argument by its sharp dualism and its suggestion of a sequence of effects (sonship leading to freedom).

John's christology is part of his inheritance. There is room for difference of opinion concerning the sources of some of his ideas[28]. But he is not trying to introduce a new doctrine. He aims to support and deepen the tradition which he has received. As far as possible he uses traditional logia as the starting point of his arguments. There are two of these in the discourse which we have studied (vv. 35 and 51-52). Both of them exhibit some degree of adaptation. But the changes which John makes are not intended to effect a radical alteration of their meaning, but to secure their relevance to the argument which they introduce.

The real basis of John's argument, however, is the Christian experience of life in Christ. It is precisely because the believers experience life in his name that Jesus, in John's view, can only be described as the preexistent Son of God. Jesus achieves what the Law (itself considered to be preexistent in Jewish speculative thought) could   286 not do[29]. The Law does not come into the argument of the present discourse, but there can be little doubt that this contrast is one reason why John is so insistent on the preexistence of Jesus. Another reason is that he thinks of Jesus as the Son of Man, designated from before the foundation of the world to be God's delegate, or agent, to carry

27. Christian belief in the preexistence of Jesus was reached early, not as a result of reflection on the sonship sayings (though these and the *Abba* address no doubt contributed to it), but as a kind of logical necessity arising from current presuppositions concerning divine mediation in the Jewish and Hellenistic world of the time (cf. Martin HENGEL, *The Son of God: The Origin of Christology and the History of Jewish-Hellenistic Religion*, Philadelphia, PA, Fortress; London, SCM, 1976). Some of these presuppositions are mentioned briefly below. John's thought represents the fruit of thorough assimilation of these ideas.

28. See the summary of recent trends in KYSAR, *Fourth Evangelist*, pp. 178-206.

29. The basic idea is already present in Sirach 24, where the preexistent Wisdom finds her ultimate expression in the Law. Severino PANCARO (*The Law in the Fourth Gospel: The Torah and the Gospel, Moses and Jesus, Judaism and Christianity according to John* [NTSuppl, 42], Leiden, Brill, 1975, pp. 367-487) has shown that John's Christology entails not only "the transferral of symbols for the Law to Jesus" (esp. pp. 452-487), but also "the metamorphosis of 'nomistic termini'" (esp. pp. 367-451), whereby expressions used in connection with the Law are now applied to Jesus.

out the eschatological functions of judgement and resurrection[30]. From this point of view the Christian experience is an anticipation of the coming age (5,24). Finally, John provides a metaphysical explanation of the preexistence of Jesus in the prologue, using the concept of the Logos, which is probably derived from Jewish Wisdom speculation[31].

But the important thing for John is that men should accept Jesus as the Son of God and thereby have life. As he says at the outset of the discourse which we have considered, he wants his readers to continue in the word of Jesus, so that they may know the truth, and thereby may be free.

30. Among the seven preexistent things recognized by the Tannaim were not only the Law but also the name of the Messiah. This is reflected in connection with the Messiah/Son of Man in *1 Enoch* 48,1-3. See Barnabas LINDARS, *Re-enter the Apocalyptic Son of Man*, in *NTS* 22 (1975-76) 52-72, and ID., *The Son of Man in the Johannine Christology*, in ID. and S.S. SMALLEY (eds.), *Christ and Spirit* (above, n. 9), pp. 43-60 (in this volume, pp. 33-50).

31. HENGEL, *Son of God*, p. 73. For a summary of the debate on this issue, see KYSAR, *Fourth Evangelist*, pp. 107-111.

NTS 38 (1992) 89-104

13

REBUKING THE SPIRIT
A NEW ANALYSIS OF THE LAZARUS STORY
OF JOHN 11

The story of the raising of Lazarus (John 11.1–44) is one of the most dramatic and impressive of the compositions in the Fourth Gospel. For this very reason it raises a host of problems for the biblical critic. There can be no dispute that it has a theological purpose which dominates the whole narrative. This is clearly set out in the first words attributed to Jesus: 'This illness is not unto death; it is for the glory of God, so that the Son of God may be glorified by means of it' (v. 4). The same point is referred to again just before the climax of the narrative in v. 40. But the more prominent the theological aim, the more difficult it becomes to view the narrative simply in terms of history. It must surely be the case that John has based his composition on a source, which was probably much simpler and briefer than the splendid story which it has become in his hands. But the source must be reconstructed before we can begin to think of it in historical terms. The modern tendency is to give up such attempts as hopeless, and to concentrate on the meaning of the text as it stands. But even that presents pitfalls to the critic. All seems well until we come to v. 33: 'Jesus . . . was deeply moved in spirit (ἐνεβριμήσατο τῷ πνεύματι) and troubled.' Unfortunately the Greek words do not mean 'deeply moved in spirit' (RSV). In his recent commentary on John in the Word Biblical Commentary, G. R. Beasley-Murray marshalls a great array of evidence to show that the meaning must be 'became angry in spirit'.[1] But why should Jesus be represented by John as angry? The effort to answer this question affects the interpretation of the whole story.

The problem is not a new one. All the major commentaries go into it in considerable detail. In the Anchor Commentary, Raymond Brown tackles it with characteristic patience, thoroughness

---

[1] G. R. Beasley-Murray, *John* (Word Biblical Commentary; Waco: Word, 1987).

and good sense.[2] Also the very full and informative discussion of Schnackenburg is especially helpful.[3]

The nature of the problem can be seen more clearly when the two competing translations of the verb ἐμβριμᾶσθαι are placed in context. Beasley-Murray points out that English-speaking exegetes have been guided by KJV 'groaned in the spirit'. Although it was known to be doubtful, the RV allowed this translation to stand, but gave as a marginal alternative 'was moved with indignation in the spirit'. But the older translation continues to be preferred, because it suits the context admirably. Jesus sees Mary and the Jews who have come with her weeping (v. 33a), he is himself affected by their emotion of grief (33b), he asks to be taken to the place where Lazarus is buried (34), and then bursts into tears (35). Naturally the Jews assume that this is an expression of grief for one whom Jesus loved greatly (36). I have myself argued that the context is decisive for this interpretation in spite of the fact that such a meaning for ἐμβριμᾶσθαι has no lexical support.[4]

The other meaning has been consistently supported by German scholars, in spite of all difficulties, because it has always been familiar from Luther's translation, *'Er ergrimmte im Geist und betriebte sich selbst'* ('he was angry in the spirit and distressed'). Other German translations give greater emphasis to the idea of anger. Beasley-Murray, giving this information, insists that the Germans are right because this is the meaning of the word. But it makes havoc of the context. What has happened to make Jesus angry? There is nothing reprehensible in showing grief. In any case Jesus weeps himself a few moments later, and this is assumed to be an expression of grief by the bystanders, who apparently do not realise that he is angry. Moreover the same verb comes again in v. 38, but this time as an inward emotion: ἐμβριμώμενος ἐν ἑαυτῷ ('in a state of anger within', Beasley-Murray). Thus there is no open expression of anger at this point, but the reader who accepts this interpretation may well detect a note of asperity in Jesus' reply to Martha in v. 40, though without this presupposition the verse has the quite different effect of preparing for the triumphant conclusion. Otherwise there seems to be no reason to mention what was in Jesus' mind.

---

[2] R. E. Brown, *The Gospel according to John* (2 vols.; The Anchor Bible; Garden City: Doubleday, 1966 and 1970).

[3] R. Schnackenburg, *The Gospel according to St John* (3 vols.; Herders theologische Kommentar zum Neuen Testament, ET, London: Burns & Oates, 1968, 1980 and 1982).

[4] B. Lindars, *The Gospel of John* (New Century Bible; London: Oliphants, 1972).

Various suggestions have been made to explain the anger of Jesus. One, which is found in patristic commentators, and will be important for our subsequent discussion, is that Jesus was displeased with the general display of grief, which is not consistent with the control of the emotions which a Christian should exercise. Thus, according to Origen,[5] Jesus first expressed anger at the people's grief, but then burst into tears himself to prove that in his humanity he had the capacity to show emotion, but finally gave an example of control by containing the anger within himself as he went to the tomb. This ingenious explanation will not do for modern exegetes, who prefer to see the anger as due to what the grief of the people signified, i.e. lack of faith. Martha has just made a profession of faith, even if she has not understood Jesus' real intentions. Now the situation of hopelessness, indicated by the extravagant mourning of the people, suggests that Jesus' previous teaching has had no effect even at this late stage in his ministry. On this view the anger of Jesus is a matter of frustration at their obtuseness. Commentators who take this line then have to regard Jesus' own tears as an expression of disappointment, against the obvious reading of it as sharing in the grief of the sisters, which is actually stated in v. 36.

An alternative suggestion, tentatively supported by Brown but rejected by Schnackenburg, is that Jesus was angry with Satan, whose opposition to the good purposes of God is a theme of the exorcisms in the Synoptic tradition, and is here apparent in the death of Lazarus. This is an important observation, as we shall see, but it is scarcely possible to accept it as an elucidation of John's purpose in the narrative as it stands, in which the theme of overcoming Satan nowhere comes to the surface. It does, however, have the advantage of removing the conflict with the tears of Jesus, which can on this view properly be regarded as the expression of Jesus' sharing of the people's grief, which only serves to increase his anger at the misery created by Satan.

A third possibility has very recently been put forward by Cullen Story.[6] He shares the insistence that the expression connotes anger, but renders it 'he rebuked (his) spirit and troubled himself' (v. 33) and 'again bearing the rebuke in himself' (v. 38). More will be said about this translation below. The novelty of this interpretation is

---

[5] *Fragmenta in evangelio Johannis* (GCS 10, *Werke*, ed. Preuschen, 1903) vol. 4, 549 (frags. 83–84). For non-biblical Greek texts in which ἐμβριμᾶσθαι occurs I am indebted to Dr Douglas de Lacey, who searched the Compact-Disc corpus of the Thesaurus Linguae Graecae on the Ibycus SC. All translations are my own, unless otherwise stated.

[6] C. I. K. Story, 'The Mental Attitude of Jesus at Bethany: John 11.33, 38', *NTS* 37 (1991) 51–66.

that both verses, and not only v. 38, are held to refer to the interior mental attitude of Jesus. Story suggests that the reproachfulness of the sisters (v. 21 and 32) and the sight of the general grief have momentarily made Jesus regret his delay in coming to Bethany, though his confidence in his intentions returns in v. 39. So Jesus is angry with himself. In my view this is no more satisfactory than the other modern interpretations, because it requires the corollary that the tears of Jesus in v. 35 are an expression of regret concerning his own inaction, against the natural meaning of the text, which suggests sharing the people's grief (cf. v. 36).

Progress towards a new solution requires a fresh look at the meaning and use of ἐμβριμᾶσθαι. It is a word that is rarely found in Greek literature, and never used by John elsewhere. It is thus most unlikely to be a part of his normal vocabulary. This is suggested further by the fact that he has felt the need to gloss it the first time with his usual word for emotional disturbance, ταράσσω (cf. 12. 27; 13.21; 14.1, 27). The two phrases ἐνεβριμήσατο τῷ πνεύματι and ἐτάραξεν ἑαυτόν are synonymous in John's presentation of the scene, as Story rightly sees. It is thus far better to suppose that John has taken the word from one of his sources for the Lazarus story, even though he has changed the meaning of it, as we shall see below. In what follows we shall first look at the meaning of ἐμβρι-μᾶσθαι. This will be followed by a fresh assessment of the sources behind the Lazarus story. Finally John's adaptation of his sources to produce the existing narrative will be elucidated.

THE MEANING OF ΕΜΒΡΙΜΑΣΘΑΙ

It is well known that the oldest occurrence of ἐμβριμᾶσθαι is in the *Seven against Thebes* of Aeschylus (6–5 cent. BCE), l. 461, where we hear of 'mares snorting (ἐμβριμώμενας) in the bridles' as they are led to their appointed place in the ambush outside the city gates. The word thus implies a physical expression of their excitement, with their breath whistling in their nostrils (l. 463–4), as they brace themselves for the rush upon the enemy. It does not denote the emotion of anger as such.

Apart from a fragment of Euripides, in which the word has no context to define its meaning, ἐμβριμᾶσθαι occurs next only in the biblical literature, and it is in connection with these passages that it is discussed in the church fathers. Before we look at these, it will be best to review other non-biblical occurrences, which in fact are very few.

In the *Epistula Ecclesiarum apud Lugdunum et Viennam* (2 cent. CE), 59–60,[7] the more vicious people in the hostile crowd 'raged (ἐνεβριμῶντο) and ground their teeth' at the bodies of the martyrs even after they had been put to death, 'as though they were trying to take some further special revenge on them'. The word suggests strongly aggressive behaviour as an expression of tremendous rage, which would not be adequately expressed in the translation 'threatened'. This has a parallel in the roughly contemporary *Necyomantia* of Lucian of Samosata, in which 'Brimo (the Terrible One, i.e. Persephone) raged (ἐνεβριμήσατο, note the pun) and Cerberus barked'.[8]

However, in the *Evangelium Bartholomaei* (3 cent. CE) 4.12 Jesus led the apostles and Mary 'from the mount of Olives, and threatened (ἐμβριμησάμενος) the angels of the underworld, and beckoned to Michael to sound his mighty trumpet'.[9] It is an expression not so much of a sudden rage as of undying hostility to the forces of evil, coming to the surface at the very sight of them.

In the fourth century the rhetorician Libanius cites in his *Declamationes* a case in which a man says that he took action whereby 'I again rebuked (ἐνεβριμώμην) the woman, but expected the man to cease from his mischief'.[10] The church writer Epiphanius (*Panarion* 66.11.7) similarly tells of one Archelaus, who 'coming up boldly, rebuked (ἐνεβριμεῖτο) the man who was holding the booty'. Later on (*Pan.* 75.2.1) he describes a confrontation between Eustathius and Aerius in which Eustathius 'flattered, exhorted, threatened, rebuked (ἐνεβριμεῖτο), and demanded, all to no effect'.[11] In the seventh century the medical writer Stephanus Atheniensis (*Scholia in Hippocratis Prognosticon* 1.4) has a story of a doctor called Erasistratos, who refuses to cure the king's protégé, although he has the skill to do so. At this 'the king became angry ... and being a tyrant, he grew indignant and threatened him (ἀπειλὰς καὶ ἐμβριμήσεις ... ἀπένεμε τῷ Ἐρασιστράτῳ), saying for example,

---

[7] Translation by H. Musurillo, *The Acts of the Christian Martyrs* (Oxford, 1972) 81. The passage is quoted *verbatim* by Eusebius, *Eccl.Hist.* 5.1.60.

[8] See Story for text and for comment on this example. I regard his use of 'censure' as a translation of ἐμβριμᾶσθαι here and elsewhere as misleading and unfortunate. Story also has a further example from Hermias' *Irrisio Gentilium Philosophorum* (2nd to 3rd century), in which Empedocles rages against his former speculations on cosmology. This text was not available to me.

[9] Translation from E. Hennecke, *New Testament Apocrypha* 1 (ET, London: SCM, 1963) 496.

[10] *Libanii Opera* (ed. R. Foerster; vol. 7; Leipzig: Teubner, 1913) 336.

[11] In another fourth-century writer, Macarius (*Apophthegmata*, MPG 34, 248), the unrecorded word ἐμβρίμιον is evidently an error through itacism for ἐμβρύμιον = 'pillow'.

"If you do not agree to cure him, I will have you executed."[12]
Evidently the ἐμβριμήσεις are menacing gestures as much as
words, which express the king's anger already mentioned.

The biblical use of the word begins in the Septuagint. It is rare,
and tends to belong to later revisions. In the standard LXX text it
occurs only three times, in Lam 2.6; Dan 11.30; and Sir 13.3. It is
doubtful if any of these represents the Old Greek. It is well known
that the text of Lamentations is heavily affected by the revision of
Aquila, and the word ἐμβρίμημα, used here, is likely to be his work,
as we shall see in a moment. In Dan 11.30 the LXX text is clearly
corrupt, so that correlation with the Hebrew is uncertain. If ἐμβρι-
μήσονται is intended to translate ונכאה (= 'suffer a rebuff', REB), it
must be a doublet alternative of ἐξώσουσιν (= 'eject'), which is a
mistranslation, but it may be influenced by the use of the root זעם
(= 'be indignant') later in the verse, or even be transferred from
Aquila's translation of that word. In Sir 13.3 the unique προσ-
ενεβριμήσατο (= 'he even adds reproaches', RSV) translates יתנוה, a
form not used elsewhere, which probably means 'boasts himself' or
'takes pride in it'. Thus the idea of anger is not present here.

In the later revisions it is clear that Aquila chose ἐμβριμᾶσθαι and
its cognates as his regular translation of Hebrew זעם (verb and
noun) = 'be indignant', often referring to the wrath of God as expressed in punitive action.[13] Though there are a couple of excep-
tions,[14] this accords with his method of distinguishing Hebrew
synonyms by using different Greek words, which are then used in
all cases. The LXX equivalent varies, but is usually ὀργή, ὀργίζω.
Symmachus follows Aquila in using ἐμβριμᾶσθαι in three places,[15]
but in Ezek 21.31(36) reads ἐμβρίμησις against Aquila, unless this is
really Aquila's reading here also. Theodotion has ἐμβρίμημα here,
but uniquely has ἐμβρίμησις in Isa 30.27 (which again may be dependent on Aquila, whose reading here is not preserved). This
leaves only one significant difference in the use of ἐμβριμᾶσθαι,
which will prove to be important for our present enquiry. This is
the fact that Symmachus uses it in Isa 7.13 for Hebrew נער = 'rebuke' (LXX ἀποσκοριάζειν, Aquila ἐπιτιμᾶν), and ἐμβρίμησις in

---

[12] Translation by J. M. Duffy, *Scholia in Hippocratis Prognosticon* (Berlin: Akademie,
1983) 60–1.

[13] Pss 7.12; 37(38).4; Jer 10.10; 15.17; Hos 7.16; probably also Num 23.8; Lam 2.6; Ezek
22.24.

[14] Ezek 21.31(36) (ἀπειλή = 'threat'); possibly Ps 7.12 (ἀπειλεῖν = 'threaten'), if this is to be
attributed to Aquila.

[15] Ps 37(38).4; Jer 15.17; Hos 7.16.

Ps 75(76).7 for the noun from the same root (LXX and Aquila ἐπιτίμησις).

The New Testament cases will be considered in more detail in the next section. This leaves only the use of the word in the church fathers. It is from their comments on the Septuagint passages that the readings of Aquila, etc., are chiefly known. In commenting on Ps 37(38).4, Basil implies that the word means rebuke by putting it in parallel with 'the threat (ἀπειλή) of your prophet Nathan', and with 'your fear' (φόβον).[16] On Ps 7.12 John Chrysostom says it means 'threatening, not punishing'.[17]

The comment of Origen on the Lazarus story, already mentioned, joins several of the above passages which show that ἐμβριμᾶσθαι with dative of the person means to rebuke. In fact it seems likely that this is how he understood ἐνεβριμήσατο τῷ πνεύματι in John 11.33, taking 'the spirit' to mean the source of the emotion of grief, which has been displayed by Mary and the Jews, but which Jesus on his part keeps within himself. So he 'rebuked (outward) emotion and upset himself (inwardly)'. However, after asking where Lazarus is laid, Jesus bursts into tears. So Origen says: 'While he is at a distance from the tomb "he rebuked the spirit". But when he has drawn near to the corpse, he no longer rebukes the spirit, but contains the rebuke in himself. So he says, "rebuking in himself (ἐμβριμώμενος ἐν ἑαυτῷ) he comes to the tomb". Again he rebukes emotion (ἐπιτιμᾷ τῷ πάθει), so that we may learn that he has become man like us unchangeably.'[18] Jesus' own expression of grief, coming between the rebuke and his self-restraint, gives an example to the people of curbing the emotions. It will be observed that Origen does not regard τῷ πνεύματι and ἐν ἑαυτῷ as synonymous phrases. Ἐμβρίμησις, as an emotion of Jesus recorded in the Gospels, comes in lists of his human passions in Epiphanius.[19] But

[16] *Hom. in Ps. 37*, MPG 30, 89–93, reproduced by Eusebius, MPG 23, 341.

[17] *Expositiones in Psalmos*, MPG 55, 95–6.

[18] My interpretation of the passage differs to some extent from Story's, who translates: 'no longer does he rebuke his spirit but he holds the rebuke in custody in himself . . . And again he rebukes (his) suffering' (οὐκέτι ἐμβριμᾶται τῷ πνεύματι, αλλὰ συνέχει ἐν ἑαυτῷ τὴν ἐμβρίμησιν . . . πάλιν δὲ ἐπιτιμᾷ τῷ πάθει). This is part of Origen's comment on v. 38. Unfortunately the comment on v. 33 has not survived, and therefore the referent of τῷ πνεύματι is not specified, and we do not know how Origen interpreted καὶ ἐτάραξεν ἑαυτὸν. But the final words, taking up πάλιν from the text, show that ἐπιτιμᾷ τῷ πάθει is his understanding of ἐνεβριμήσατο τῷ πνεύματι, and the fact that this is now something that Jesus does within himself suggests that the previous rebuke related to an outward act, whereas now it is his own example of self-restraint which constitutes a further rebuke.

[19] *Panarion* 69.19.7; 77.26.7.

Chrysostom, in his homilies on John, is clearly directly indebted to Origen and supports the above interpretation. On v. 33 he says: 'Then, rebuking passion (for that is what "he was angry at the spirit" means), he checked the emotion . . .'.[20] The last phrase appears to be his interpretation of καὶ ἐτάραξεν ἑαυτόν, for he goes on to say that Jesus asked where Lazarus was laid in a way that avoided any expression of grief. However, Jesus then wept and subsequently again rebuked the emotion in himself, thus proving his real humanity. Chrysostom gives a more descriptive idea of his understanding of ἐμβριμᾶσθαι in his comment on Matt 9.30: 'Then after the healing he ordered them not to speak to anyone; and not simply ordered, but with much vehemence. For, it says, Jesus rebuked (ἐνεβριμήσατο) them . . .'.[21]

This survey has shown that ἐμβριμᾶσθαι and its cognates refer to an aggressive style of behaviour rather than to the emotion of anger as such. The emphasis is on outward expression rather than on inward feeling. It is not to be assumed that it is always an expression of anger, for it may be used in connection with a stern warning. In his commentary on Aristotle's *Nichomachean Ethics*, Eustratius (11–12 cent.) places 'rebuke' (ἐπιτίμησις) between the more serious 'admonition' (νουθέτησις) and the milder 'exhortation' (παράκλησις). He then explains that '"admonition" is a sort of schoolmasterly discipline of persons, correcting the emotion, but "rebuke" is a sort of authoritative ἐμβρίμησις, frightening the unreasonably passionate person to curb desire, while "exhortation" is a word lovingly offered and gently bringing one back from the domination of uncontrolled passions.'[22] We have seen the same close connection of the word with the idea of administering a rebuke in several of the passages cited above, both biblical and secular. This does not really suit the usage in the Lazarus story as it stands in John. Even when the phrase is treated as verb and object (rebuking the spirit), the efforts of scholars both ancient and modern to make sense of it in the context are far from convincing. On the other hand this does provide the key to a fresh understanding of the underlying source.

---

[20] MPG 59, 350: Εἶτα ἐπιτιμήσας τῷ πάθει (τὸ γὰρ, 'Ενεβριμήσατο τῷ πνεύματι, τοῦτό ἐστιν) ἐπέσχε τὴν σύγχυσιν . . .

[21] *Hom. in Mattheum*, MPG 57, 378. The spurious *Hom. in Lazarum* 2, MPG 62, 777–8, understands the phrase to mean 'troubled in spirit'. It was then that Jesus prayed (referring to v. 41, which implies that Jesus has prayed earlier).

[22] *Commentary on the Nichomachean Ethics*, ed. G. Heylbut (1892) 119.

THE SOURCES OF THE LAZARUS STORY

The story of the raising of Lazarus is a brilliant and dramatic composition, which has clearly been built up by John from several sources. It is unnecessary for the purpose of this article to review the large number of theories which have been proposed, and which are summarized in the major commentaries. Here it need only be said that the setting of the family of Mary and Martha and Lazarus in Bethany presupposes that the anointing of Jesus at Bethany (John 12.3–8, closely parallel to Mark 14.3-9) has already been linked with Luke's story of Mary and Martha in Galilee (John 12.1–2, cf. Luke 10.38–42), and that the addition of Lazarus may well be derived from Luke's parable of the Rich Man and Lazarus (Luke 16.19–31), which includes the theme of resurrection from the dead. Neither of these, however, is enough to account for the actual story of the raising of a dead man by Jesus. The raising of Jairus' daughter (Mark 5.21–43) and of the son of the widow of Nain (Luke 7.11–17) provide precedents, but cannot be regarded as literary sources.

There has therefore been a tendency to assume that John had a special source which contained the nucleus of the Lazarus story in very much the same form as we have it now, but without the dialogues between Jesus and the disciples (11.4–16) and Martha (v. 20–27). On this view it is assigned to the Signs Source, which it is believed was a collection of miracle stories used by John for the narrative parts of the Gospel.[23] I do not wish to dispute the possibility that John used such a source, but I have always felt that it is a mistake to suppose that John has preserved what he found in the source almost intact, because that seriously underestimates the extent of his rewriting and recasting of his sources, which is everywhere apparent in the Gospel. In my own commentary on 11.1–44 I refused to trace any part of the central feature of raising the dead man to a source of this kind with the one exception of the verb ἐμβριμᾶσθαι. That seemed to me to be the only trace left of a pre-Johannine raising story.[24] In the light of our study of this word it now becomes possible to discover a little more of it. We shall see that it has a profound effect on our understanding of John's use of sources, and also opens the way to a much needed correction to the Signs Source theory as well.

---

[23] See most recently R. T. Fortna, *The Fourth Gospel and its Predecessor* (Edinburgh: T. & T. Clark, 1989) 94–109.

[24] *The Gospel of John*, 398; also *Behind the Fourth Gospel* (London: SPCK, 1971) 58.

Let us first turn our attention to the three places where the word is used in the Synoptic Gospels and to comparable passages, beginning with Mark. The most straightforward passage, interestingly, is in the anointing at Bethany, Mark 14.5. Some people were indignant at the waste of the costly ointment, and they ἐνεβριμῶντο αὐτῇ ('reproached her', RSV). It is the normal construction of the verb with dative of the person, meaning to rebuke someone, and to do so vehemently, as Chrysostom pointed out in another context.

Mark 1.43 is more complex. Here Jesus has just cleansed a leper, and then we are told, 'rebuking him (ἐμβριμησάμενος αὐτῷ), he at once cast him out'. This is such a rough way of treating the man, that it has to be assumed that Mark means that Jesus 'sternly charged him and sent him away at once' (RSV). The man is told to tell no one about the miraculous cure. Those who are familiar with the criticism of Mark will know at once that we have here one of the great themes of Mark's Gospel, the messianic secret. Mark shows Jesus as hiding his messianic identity, which is only gradually revealed to the disciples. On the other hand the demons know who he is, and when confronted by Jesus say so. There has just been an example of this in Mark 1.24. Jesus is about to exorcize an unclean spirit (πνεῦμα ἀκάθαρτον, v. 23), and so in the next verse we are told that he 'rebuked it (ἐπετίμησεν αὐτῷ), and said, "Be silent and come out of him".' In the light of this parallel we should seriously consider the possibility that this is the proper context of Jesus' rebuke in v. 43 in Mark's source. He has dropped the idea that the leper's disease was caused by an unclean spirit or demon, and transferred Jesus' address to the spirit to the man himself in order to take further his theme of the messianic secret. The vocabulary of v. 25 and v. 43 is almost identical, and the words are far more suitable as a rebuke to the demon than as an unreasonably aggressive warning to the man who has just been cured. In fact the whole verse makes better sense if it is applied to the unclean spirit: Jesus 'rebuked it and at once cast it out' (cf. v. 39). If this is correct, the publicity mentioned in v. 43 was not originally an act of disobedience on the man's part, but simply the normal reaction to a miracle of this kind.

Matthew does not use ἐμβριμᾶσθαι in his parallel to Mark 1.43 (i.e. Matt 8.4), but he introduces it in a similar way in Matt 9.30. This story of the healing of two blind men is peculiar to Matthew, and may well be a substitute for the gradual healing of a blind man in Mark 8.22–26, which Matthew omits. It appears to be a pastiche of several healing traditions in Mark, and so its value as independent evidence for the use of the word is doubtful. The anecdote ends with a warning to the men to keep silence, as in the Marcan tradition at Mark 8.26, but using the vocabulary of Mark 1.43–5: 'And Jesus ἐνεβριμήθη them, saying, "See that no one knows it!" But they went out and published (διεφήμισαν, cf. Mark 1.45) [the news about] him throughout that country.' Matthew had omitted Mark 1.45 in his parallel at 8.4. The meaning in Matt 9.30 can only be a solemn warning or threat. The two men have been cured as a result of their confession of faith, which is the chief motif of the composition.[25] There are no possible grounds for anger on the part of Jesus. Thus Matthew has taken over from Mark 1.43 not only the word, but also the context and meaning of it, which, as suggested above, was probably not its meaning in Mark's source. On the other hand it is not a misuse of the word, which, as we have seen in the examples above, can denote a threat or threatening behaviour.

If we are right in assuming that the verb was originally applied to the casting out of an unclean spirit, the choice of this rare word is more easily accounted for. Elsewhere the usual word for 'rebuke' (ἐπιτιμᾶν) is used, but ἐμβριμᾶσθαι conveys a more vivid idea of the energy and forcefulness with which Jesus confronted the demons which were popularly supposed to be responsible for sickness.[26] This suggests that the whole of John's phrase, ἐνεβριμήσατο τῷ πνεύματι, is derived from John's source, which was an exorcism story in which Jesus 'rebuked the spirit'. It will now be argued that a closer look at two exorcisms in Mark can contribute further to the reconstruction of John's source.

First, we may refer again to Mark 1.23–6. Here words which are relevant to the reconstruction are italicised (translation from RSV):

> There was in their synagogue *a man with an* unclean *spirit*; and he *cried out* . . . But Jesus *rebuked* (ἐπετίμησεν) *him*, saying, 'Be silent, and *come out* of him!' And the unclean spirit, convulsing him and *crying with a loud voice*, came out of him.

All these features are also found in the more elaborate exorcism of the epileptic boy in Mark 9.14–29. The final verses (25–9) are relevant:

> Jesus . . . *rebuked the* unclean *spirit*, saying to it, 'You dumb and deaf spirit, I command you, *come out* of him, and never enter him again.' And after *crying out* and convulsing him terribly, it *came out*, and the boy was

---

[25] Cf. the redaction-critical analysis of Held in G. Bornkamm, G. Barth and H. J. Held, *Tradition and Interpretation in Matthew* (London: SCM, 1963) 223–5.

[26] C. Bonner, 'Traces of Thaumaturgic Technique in the Miracles', *HTR* 20 (1927) 171–81, cited classical examples for such abnormal energy, which he felt was readily comprehensible in the case of the Lazarus story in view of the 'portentous miracle' involved.

like a *corpse*; so that most of them said, '*He is dead*.' But Jesus took him by the hand and *lifted him up* (ἤγειρεν), *and he arose* (ἀνέστη) . . . And he said to them, 'This kind cannot be driven out by anything but *prayer*.'

In this second example the expulsion of the spirit is combined with an act which is comparable to (and actually thought to be) a case of the raising of a dead person. The use of ἤγειρεν and ἀνέστη in v. 27 suggests that the comparison is deliberate. If a similar episode lies behind the Lazarus story, it must be assumed that the rebuke to the spirit and the command to come out of the boy, which is followed by the raising of the boy as if from death, have been adapted as follows: (a) The rebuke (ἐνεβριμήσατο τῷ πνεύματι, v. 33) becomes Jesus' own emotional reaction in the face of the general grief. (b) The command to the spirit to come out of the boy becomes a command to Lazarus to come out of the tomb (ἐξῆλθεν, v. 44, cf. Mark 1.26; 9.25, 26). (c) The loud voice is transferred from the spirit speaking through the boy to Jesus himself (φωνῇ μεγάλῃ ἐκραύγασεν, v. 43, cf. Mark 1.23, 26; 9.26). (d) The coming out of the spirit and the raising up of the boy have been combined in the coming out of Lazarus from the tomb (v. 44). (e) The 'death' and 'resurrection' of the boy have been used earlier in the dialogue of Jesus and Martha (vv. 21–7). (f) The connection of the exorcism with prayer is referred to in v. 41–2.

It can thus be conjectured that John's story retains traces of a tradition of an exorcism by Jesus, in which the crippling effect of the spirit or demon, and the new life resulting from the exorcism, have already been compared with death and resurrection, no doubt in connection with the use of the story in catechesis. Although these traces have been isolated by comparison with passages in Mark, it is clear that John was not building directly on Mark, as Neirynck maintains.[27] For the crucial phrase for rebuking the spirit (ἐνεβριμήσατο τῷ πνεύματι) appears in Mark only in a secondary position (ἐμβριμησάμενος αὐτῷ, 1.43), where Mark has abandoned the connection of the healing with exorcism and transferred the rebuke to form a warning to the man who has been cured. John has it in its proper connection with an exorcism, though he has used it differently. This is thus a case where it can be asserted with a high degree of confidence that John had access to Synoptic-type traditions which were not identical with the forms of the same or similar traditions in the Synoptic Gospels themselves.[28]

---

[27] F. Neirynck, 'John and the Synoptics', *L'Évangile de Jean* (ed. M. de Jonge; BETL 44; Gembloux: Duculot, 1977) 73–106 [= *Evangelica*, 1982, 365–389].

[28] Cf. B. Lindars, 'John and the Synoptic Gospels: A Test Case', *NTS* 27 (1981) 287–94. It is

These observations on the sources of the Lazarus story need to be taken into account in further work on the theory of a Signs Source. It is one of the weaknesses of current reconstructions of the source that it is supposed not to have included an exorcism, simply because none is reproduced in John. But if it was a collection of popular memories of Jesus it is altogether probable that at least one of the stories was of this type, seeing that casting out demons is such a prominent feature of the Synoptic tradition.[29] Moreover recognition of the possibility that the Lazarus story is based on such a tradition points to the need for a far more rigorous and radical approach to the question of the sources behind the Fourth Gospel.

JOHN'S USE OF THE TRADITION

John created the story of Lazarus out of several items in the tradition with which he was familiar, using all his skill to make the most impressive demonstration of the lordship of Jesus as Son of God (11.4) over life and death. If the sources available to him included a story comparable to Mark 9.14–29, he had a tradition which had already been adapted to illustrate the Christian teaching on death and resurrection. But instead of describing the cure of a demon-possessed boy as a model which is then applied to death and resurrection, John adapted the tradition to depict an actual case of raising a dead man. It is not necessary to assume that he disapproved of attributing exorcism to Jesus, for he uses the language of demon possession without difficulty in 8.48, and Jesus' own death and resurrection win the victory over Satan (12.31). It is enough to suppose that the exorcism account was the best tradition for his purpose which was available to him. However it could not be used without considerable adaptation. Lazarus must be really dead, not a demon-possessed man looking as if he is dead. To expel the demon would not necessarily bring him back to life again. The object is achieved, not by a command to the demon to come out of the man, but by a command to the man himself to come out of

---

of course true that Mark has ἐνεβριμῶντο αὐτῇ in the anointing at Bethany (Mark 14.5), which is one of the sources for the scenario of the Lazarus story. But it seems to me very unlikely that he would take the word from this source and substitute it for ἐπιτιμᾶν in the exorcism story. As so often in Johannine study, complete certainty is impossible to attain.

[29] It is the basis of the Beelzebul controversy, Mark 3.22–30, combined with Q parallels in Matthew 12 and Luke 11, and is the subject of numerous editorial summaries. In general on this issue see Morton Smith, *Jesus the Magician* (London: Gollancz, 1978).

the grave. John agrees with the source that Jesus can do this only because of reliance on prayer to God.

According to the source, Jesus rebuked the spirit before commanding it to come out of the man. This is not possible in John's adaptation. Instead he uses this item as part of the build-up towards the climax. Thus, in spite of the interruptions in vv. 34–7 and 38b–42, he is aware of the connection between it and the command which follows it.[30] In fact what he has done is to build up this item into a separate motif. Jesus' energetic rebuke of the spirit becomes a display of emotion which serves a different function in the story. Here it must be insisted again that the context is decisive for the translation 'deeply moved', in spite of all the arguments to the contrary. Disregarding the fact that the phrase clearly meant 'rebuking the spirit' in the source, John builds around it a scene of grief. It is designed to bring Jesus to the tomb without revealing his real intention until the last possible moment. Everyone weeps, including Jesus himself. This naturally evokes the opinion that he has been powerless to save Lazarus (v. 37). It also provides a pretext for Jesus to ask to be taken to the tomb (v. 34), and even to have the stone removed from the entrance (v. 39), for it can be assumed that his motive is only to take a last look at his friend. Only then does Jesus reveal that the people are about to see a display of the glory of God, and he prays that it may not fail in its evangelistic purpose (vv. 40–2). From a narrative point of view these verses hide Jesus' intention from the bystanders, but from the point of view of the readers, who know what Jesus is going to do, they create suspense and add to the effectiveness of the climax. The motif of anger does not come into the story.

That John wishes ἐνεβριμήσατο τῷ πνεύματι to mean 'moved in spirit', treating the dative as adverbial and not as the object, is indicated by the addition of the synonymous phrase καὶ ἐτάραξεν ἑαυτόν ('and he troubled himself') immediately after it. The two phrases are then combined in the words ἐμβριμώμενος ἐν ἑαυτῷ ('being moved in himself') in v. 38. John always uses ταράσσειν elsewhere to denote inward anxiety or grief (12.27; 13.21; 14.1, 27).

The question which must now be asked is whether John simply misunderstood the source and reproduced what he thought that it meant, or deliberately altered the meaning, and the syntax of

---

[30] Schnackenburg suggests that the repetition of ἐμβριμᾶσθαι in v. 38 is a sign that the intervening verses 34–7 are an insertion into the source, which is here resumed from v. 33. But the composition seems to me to require a more radical interpretation.

the phrase, for the sake of his composition. It is possible that he genuinely thought that τῷ πνεύματι was adverbial, as he could have taken it to mean that Jesus was moved in spirit when giving the command to the demon to come out of the man in the original tradition. On the other hand this may be a case where he has taken advantage of an ambiguity in the Greek to build up the source into what he needs for his dramatic presentation. For he seems to have done the same thing in 3.3–5, where ἄνωθεν probably meant 'again' in his source, but is used by John to mean 'from above', which is the crucial idea for the whole of the discourse which then follows.[31]

Our study of ἐμβριμᾶσθαι has shown that, though the word often refers to anger or indignation, its primary application is to vehement expression of emotion, and can denote behaviour of this kind without necessarily revealing the inward state of the subject. Thus it is used in contexts where the action is a threat or verbal rebuke, which may be a stern approach required by the situation, but is not necessarily prompted by a feeling of anger at all. This is surely true of the occasions when Jesus rebuked the unclean spirits, opposing them with great forcefulness and authority, but prompted inwardly, not by anger, but by compassion for the sufferer. As the exorcisms are popular impressions of the impact of Jesus on society in his preaching ministry, we cannot tell how far they represent what actually happened, how they relate to healing mechanisms in the light of modern medical knowledge, or what was really Jesus' state of mind in performing them. His vehement rebuke of the demons, in so far as it is historical, attests a factual matter, not a mental state.

John could have created this dramatic scene without using the disputed ἐμβριμᾶσθαι at all. But it is characteristic of his method of narrative composition to build on words or phrases in his sources, and when he does so he usually makes use of such a word more than once.[32] Hence the repetition of ἐμβριμᾶσθαι in v. 38. In this case he has been inspired to build a magnificent demonstration of the power of Jesus over life and death at a climactic point in his theological presentation of the gospel message, using an example of

---

[31] This is argued in my article referred to in n. 28 above [in this volume, pp. 105-112].

[32] Thus 'your son lives' in 4.50 is the basis of the additional episode, giving confirmation of the miracle, in vv. 51–3, in which the same words are repeated twice. In 20.24–9 the Thomas episode has been created out of a tradition closely related to Luke 24.36–43, and has repetitions in vv. 25 and 27 of words used in v. 20, cf. my 'The Composition of John 20', *NTS* 7 (1960) 142–7 [in this volume, pp. 3-9].

exorcism from the tradition which has already been pressed into service to make this point, as in Mark 9.26–7. It is because he changed the force of the traditional information that Jesus 're-buked the spirit' that his words have caused so much controversy among modern commentators. Perhaps this new study of the problem will exorcize this particular spirit at last.

14

CAPERNAUM REVISITED
JOHN 4,46-53 AND THE SYNOPTICS

In his opening address at the Colloquium Biblicum Lovaniense, 1990, Frans Neirynck referred to his own position with regard to the vexed question of the relationship between the Fourth Gospel and the Synoptic Gospels. He made it clear that, although he thinks that sections of the Fourth Gospel are directly indebted to one or other of them, he does not exclude the use of oral tradition and other source material. He concluded his paper with the thought that redaction criticism of John has revealed the complexity of John's use of sources, but this does not exclude his use of the Synoptics. This possibility must still be addressed by source critics. "The Johannine redaction", he said, "will appear to be a more complex process of gospel writing, but this complexity has its own attractiveness, at least to me". It is in response to this judgment, and in grateful recognition of Neirynck's distinguished work in the field of gospel criticism, that I have pleasure in offering this essay as a contribution to the collection in his honour.

It is my belief that progress in the source criticism of the Fourth Gospel can be made only by a more rigorous analysis of John's compositional methods in relation to sources than has been attempted hitherto. For this purpose it is necessary to begin with the synoptic parallels, because these alone provide the possibility of objective comparisons. Moreover, it is necessary to start with a completely open mind about the question of dependence, so as not to prejudge the issues. The situation is not like the triple tradition, in which (according to the two-source hypothesis) we have in Mark the source which has been redacted independently by Matthew and Luke, but more like Q, in which the common source has to be reconstructed by applying the results of redaction criticism.

From this point of view the story of the Healing of the Official's Son (Jn 4,46-53) is particularly interesting. The synoptic parallel, the story of the Healing of the Centurion's Servant, is the only miracle story in Q (Mt 8,5-13 = Lk 7,1-10). There are considerable differences between the two versions of it in Matthew and Luke, apart from the main speech of the centurion and Jesus' response, which are almost word-for-word the same. This has led a number of scholars to assert that this section is the only part of the story which was found in Q, so that each evangelist has supplied his own introduction and conclusion. As this section appears to be completely missing from John 4,46-53, it can then be assumed that there is no connection between John and the Q story at all. On the other hand it is hard to deny that they are different versions of the same tradition. In fact a fresh examination of the relationship between them, which was intended to clarify John's use of sources, has opened the way to a new reconstruction of the Q story itself, as will be shown below. John thus appears to be on a level with Matthew and Luke as far as this pericope is concerned, making his own contribution to research into Q, which has been largely conducted without his aid. At the same time this comparative study has consequences for further research into the relationship between the Fourth Gospel and the sources which lie behind it.

It may be thought unduly bold to trespass on ground which Neirynck has himself worked over, producing results with which I find myself in agreement to a considerable extent[1]. But more needs to be said, and it is for this reason that it has seemed right to make a fresh visit to Capernaum and explore once more the underlying layers of this memorable tradition[2].

I. FALSE TRACKS

Though a connection between these stories in John and Q has been often claimed, the tendency of recent study has been to deny that this is close enough for fruitful verbal comparisons to be made. For instance, the major work of Schulz on Q gives eleven pages to the reconstruction of the story underlying Matthew and Luke, but makes no mention of John's story at all[3]. Similarly neither Polag nor Schenk take John into account[4]. Wegner, on the other hand, examines the obvious verbal parallels between John and Matthew/Luke, but concludes, in line with most commentators on the Fourth Gospel, that John is independent of the Synoptic tradition and so makes no contribution to the recovery of Q[5]. It does not seem to occur to any of these scholars that, if John is independent of the Synoptics, he may preserve traces of the original which might have a bearing on the reconstruction of Q.

1. F. NEIRYNCK, *John 4,46-54. Signs Source and/or Synoptic Gospels*, in *ETL* 60 (1984) 367-375 (= *Evangelica II*, 1991, pp. 677-687, 687-688: Additional Note).
2. For a brief preliminary visit, see B. LINDARS, *Traditions behind the Fourth Gospel*, in M. DE JONGE (ed.), *L'Évangile de Jean. Sources, rédaction, théologie* (BETL, 44), Gembloux, Duculot - Leuven, University Press, 1977 (²1987), pp. 109-124; ID., *The Gospel of John* (NCB), London, Oliphants, 1972, *ad loc.*
3. S. SCHULZ, *Q. Die Spruchquelle der Evangelisten*, Zürich, Theologischer Verlag, 1972, pp. 236-246.
4. A. POLAG, *Fragmenta Q. Textheft zur Logienquelle*, Neukirchen-Vluyn, Neukirchener, ²1982; W. SCHENK, *Synopse zur Redenquelle der Evangelien*, Düsseldorf, Patmos, 1981.
5. U. WEGNER, *Der Hauptmann von Kapernaum* (WUNT, II/14), Tübingen, Mohr, 1985, pp. 33-37.

Recognition of the value of John from this point of view has been hindered by presuppositions of Johannine study which have almost been raised to the status of unquestionable principles. In the first place, the popularity of the Signs Source theory has led most scholars to assume that John drew the story from this source and not from Q. Of course it is this very story which is the most potent reason why the Signs Source theory has been so widely accepted, because it is explicitly related to the Marriage at Cana and listed as the second sign (Jn 4,54). However, even if the theory of a Signs Source is accepted (and I agree with Neirynck in regarding it as very doubtful), this verse is clearly editorial, whether it belongs to the source or not[6], and must be set aside in analysing the pericope in relation to both source criticism and form criticism. This initial presupposition has led to a tendency to emphasize the differences between John and Q, so that little attempt has been made to estimate the full extent of the links between them. This tendency can be seen in Dodd's *Historical Tradition in the Fourth Gospel*, which has exerted considerable influence, especially among English-speaking scholars[7]. However, Fortna's reconstruction of the Signs Source interestingly does make some use of the synoptic story to fill in gaps left by the exclusion of obvious Johannisms, but it fails to convince, because it depends on unsatisfactory criteria for isolating the source from the extensive rewriting and recasting which is characteristic of John[8]. Emphasis on the differences between John and the Synoptics is bad methodology, because John's source is an unknown quantity, and there is no intrinsic reason why the version of the tradition available to him should not have been virtually identical with Q. The common material between John and the Synoptics is more likely to form a basis for reconstruction than the differences, which may be due to the redactional work of any of the three evangelists concerned and not to a different form of the source.

The preoccupation with special sources for John also leads to very complex theories, such as those of Heekerens and Dauer, which presuppose an intermediate stage between the Synoptic Gospels (or Q) and the final Johannine redaction[9]. The criticism of these theories by Neirynck

6. It is attributed to John himself, along with 2,11, by W.J. BITTNER, *Jesu Zeichen im Johannesevangelium* (WUNT, II/26), Tübingen, Mohr, 1987, p. 6.

7. C.H. DODD, *Historical Tradition in the Fourth Gospel*, Cambridge, University Press, 1963, pp. 188-195.

8. R.T. FORTNA, *The Gospel of Signs. A Reconstruction of the Narrative Source Underlying the Fourth Gospel* (SNTS MS, 11), Cambridge, University Press, 1970; ID., *The Fourth Gospel and Its Predecessor. From Narrative Source to Present Gospel*, Edinburgh, Clark, 1989.

9. H.-P. HEEKERENS, *Die Zeichen-Quelle der johanneischen Redaktion. Ein Beitrag zur Entstehungsgeschichte des vierten Evangeliums* (SBS, 113), Stuttgart, Katholisches Bibelwerk, 1984; A. DAUER, *Johannes und Lukas. Untersuchungen zu den johanneisch-lukanischen Parallelperikopen Joh 4,46-54 / Lk 7,1-10 – Joh 12,1-8 / Lk 7,36-50; 10, 38-42 – Joh 20,19-29 / Lk 24,36-49* (FzB, 60), Würzburg, Echter, 1984.

in the article already mentioned is entirely on the right lines, and makes it unnecessary for me to deal with them here.

Another factor which has inhibited progress is the tendency to confuse source criticism and form criticism. Dodd pointed out that John's story has a formal resemblance to the story of the Syrophoeni-cian's Daughter in Mk 7,24-30 = Mt 15,21-28[10]. Thus the sick girl is not present when her mother makes her appeal for help. Jesus' first response amounts to a rebuff. The mother persists in her appeal, and Jesus commends her persuasive wit (in Matthew her great faith), and grants her request. On her return home she finds that her daughter is cured. It can be argued that this story has provided the form of John's retelling of the tradition. Boismard, who accepted from Dodd the idea of a connection between them[11], has recently restated the case for John's dependence on it even more strongly, claiming that it is his primary source, and the Q story is only a secondary influence[12]. However, it must be objected that this can be true only in the sense that the Syrophoenician's Daughter may have provided the basic *model* for John's composition. It is not a source in the sense of a literary unity which has been taken over and adapted by means of editorial changes. The verbal contacts are minimal. But we shall need to keep it in mind for comparative purposes, because redactional elements are liable to be repeated by the same evangelist (e.g., Mt 8,13 is almost identical with Mt 15,28), and there can be cross-fertilization from one pericope to another. So we shall also see the influence of Mk 5,25-43 on the redaction of the Centurion's Servant in Matthew and Luke.

II. JOHN AND THE CENTURION'S SERVANT

These reflections lead to the conclusion that the best approach is to start from the assumption that John's story is based on a written form of the Centurion's Servant, similar to the forms which were available in Matthew and Luke, if not identical with one of them. Before coming to detailed comparisons we may observe the chief distinguishing features of John's composition.

10. Bultmann (*The History of the Synoptic Tradition*, Oxford, University Press, 1968, pp. 38f.) had already drawn attention to the parallel between this story and the Centurion's Servant, and even suggested that "the two stories are variants", but he did not refer to John. In the commentary (*The Gospel of John*, Oxford, University Press, 1971, p. 205) he mentions the parallel, but assumes that John has adapted a version of the Centurion's Servant which cannot now be recovered.

11. M.-É. BOISMARD, *Saint Luc et la rédaction du quatrième évangile (Jn iv, 46-54)*, in *RB* 69 (1962) 185-211.

12. *Jn 4,46-54 et les parallèles synoptiques*, in A. DENAUX, *John and the Synoptics* (BETL, 101), Leuven, University Press - Peeters, 1992, pp. 239-259.

In the first place, it is evident that John wishes to exclude the issue of Jesus' attitude to the Gentiles, which is a principle motive in the Q story. He uses the story in a context of universal mission in which the distinction between Jew and Gentile is no longer relevant (Jn 4,21-24.42). This explains the change from ἑκατοντάρχης to βασιλικός, as the former would certainly be a Gentile, but the latter might just as well be a Jew[13]. The same factor also accounts for the omission of Jesus' commendation of the centurion's faith, in which the contrast with the Jews is expressed. Secondly, faith remains an essential motif for John, and is even enhanced by him, but the object of faith differs. In the Q story it is faith *that* Jesus can cure the patient without even going to the house. Jesus marvels at the centurion's faith, but the reader marvels at Jesus' miraculous power. But for John faith is directed *to* Jesus as the giver of life, and the episode is intended to evoke confession of faith in him as the saviour of the world (cf. v. 42). This different concept of faith explains the actual treatment of faith in John's revised form of the story. He brings the issue to the front by making it the subject of Jesus' response to the initial request for healing (v. 48). Finally, John stresses the decisive character of the miracle by increasing the distance between Jesus and the sick boy, which provides the opportunity for a confirmatory episode to prove that his recovery was simultaneous with Jesus' response to the official.

In spite of these drastic changes, comparison with the Synoptics shows that John has retained a great deal of the wording of the source. In the following tables allowance has been made for necessary changes, e.g., second-person pronouns and verb forms are treated as equivalents of third-person forms if the redaction does away with direct speech. On this basis the words underlined in the John column can be regarded as taken from the source. Italic with underlining denotes a Johannine substitute for a word with similar meaning in the source. In the Matthew and Luke columns the corresponding words are underlined if they belong to the source, and substitute-words are italic with underlining, but no attempt has been made to account for words which have no counterparts in John.

The official's request (Jn 4,46-47)

Mt 8,5-7	Lk 7,1-3	Jn 4,46-47
5 εἰσελθόντος δὲ αὐτοῦ εἰς Καφαρναούμ προσῆλθεν αὐτῷ	1 ... εἰσῆλθεν εἰς Καφαρναούμ	46 *ἦλθεν* οὖν πάλιν εἰς *τὴν Κανὰ τῆς Γαλιλαίας* ὅπου ἐποίησεν τὸ ὕδωρ οἶνον

---

13. Cf. C.K. Barrett (*ad loc.*), suggesting that the word could refer to a civilian in the service of Herod Antipas.

ἑκατόνταρχος	2 ἑκατοντάρχου δέ τινος	καὶ ἦν τις βασιλικὸς
παρακαλῶν αὐτὸν		
6 καὶ λέγων·		
κύριε, ὁ παῖς μου	δοῦλος	οὗ ὁ υἱὸς
βέβληται ἐν τῇ οἰκίᾳ	κακῶς ἔχων	ἠσθένει
παραλυτικὸς	ἤμελλεν τελευτᾶν ...	ἐν Καφαρναούμ
δεινῶς βασανιζόμενος	3 ἀκούσας δὲ περὶ τοῦ	47 οὗτος ἀκούσας ὅτι
7 λέγει αὐτῷ· ἐγὼ	Ἰησοῦ ... ἐρωτῶν αὐτὸν	Ἰησοῦς ἥκει ἐκ τῆς Ἰου-
		δαίας εἰς τὴν
ἐλθὼν	ὅπως ἐλθὼν	Γαλιλαίαν, ἀπῆλθεν πρὸς
		αὐτὸν καὶ ἠρώτα
θεραπεύσω	διασώσῃ	ἵνα καταβῇ καὶ ἰάσηται
αὐτόν.	τὸν δοῦλον αὐτοῦ.	αὐτοῦ τὸν υἱὸν ἤμελλεν
		γὰρ ἀποθνῄσκειν.

In Jn 4,46 the alteration of Jesus' movements explains ἦλθεν for the original εἰσῆλθεν and the transference of Καφαρναούμ to the end of the verse. On the other hand John's καὶ ἦν τις may well be original, as it is a good narrative opening (cf. Jn 1,6; 11,1). If so, Luke has improved the style by using the genitive. Matthew as usual abbreviates the source. After making the opening words a genitive absolute, he brings the centurion to Jesus without any explanation of the circumstances, which then have to be included in the centurion's request. For the sick person it is widely held that Matthew preserves the original παῖς, varied to δοῦλος in Luke and υἱός in John, though both retain παῖς at other points in the story. The description of the sickness in Matthew is not likely to be original (see next paragraph). The colloquial expression κακῶς ἔχων in Luke should be accepted, as he retains it in 5,31 when reproducing a source (i.e., Mk 2,17), but does not introduce it elsewhere, whereas John's ἠσθένει is his regular word for sickness (cf. 11,1-6).

It is difficult to decide whether Luke's ἤμελλεν τελευτᾶν is correctly placed, or John's position is original, where it adds urgency to the man's request. But τελευτᾶν is not common in Luke (only here and Acts 2,29; 7,15), whereas John's ἤμελλεν ἀποθνῄσκειν reappears in 11,51; 12,33; 18,32 (τελευτᾶν only in 11,39). Matthew's δεινῶς βασανιζόμενος could well be a substitute for this phrase (cf. 8,29, derived from Mk 5,7), and ἐν τῇ οἰκίᾳ may be taken from a sentence which he has omitted, as will be shown below.

In Jn 4,47 ἀκούσας comes from the source, as shown by the Lucan parallel, but the ὅτι clause represents a rewriting of the opening in v. 46. This alters the meaning, as the news is not the fame of Jesus as a healer (John takes this for granted), but his return to the locality. It is probable that Matthew has suppressed this item for the sake of brevity. Moreover Matthew's προσῆλθεν αὐτῷ accords with Matthean usage, and so has less claim to originality than John's ἀπῆλθον πρὸς αὐτόν, which is very common in Matthew, used rarely by Mark and Luke, but found elsewhere in John only at 12,21. Luke's evidence fails at this point because of his insertion of the deputation of Jews. After this, Luke and John agree in the use of ἐρωτάω against Matthew παρακαλῶν αὐτόν, which, however, is more likely to be original. The agreement could be due to John's use of Luke, but this cannot be regarded as certain, because both evangelists frequently use ἐρωτάω, whereas παρακαλέω is never used by John and Luke uses it in the sense of making a request only in Lk 8,31.32.41, where he is reproducing Mark. Elsewhere in Luke it has the sense of urge or exhort, as also often in Acts, and he actually uses it in this way here in Lk 7,4, presumably by the influence of the source. Moreover John differs from Luke in omitting the object αὐτόν. John's form of the final clause naturally has καταβῇ for ἐλθών of the source.

Of the three words for healing John's ἰάσηται may well preserve the original verb against the others. Matthew retains it in verses 8 and 13 (cf. Lk 7,7), but otherwise has it only in a quotation in 13,15 and in the ending of the Syrophoenician's Daughter, 15,28 probably dependent on 8,13. His usual word is θεραπεύω, as here. Luke's διασώσῃ, also found only here in the gospel, is used five times in Acts, and in both books σῴζω is common as an alternative (Matthew has διασώζω only at 14,36 = Mk 6,56, σῴζω). Luke likes variation, and uses both ἰάομαι and θεραπεύω several times.

Jesus demurs (Jn 4,48-49)

Mt 8,10	Lk 7,9	Jn 4,48-49
10 ἀκούσας δὲ	9 ἀκούσας δὲ ταῦτα	48 εἶπεν οὖν ὁ Ἰησοῦς πρὸς αὐτόν· ἐὰν μὴ
ὁ Ἰησοῦς ἐθαύμασεν	ὁ Ἰησοῦς ἐθαύμασεν	σημεῖα καὶ τέρατα ἴδητε,
καὶ εἶπεν τοῖς	αὐτὸν καὶ στραφεὶς τῷ	οὐ μὴ πιστεύσητε
ἀκολουθοῦσιν·	ἀκολουθοῦντι αὐτῷ ὄχλῳ	49 λέγει πρὸς αὐτὸν ὁ
ἀμὴν λέγω ὑμῖν, παρ'	εἶπεν· λέγω ὑμῖν,	βασιλικός· κύριε, κατάβηθι
οὐδενὶ τοσαυτὴν πίστιν	οὐδὲ ἐν τῷ Ἰσραὴλ	πρὶν ἀποθανεῖν τὸ
ἐν τῷ Ἰσραὴλ εὖρον.	τοσαυτὴν πίστιν εὖρον.	παιδίον μου.

John's version of Jesus' response demands explanation. At first sight it has no basis in the Q story. However, the clue is provided by the theme of faith, which comes near the end in Q. John takes this up, using, as always, the verb (cf. Mt 8,13 ἐπίστευσεν). But the same verse also includes the idea of wonder. From this point of view John's σημεῖα καὶ τέρατα ἴδητε is a substitute for ἐθαύμασεν in the source. John has transferred the idea from Jesus himself to the wider audience. The plural verbs indicate that the words are spoken τῷ ἀκολουθοῦντι αὐτῷ ὄχλῳ (cf. the plural verbs in 1,51; 3,11). 'Signs and wonders' is a conventional phrase in the vocabulary of mission (cf. Acts 2,22.43; 4,30; 5,12, etc., Rom 15,19; 2 Cor 12,12; Heb 2,4), and so relates to the larger context of John 4.

There has been much discussion about the relationship between this apparently unsatisfactory form of faith and the faith which is the climax at the end of the pericope (v. 53). Brown (Anchor Bible ad loc.) traces a progression towards full faith, which the episode is intended to teach, but v. 50 already shows the true response. The real point in v. 48 is that it is faith based on sight (ἴδητε). People may 'believe into' Jesus in the Johannine sense, and so have what appears to be full faith, if they actually see him perform a miracle, such as the official has requested. But what Jesus requires is faith in him as the giver of life even when there is no visible action on his part. Hence his refusal to go down to Capernaum. Thus the motif is in line with the central feature of the underlying story, in which the centurion refuses to allow Jesus to enter his house. John has created an alternative to this crucial item in order to adapt the story to promote his own concept of faith. But his version presupposes the dialogue of Mt 8,8-10 = Lk 7,6-9 as its point of departure.

Having inserted this intervention of Jesus into the source, John must also make the official respond to him. Characteristically John does this in v. 49 by reproducing the source-material which he has already used in v. 47. However, the repetition serves a positive purpose, because it emphasizes the imminent death of the boy. John is not really interested in the story as a miracle of healing, but as an example of the lordship of Jesus over death and life. This at once becomes apparent in the following verse.

Jesus gives life (Jn 4,50-51)

Mt 8,8-9	Lk 7,6-8	Jn 4,50-51
	6 ὁ δὲ Ἰησοῦς ἐπορεύετο σὺν *αὐτοῖς*. ἤδη δὲ αὐτοῦ οὐ μακρὰν ἀπέχοντος ἀπὸ	
8 ἀποκριθεὶς δὲ ὁ ἑκατόνταρχος ἔφη· κύριε,	τῆς οἰκίας, ἔπεμψεν φίλους ὁ ἑκατοντάρχης λέγων αὐτῷ· κύριε, μὴ	50 λέγει αὐτῷ ὁ Ἰησοῦς·
οὐκ εἰμὶ ἱκανὸς ἵνα μου ὑπὸ τὴν στέγην εἰσέλθης·	σκύλλου· οὐ γὰρ ἱκανός εἰμι ἵνα ὑπὸ τὴν στέγην μου εἰσέλθης· 7 διὸ οὐδὲ ἐμαυτὸν ἠξίωσα πρὸς σὲ	πορεύου, ὁ υἱός σου ζῇ· ἐπίστευσεν ὁ ἄνθρωπος τῷ λόγῳ ὃν εἶπεν αὐτῷ ὁ Ἰησοῦς, καὶ ἐπορεύετο·
ἀλλὰ μόνον εἰπὲ λόγῳ, καὶ ἰαθήσεται ὁ παῖς μου. 9 καὶ γὰρ ἐγὼ ἄνθρωπός εἰμι ὑπὸ ἐξουσίαν,	ἐλθεῖν· ἀλλὰ εἰπὲ λόγῳ, καὶ ἰαθήτω ὁ παῖς μου. 8 καὶ γὰρ ἐγὼ ἄνθρωπός εἰμι ὑπὸ ἐξουσίαν τασσόμενος,	51 ἤδη δὲ αὐτοῦ καταβαίνοντος οἱ δοῦλοι ὑπήντησαν αὐτῷ λέγοντες ὅτι ὁ παῖς αὐτοῦ ζῇ

ἔχων ὑπ᾽ ἐμαυτὸν   ἔχων ὑπ᾽ ἐμαυτὸν
στρατιώτας, καὶ λέγω   στρατιώτας, καὶ λέγω
τούτῳ· πορεύθητι, καὶ   τούτῳ· πορεύθητι, καὶ
πορεύεται, καὶ ἄλλῳ·   πορεύεται, καὶ ἄλλῳ·
ἔρχου, καὶ ἔρχεται, καὶ   ἔρχου, καὶ ἔρχεται, καὶ
τῷ δούλῳ μου· ποίησον   τῷ δούλῳ μου· ποίησον
τοῦτο, καὶ ποιεῖ.   τοῦτο, καὶ ποιεῖ.

This section contains the crucial point of the Q story, expressed in compelling and memorable form, and it is no accident that Matthew and Luke have reproduced it almost word for word. It seems very regrettable that John should abandon it, but obviously he did so deliberately. The reason is not, as some might think, that he objected to the thought that the centurion tells Jesus what to do, but that he wishes to capitalize what it actually is, an outstanding expression of faith, and use it to promote his concept of faith, as we have just seen. In my view he actually takes words from this section, in which the centurion gives examples of a military officer's commands which are instantly obeyed. But he applies this motif to Jesus himself, who in v. 50 issues one of the centurion's typical commands, which the official promptly carries out. Moreover, as the official believes 'the word' (τῷ λόγῳ) of Jesus, it is clear that he now understands that Jesus needs only to 'speak by word' of mouth (εἰπὲ λόγῳ) to perform the cure, and has no need to go down with him to Capernaum. The reference to him as ὁ ἄνθρωπος in v. 50b provides another contact with this part of the source (Mt 8,9 = Lk 7,8).

It is commonly recognised that Jesus' healing words, ὁ υἱός σου ζῇ, are identical with words attributed to Elijah in 1 Kings 17,23, and this has suggested a typological relationship between the stories. But it is much more likely that the similarity is nothing more than chance. In the Elijah story the words report the restoration of the boy to life after the miracle has been done. All the circumstances are entirely different. The saying is much too brief to require literary dependence. The application of ζάω to recovery of a dying person occurs in Mk 5,23. John requires it here to make the contrast with the idea of death in the preceding verses. Thus it is likely to be a substitute-word for a word for healing, and the whole phrase represents ἰαθήσεται (-ήτω) ὁ παῖς μου in the source, and no other influence is needed to account for it. The fact that Jesus uses the present tense rather than the future is significant in the light of what follows.

Precisely the same words are used by the servants who meet the official on his journey home (v. 51), and then repeated again in the conclusion (v. 53). The meeting with the servants begins the special Johannine feature of the confirmation of the miracle, which is aimed at ensuring that the correct lesson is drawn from the story. This section appears to have no basis in the source, and at first sight looks as if it might have been influenced by Luke's second deputation (cf. Mk 5,35 = Lk 8,49, which is responsible for Luke's insertion of μὴ σκύλλου). However, a closer look at the relation between John and Luke suggests another possibility. The beginning of Luke's second deputation uses words which may be derived from the source, where they referred to Jesus' movement. For ὁ δὲ Ἰησοῦς ἐπορεύετο σὺν αὐτοῖς (adapted from an original αὐτῷ) in Lk 7,6 follows naturally from the centurion's appeal to Jesus to come in Lk 7,3 = Mt 8,7, and the further note, that it was not until Jesus was near the house (ἤδη δὲ αὐτοῦ οὐ μακρὰν ἀπέχοντος ἀπὸ τῆς οἰκίας) that the centurion spoke again, follows naturally on that. There is really a lacuna in Matthew's account, for the centurion asks Jesus to come, and then, as soon as Jesus agrees to do so, tells him not to come after all. It is for this reason that many commentators treat Mt 8,7 as a question, so that the reply amounts to a rebuff (as in the Syrophoenician's Daughter and Jn 4,48). It then has to be assumed that Jesus is unwilling to enter a Gentile's house in spite of the urgency of the request, and the centurion's further response is aimed at overcoming his reluctance to help. But the story makes much better sense if Jesus showed no unwillingness, but the centurion began to have doubts about the propriety of expecting him to enter his house when they had already gone part of the way. It is this delicacy of feeling which Luke has picked up and elaborated (to the detriment of the story, in my opinion) by making the centurion work entirely through messengers. Once it is realised that Matthew has omitted this item, the argument for treating Mt 8,7 as a question becomes unnecessary, as we are dealing here, not with the original form of the story, but with Matthew's slightly inept abbreviation of it. John thus contributes to the reconstruction of this part of the story, because he has retained ἤδη δὲ αὐτοῦ from the source, though he has adjusted the verb to suit the distance and applied the phrase to the centurion, who alone goes to the house in his recasting of the story. It remains to be said that Luke's οὐ μακρὰν ἀπέχοντος ἀπὸ τῆς οἰκίας is a typically Lucan expression[14], and perhaps replaces a simpler phrase ἐγγίζοντος τῇ οἰκίᾳ in the source. Finally John's description of the messengers as δοῦλοι cannot be traced to either of the two deputations in Luke, but could have been suggested by the use of δοῦλος by the centurion in Mt 8,9 = Lk 7,8. So John knows from the source that the centurion employs at least one δοῦλος, and there is no confusion with the ambiguous word παῖς. For ὑπήντησαν cf. Jn 11,20.

14. Cf. especially Lk 15,20; 24,13. A. Plummer (ICC, ad loc.) notes that Luke has a liking for οὐ + adjective or adverb.

The miracle confirmed (Jn 4,52-53)

Mt 8,13	Lk 7,10	Jn 4,52-53
13 καὶ εἶπεν ὁ Ἰησοῦς τῷ ἑκατοντάρχῃ· ὕπαγε, ὡς ἐπίστευσας γενηθήτω σοι. καὶ ἰάθη ὁ παῖς ἐν τῇ ὥρᾳ ἐκείνῃ	10 καὶ ὑποστρέψαντες εἰς τὸν οἶκον οἱ πεμφθέντες εὗρον τὸν δοῦλον ὑγιαίνοντα	52 ἐπύθετο οὖν τὴν ὥραν παρ' αὐτῶν ἐν ᾗ κομψότερον ἔσχεν· εἶπαν οὖν αὐτῷ ὅτι ἐχθὲς ὥραν ἑβδόμην ἀφῆκεν αὐτὸν ὁ πυρετός. 53 ἔγνω οὖν ὁ πατὴρ ὅτι ἐκείνῃ τῇ ὥρᾳ ᾗ εἶπεν αὐτῷ ὁ Ἰησοῦς· ὁ υἱός σου ζῇ, καὶ ἐπίστευσεν αὐτὸς καὶ ἡ οἰκία αὐτοῦ ὅλη.

Although the possibility that John here incorporates an item from another tradition cannot be excluded in the light of the similar story of R. Hanina b. Dosa[15], his composition still keeps as close as possible to the vocabulary of the main source. Hence such a tradition (which was not in Greek) can be regarded only as a model for what was not provided in the source, and should not be taken as a second source. Unfortunately we have no access to the full detail of the original conclusion in the source, because Matthew can be expected to have abbreviated it, and Luke has rewritten it to accommodate his device of the second deputation. John here obviously agrees with Matthew. He has already represented ὕπαγε, ὡς ἐπίστευσας in πορεύου ... ἐπίστευσεν in v. 50, and the last word is repeated in the final sentence of v. 53. Otherwise the main variations are the two expressions for the recovery of the boy. The first, κομψότερον ἔσχεν, reverses κακῶς ἔχων (Lk 7,2), which we have seen may have stood in the source rather than John's ἠσθένει. The second, ἀφῆκεν αὐτὸν ὁ πυρετός, has a parallel in the rabbinic story, but the same Greek words occur in the case of Peter's mother-in-law, which immediately follows the Centurion's Servant in Mt 8,15 (= Mk 1,31). Though it is tempting to see here more than coincidence, it is likely to be another instance of a phrase which is too commonplace to compel the conclusion that John is directly indebted to Matthew for it. It no doubt denotes a turn for the better, because the reduction of a high temperature, which is easily observable, makes possible a fair estimate of the exact time when the healing process can be said to have begun. It should thus be regarded as a further substitute for ἰάθη (cf. Mt 8,13). At the end John uses οἰκία, which was probably

---

15. *Berakoth*, 34b. Translation in BARRETT, *The Gospel according to St. John*, London, SPCK, ²1978, p. 249. The most striking resemblances are the rabbi's instruction to the messengers, "Go, for the fever has left him", and their discovery on their return that "in that hour the fever left him".

in his source for v. 51a (= Lk 7,6a, cf. Mt 8,6), but he applies it to the household in line with missionary usage (cf. Acts 16,32). In v. 53 πατήρ is another substitute for ἑκατοντάρχης. For the question whether ἐκείνη τῇ ὥρᾳ requires a debt to Matthew's redaction see next section.

III. The Underlying Story

The above analysis has confirmed the impression that John's story of the Official's Son is an adaptation of the story of the Centurion's Servant in Matthew and Luke, which is generally attributed to Q. But it has also indicated that, because John tends to retain as much as possible of his source, in spite of recasting it radically, he has more to contribute to the reconstruction of the source than has previously been recognised.

In order to facilitate comparison, I give here a tentative reconstruction of the source based on the critical evaluation of the form in all three Gospels which has just been made. All the words are found in one or other of the three texts except [ἐγγίζοντος].

εἰσῆλθεν ὁ Ἰησοῦς εἰς Καφαρναούμ. καὶ ἦν τις ἑκατόνταρχος οὗ ὁ παῖς κακῶς ἔχων ἤμελλεν τελευτᾶν. ἀκούσας δὲ περὶ τοῦ Ἰησοῦ, ἀπῆλθεν πρὸς αὐτὸν καὶ παρεκάλεσεν αὐτὸν ἵνα ἐλθὼν ἰάσηται αὐτοῦ τὸν παῖδα. ὁ δὲ Ἰησοῦς ἐπορεύετο σὺν αὐτῷ. ἤδη δὲ αὐτοῦ [ἐγγίζοντος] τῇ οἰκίᾳ, λέγει πρὸς αὐτὸν ὁ ἑκατόνταρχος· κύριε, οὐκ εἰμι ἱκανὸς ἵνα μου ὑπὸ τὴν στέγην εἰσέλθῃς· ἀλλὰ μόνον εἰπὲ λόγῳ, καὶ ἰαθήσεται ὁ παῖς μου. καὶ γὰρ ἐγὼ ἄνθρωπός εἰμι ὑπὸ ἐξουσίαν, ἔχων ὑπ' ἐμαυτὸν στρατιώτας, καὶ λέγω τούτῳ· πορεύθητι, καὶ πορεύεται, καὶ ἄλλῳ· ἔρχου, καὶ ἔρχεται, καὶ τῷ δούλῳ μου· ποίησον τοῦτο, καὶ ποιεῖ. ἀκούσας δὲ ταῦτα ὁ Ἰησοῦς ἐθαύμασεν αὐτὸν καὶ στραφεὶς τῷ ἀκολουθοῦντι αὐτῷ ὄχλῳ εἶπεν· ἀμὴν λέγω ὑμῖν, παρ' οὐδενὶ τοσαυτὴν πίστιν ἐν τῷ Ἰσραὴλ εὗρον.

καὶ εἶπεν ὁ Ἰησοῦς τῷ ἑκατοντάρχῃ· ὕπαγε, ὡς ἐπίστευσας γενηθήτω σοι. καὶ ἰάθη ὁ παῖς ἐν τῇ ὥρᾳ ἐκείνῃ.

In this reconstruction the first paragraph, based almost exclusively on Luke and John, contains 50 words. The extent of Matthew's abbreviation can be realised when the same introductory material is compared (down to ὁ ἑκατόνταρχος ἔφη in Mt 8,8). He has reduced it by about one third to 34 words. This is consistent with the scale of reduction in his treatment of many pericopae in the triple tradition. The reduction has been achieved in the following manner: (a) the description of the servant's sickness replaces the request for healing in the centurion's speech; (b) the information that the centurion heard of Jesus' reputation before going to him has been omitted; (c) a brief response of Jesus incorporates the request for healing and his decision to go to the house; (d) the information that they were near the house when the centurion had second thoughts and began his main speech is omitted. It is possible that ἐν τῇ οἰκίᾳ in Mt 8,6 is a relic of (d). Also in the same verse δεινῶς βασανιζόμενος may be a substitute for ἤμελλεν τελευτᾶν, as suggested above. Matthew uses βασανίζω elsewhere only at 8,29; 14,24, both from Mark (5,7; 6,48).

In the same paragraph Luke has changed παῖς to δοῦλος, possibly for consistency with the centurion's speech (Lk 7,8), and added ὃς ἦν αὐτῷ ἔντιμος to explain why the centurion was specially interested in his welfare (John has achieved the same object by changing παῖς to υἱός). Luke has also introduced the deputation of Jewish elders in vv. 3-5. This has necessitated changing ἀπῆλθεν πρὸς αὐτὸν καὶ παρεκάλει αὐτόν (cf. Jn 4,47) to ἀπέστειλεν πρὸς αὐτὸν πρεσβυτέρους τῶν Ἰουδαίων ἐρωτῶν αὐτόν. The use of διασῴζειν seems to be a stylistic alteration to increase the sense of urgency (cf. Acts 23,24; 27,43-44; 28,1.4). In v. 4 there is virtual repetition of ἀπῆλθεν πρὸς αὐτὸν καὶ παρεκάλει αὐτόν in οἱ δὲ παραγενόμενοι πρὸς τὸν Ἰησοῦν παρεκάλουν αὐτόν.

In v. 6 Luke is once more closer to the source. He has of course changed σὺν αὐτῷ to σὺν αὐτοῖς. In the next words we have the evidence of John's ἤδη δὲ αὐτοῦ καταβαίνοντος (Jn 4,51) to suggest that Luke preserves the original motif, which John has altered to suit his recasting of the story. But οὐ μακρὰν ἀπέχοντος is much too characteristic of Luke's style to be accepted as the original text, and so it has seemed probable that both Luke and John have altered the common verb ἐγγίζοντος with dative or εἰς. Luke uses this verb frequently, but his alteration of it here adds vividness to the narrative.

The contribution which John can make to reconstruction of this part of the source has gone unrecognised because John has transferred the movement of Jesus with the centurion towards the house (which does not apply in his recasting of the story) to the journey of the centurion alone towards Capernaum. This transference of source-material actually produces an interesting triple overlap in his treatment of the source. In Jn 4,50-51 Jesus' command and the man's response, πορεύου ... καὶ ἐπορεύετο (v. 50) corresponds, as we have seen, with the centurion's order πορεύθητι, καὶ πορεύεται. But the same verses *also* reflect, firstly, Matthew's *conclusion* of the story in the words πορεύου ... ἐπίστευσεν at the beginning of v. 50, cf. Mt 8,13 ὕπαγε, ὡς ἐπίστευσας, and, secondly, the words which we have just referred to in Lk 7,6, ἐπορεύετο ... ἤδη δὲ αὐτοῦ, in v. 50-51.

The second paragraph is so well preserved in Matthew and Luke that further comment is unnecessary. In my reconstruction obvious Lucan additions have been omitted, but some words only found in Matthew have been retained. John has availed himself of some of the ideas and vocabulary of this section in ways that have not hitherto been satisfactorily expounded.

The concluding paragraph cannot be reconstructed with confidence, because Matthew has to be used as basis, and we cannot tell how far he has abbreviated what lay before him. Matthew has very similar conclusions in 9,22b; 9,29; 15,28; 17,18b. As he tends to repeat himself, it is arguable that the present passage lies behind all of these. At least ὕπαγε, ἐπίστευσας, ἰάθη ὁ παῖς, and ἐν τῇ ὥρᾳ ἐκείνῃ, which are paralleled in John, can well be accepted as original. It is noteworthy that Matthew has ἐν τῇ ὥρᾳ ἐκείνῃ only here, as he uses the preposition ἀπό in the other passages. Luke's ending, on the other hand, has no words in common with John, and is clearly an adaptation of the source to accommodate the deputations. He has taken words from his previous text (οἶκον, cf. οἰκίαν, v. 6, πεμφθέντες, v. 6, εὗρον, v. 9, δοῦλον, v. 2), and reduced the original definite statement of the servant's recovery to the feeble and colourless ὑγιαίνοντα (cf. Lk 5,31 ὑγιαίνοντες for Mt/Mk ἰσχύοντες).

IV. Concluding Reflections

Our visit to Capernaum has gone over old ground, but by digging deeper into John's version of the story we have brought to light some small facets of the source which have not previously been sufficiently stressed. This story is a rare case where synoptic criticism can be applied to John almost on equal terms with the Synoptics. The impetus to undertake this new study came from my previous work on the Lazarus story of John 11, where investigation of the problem of the meaning of ἐμβριμάομαι led to a new theory of the relationship between John's narrative and the underlying source for the miracle[16]. It appeared that John had adapted an exorcism tradition, which had already been interpreted as a model of death and resurrection, like the story of the Epileptic Boy in Mk 9,14-29. John took from the source the whole phrase ἐνεβριμήσατο τῷ πνεύματι (v. 33), though he gave it a different meaning. In the original it referred to Jesus' rebuke of the unclean spirit, which is a feature of exorcism (cf. Mk 1,25, 9,25). Once this form of story had been identified as the basis, further words from the source could be detected in John's narrative, mostly common

16. B. LINDARS, *Rebuking the Spirit. A New Analysis of the Lazarus Story of John 11*, in *NTS* 38 (1992) 89-104 [in this volume, pp. 183-198]; A. DENAUX (ed.), *John and the Synoptics* (BETL, 101), Leuven: University Press – Peeters, 1992, pp. 542-547.

words, which would not have been perceived as source-material if the original context of the very distinctive ἐμβριμάομαι had not been identified first.

In the present case the recasting of the narrative is much less drastic than in the Lazarus story, and the relation to the underlying source is accordingly much closer. But both examples illustrate features of John's treatment of his sources which are interesting in themselves and may well have significance for further study. Of course some of these features have long been recognised.

(a) John always has a strong sense of purpose in using traditional material, and nothing is reproduced only because it is an accepted part of the story of Jesus. His teaching on Jesus as the agent of resurrection in chapter 11 required a raising story, but apparently John had nothing suitable in his stock of traditions, and so he used an exorcism story which was relevant to the theme. In chapter 4 he wished to round off the teaching with an example of believing in Jesus as the giver of life. In the missionary context of the chapter this case of healing at a distance helps the reader to see how those who believe in Jesus at any time and place can experience his response to human need as the saviour of the world. This is an essential aspect of John's christology.

(b) In his new version of the story John makes use of the vocabulary and ideas of the source as far as possible, but not necessarily in the same order. He also transfers words and actions from one character to another. In the Lazarus story the command to the unclean spirit to come out of the possessed person in the source becomes Jesus' command to Lazarus to come out of the grave. Here the movement of Jesus to the centurion's house is transferred to the official alone.

(c) Where John introduces new material he continues to use the vocabulary of the source, thus causing repetition. But this is intentional, for the repeated stress on the imminent death of the boy is balanced by the threefold statement that he lives, which is the whole point of the story.

(d) John's debt to the source can also be observed when his own word or phrase, needed for his version of the story, constitutes a substitute for a word or phrase in the source, e.g., ζάω for ἰάομαι. When allowance is made for this kind of substitution, the relation of his composition to the source can be seen to be much closer than it appears at first sight.

(e) Another kind of debt is the use of a theme from the source. It has been argued above that Jesus' reference to 'signs and wonders' is based on Jesus' own amazement in the source. John has also taken the theme of faith from the end of the story and given it new emphasis by attaching it to each phase of the story (vv. 48.50.53).

(f) The major change involved in placing Jesus in Cana, while keeping the official's home in Capernaum, is also purposeful, for it provides the opportunity for the confirmatory episode at the end. It is possible that John here incorporates a theme or actual words from another source. This certainly seems to be the case in Jn 5,8.

With regard to Synoptic study, this pericope is a remarkable case in which John gives positive help towards the recovery of the common source behind Matthew and Luke. Luke's expansions of the source have obscured aspects of the opening part of the story which Matthew has edited out for the sake of brevity. John enables us to disentangle these elements and to restore them to the source. In expanding the story Luke has shifted the emphasis away from the issue of faith (still mentioned, but not emphasized, in Lk 7,9) to the character of the centurion as an ideal Gentile convert, surpassing the Jews, with the result that the ending is weak and lacking in emotional effectiveness. On the other hand Matthew's emphasis on faith might be attributed to his editorial interests, but John's version suggests that he had no need to build up this aspect, as it was sufficiently prominent in the source. It remains true, however, that even if Matthew gives the best form of the conclusion, we do not have the means to reconstruct the original with confidence.

Was John's source Q? That is a question which must be left to Synoptic and Johannine scholars to ponder on future visits to Capernaum.

INDEX OF AUTHORS

INDEX OF BIBLICAL REFERENCES

28,10	5			
28,8	5			
28,9-10	3			
28,19-20	59			
Mark				
1,4	55			
1,8	56			
1,10	156			
1,23-26	193			
1,23	192 194			
1,24	192			
1,25	192 212			
1,26	194			
1,31	209			
1,39	192			
1,40-44	19			
1,43-45	193			
1,43	192 193 194			
1,45	193			
2,10	48			
2,15-17	16			
2,17	204			
2,18-22	17			
2,18-20	15			
2,18-19	19 114			
2,18	16 18			
2,19	16 17			
2,22	10 12			
2,28	48			
3,23-26	107			
3,19	171			
3,22-30	195			
4,12	111			
4,22	20			
5,7	204 211			
5,21-43	191			
5,23	207			
5,25-43	202			
5,35	208			
6,14-15	35			
6,48	211			
6,50	44			
6,56	205			
7,5	19			
7,6-23	19			
7,19	19			
7,24-30	89 202			
8,11-12	97			
8,22-26	192			
8,26	193			
8,28-29	35			
8,31	39 116 153			
9,1	45 107 125 126 128 179			
9,14-29	193 195 212			
9,25-29	193			
9,25	194 212			
9,26-27	198			
9,26	194			
9,27	194			
9,30	117			
9,33-37	105 106 112			
9,33	174			
9,35	105			
9,37	38 105 106			
10,13-16	105 112			
10,14	106			
10,15	105 106 111 115 179			
10,16	105			
10,17	105			
10,33	117			
10,43-44	105			
10,44	173			
10,45	81			
11,12-14	10			
11,14	171			
11,20-25	10			
11,29-32	35			
13	135			
13,5-31	135			
13,9-13	134			
13,9	135			
13,10	135			
13,13	141			

	172 175 179	9	45 58 81 137
8,32	23 170	9,1-7	94
8,33	120 123 163 164	9,1-34	58
	170 177 179	9,2-3	92
8,34-36	124 178	9,3	24 45 159
8,34	124 126 163 167	9,5	45 163
	169 170 178	9,14	92
8,35	9 97 122 126 127	9,22	132 133
	167 168 169 170	9,31	23
	171 172 174 177	9,34	132
	181	9,35-37	160
8,36-37	126	9,35	34 45 58 159
8,36	124 125 127 170	9,36	160
	175 176 179	9,38-39	159
8,37-47	170 172	9,38	58
8,37	56 120 163 177	9,39	58
	178	9,41	26
8,38	121 125 177	10	58 81
8,39-47	123 125	10,1-18	45 137
8,39	163 177	10,1-5	62 97
8,40	62 120 177	10,1-3	97
8,41	112	10,3-5	97
8,42	163 177	10,7-18	62
8,44-46	124	10,10-18	24
8,44	23 26 177	10,11	58 70
8,46	25 26	10,15	58 70
8,47	127	10,17-18	58 81
8,48-58	170	10,17	24 83
8,48	195	10,19-21	137
8,51-52	45 97 107 126	10,22-39	45 68 144
	127 128 129 156	10,24	45
	172 177 181	10,25	81 144
8,51	23 100 125 126	10,26-29	137
	170 177 178 179	10,27-29	46
8,52	125 179	10,29	81
8,53	177	10,30	46 58 81 144
8,54	163	10,32	144
8,56-58	120	10,33	46 58 81 170
8,57	126 180	10,34	46 144
8,58	44 45 58 100 126	10,36-38	58
	127 129 169 170	10,36	45 46 163 164
	176 180	10,37-38	84 144
8,59	170	10,38	46 81

13,23	5		15,9-10	24 83	
13,27	7		15,11	17 147	
13,28	78		15,12-18	84	
13,31-32	47 58 71 80		15,13	64 70 151	
13,31	34 80 155 166		15,15	53 121 172	
13,32	80 82		15,16	30 140 142	
13,33	84		15,18–16,15	138	
13,34-35	23 53 64 84		15,18–16,4	84 131 134 136	
13,37-38	70			137 149 150	
13,38	126 148 156		15,18-25	137 138 145 146	
14–16	138			147	
14,1-7	84		15,18-20	138 145 149	
14,1	186 196		15,18-19	145	
14,2-3	84		15,18	138 139 140 141	
14,6-7	84			142 151	
14,6	6 23		15,19	139 139 140 141	
14,10-11	83			142 151	
14,12	144		15,20	131 138 142 143	
14,15	23			145 146	
14,16-17	28 59 146		15,21-25	138	
14,17	146		15,21-24	143 145 148 152	
14,18-24	53		15,21	139 140 143 150	
14,18-23	58 84		15,22	139 140 141 142	
14,19	24			143 144 145	
14,20	83		15,23	139 140 143	
14,21	23		15,24	139 140 141 142	
14,23-24	23			143 144	
14,25	147		15,25	139 140 144	
14,26	59 146 147		15,26–16,11	138	
14,28	28 84		15,26-27	59 137 145	
14,27	6 186 196		15,26	28 145 146	
14,30	84		15,27–16,7	138	
14,31	83 136		15,27	145 146	
15-17	136		16	35 146	
15-16	136 147 149		16,1-4	137 145	
15	35 146		16,1	147 148	
15,1-17	138		16,2	132 133 137 147	
15,1-10	53 58 84			148	
15,1	98		16,3	147 148	
15,2	56		16,4	147 148	
15,3	56		16,4-7	137	
15,5	8		16,5-15	59	
15,8	30		16,5-7	58	

STUDIORUM NOVI TESTAMENTI AUXILIA

Edited by F. Neirynck

Available:

LEUVEN UNIVERSITY PRESS - UITGEVERIJ PEETERS